Baptism

 McMaster Divinity College Press
McMaster Theological Studies Series

Defining Issues in Pentecostalism: Classical and Emergent (2008)

Pentecostalism and Globalization: The Impact of Globalization on Pentecostal Theology and Ministry (2009)

You Mean I Don't Have to Tithe?: A Deconstruction of Tithing and a Reconstruction of Post-Tithe Giving (2009)

Baptism

Historical, Theological, and Pastoral Perspectives

edited by
GORDON L. HEATH
and
JAMES D. DVORAK

PICKWICK *Publications* • Eugene, Oregon

BAPTISM
Historical, Theological, and Pastoral Perspectives

McMaster Divinity College Press Theological Study Series 4

Copyright © 2011 Wipf and Stock Publishers. All rights reserved. Except for brief quotations in critical publications or reviews, no part of this book may be reproduced in any manner without prior written permission from the publisher. Write: Permissions, Wipf and Stock Publishers, 199 W. 8th Ave., Suite 3, Eugene, OR 97401.

Scripture quotations from the *New Revised Standard Version Bible*, © 1989, Division of Christian Education of the National Council of Churches of Christ in the United States of America. Used by permission. All rights reserved.

McMaster Divinity College Press
1280 Main Street West
Hamilton, Ontario, Canada
L8S 4K1

Pickwick Publications
An Imprint of Wipf and Stock Publishers
199 W. 8th Av.e, Suite 3
Eugene, OR 97401

www.wipfandstock.com

ISBN 13: 978-1-60899-486-1

Cataloging-in-Publication data:

Baptism : historical, theological, and pastoral perspectives / edited by Gordon L. Heath and James D. Dvorak.

xviii + 272 p. ; 23 cm. Includes bibliographical references and indexes.

McMaster Divinity College Press Theological Study Series 4

ISBN 13: 978-1-60899-486-1

1. Baptism — History of doctrines. I. Heath, Gordon L. II. Dvorak, James D. III. Title. IV. Series.

BV811 B25 2011

Manufactured in the U.S.A.

Contents

List of Contributors / vii

Introduction—Gordon L. Heath and James D. Dvorak / *xiii*

1   Baptism in Orthodox Christianity
    —*Irenaeus M. C. Steenberg* / 1

2   Baptism in the Roman Catholic Church—*Gerard Kelly* / 26

3   The Lutheran Theology of Baptism—*Robert Kolb* / 53

4   Baptism in the Reformed Tradition—*John Vissers* / 76

5   Baptism in the Anglican Communion—*Alan L. Hayes* / 111

6   Baptism among Baptists—*Anthony R. Cross* / 136

7   Baptism and Quakers—*Howard R. Macy* / 156

8   Baptism in the Restoration Movement—*Curt Niccum* / 174

9   Baptism among Pentecostals—*Steve Studebaker* / 201

Conclusion: Author Responses / 225

Bibliography / 245

Name Index / 259

Scripture Index / 265

Contributors

EDITORS

JAMES D. DVORAK is associate professor of Greek and New Testament at Oklahoma Christian University. He is currently a PhD Candidate at McMaster Divinity College, specializing in Biblical Greek Language and Linguistics. He is a research partner with OpenText.org and has authored a number of peer-reviewed journal articles. He is currently co-editing a volume on New Testament ecclesiology. He is a minister with the fellowship of non-denominational Churches of Christ.

GORDON L. HEATH is associate professor of Christian History at McMaster Divinity College, and also serves as Director of the Canadian Baptist Archives. He received his PhD from St. Michael's College at the University of Toronto. His publications include *A War with a Silver Lining: Canadian Protestant Churches and the South African War, 1899–1902* (McGill-Queens University Press, 2009), *Doing Church History: A User-Friendly Introduction to Researching the History of Christianity* (Clements, 2008), and *The Lost Gospel of Judas: Separating Fact from Fiction* (co-authored by Stanley E. Porter; Eerdmans, 2007). He is an ordained minister with the Convention of Atlantic Baptist Churches.

AUTHORS

ANTHONY R. CROSS, PhD, is Director of the Centre for Baptist History and Heritage, and a Research Fellow, Regent's Park College, Oxford, and Member of the Faculty of Theology, University of Oxford. Cross trained for the Baptist ministry at Bristol and South Wales Baptist Colleges, and studied at the Universities of Bristol, University College Cardiff, and Keele before holding pastorates in Cambridge and Wiltshire. From 1998 to 2001 he was a Research Fellow at the Centre for Advanced Theological

Research, University of Roehampton, London, and a Fellow of the Centre for Baptist History and Heritage from 2003 to 2009. In 2009 he succeeded Professor John H. Y. Briggs as Director of the Centre. He has lectured widely in church history, theology and Baptist history, and written, co-authored, and edited over a dozen volumes, and published numerous chapters and articles in books and journals. He specializes in Baptist history and theology, with a specific interest in the theology and practice of baptism and evangelical sacramentalism. Since 2000 he has been a Consultant for Paternoster and their six academic monograph series, and he conceived and developed Paternoster's Studies in Baptist History and Thought series, for which he is co-ordinating editor. He is ordained with the Baptist Union of Great Britain.

ALAN L. HAYES is professor of the history of Christianity in the Bishops Frederick and Heber Wilkinson Chair at Wycliffe College, University of Toronto, and director of the Toronto School of Theology. He received his BA from Pomona College, Claremont, California, and his BD and PhD at McGill University. He specializes in Canadian church history. His most recent book is *Anglicans in Canada: Controversy and Identity in Historical Perspective* (University of Illinois Press, 2004). He is an editor of *Anglican and Episcopal History*. He is ordained as a priest in the Anglican Church of Canada.

GERARD KELLY was first appointed lecturer in systematic theology in 1986 at the Catholic Institute of Sydney (CIS), one of the founding member institutions of the Sydney College of Divinity. In 2004 he was appointed the President of CIS. He was ordained a priest for the Roman Catholic Archdiocese of Sydney in 1980. In 1992 he completed the PhD(Th) at the Collège dominicain de philosophie et de théologie in Ottawa, Ontario. The dissertation, which had been prepared under the direction of noted ecumenist J. M. R. Tillard, was subsequently published as *Recognition: Advancing Ecumenical Thinking* (Peter Lang, 1996). Gerard Kelly has been involved in ecumenical dialogues since the early 1990s, and was a member of the Roman Catholic delegation at the Fifth World Conference on Faith and Order held in Santiago de Compostela, Spain, in 1993. In 1997 he was appointed to the Lutheran–Roman Catholic Dialogue in Australia and in 2009 became the co-chair. In 1999 he was appointed to the Faith and Unity Commission of the National Council of Churches in Australia and became the chair in 2007. His theological interest in baptism began when, as an undergraduate, he read the baptismal homilies of St. John Chrysostom. Later, while ministering in a parish, more urgent pastoral questions around baptism surfaced. In recent years he has been exploring the ecumenical implications of a baptismal ecclesiology.

ROBERT KOLB is Missions Professor of Systematic Theology emeritus at Concordia Seminary, Saint Louis, Missouri, USA. After doctoral studies at the University of Wisconsin (1973) and directing the Center for Reformation Research, Saint Louis (1972–1977), he taught at Concordia College, Saint Paul, Minnesota (1977–1993). He has served since 1993 as a member of the continuation committee of the International Congress for Luther Research. Former associate editor and co-editor of *The Sixteenth Century Journal* (1973–1998), he is co-editor (with Timothy J. Wengert) of *The Book of Concord, the Confessions of the Evangelical Lutheran Church*, (Augsburg Fortress, 2000), editor of *Lutheran Ecclesiastical Culture, 1550–1675*, (Brill, 2008), editor and author of *Make Disciples, Baptizing, God's Gift of New Life and Christian Witness* (Concordia Seminary, 1997), *Martin Luther, Confessor of the Faith* (Oxford University Press, 2009), (with Charles P. Arand) *The Genius of Luther's Theology: A Wittenberg Way of Thinking for the Contemporary Church* (Baker Academic, 2008), *Bound Choice, Election, and Wittenberg Theological Method from Martin Luther to the Formula of Concord* (Eerdmans, 2005), *Martin Luther as Prophet, Teacher, and Hero. Images of the Reformer, 1520–1620* (Baker, 1999), as well as other books and articles. He regularly teaches overseas, having offered instruction or lectured in eighteen countries in Europe and Asia since 1994.

HOWARD MACY is Professor of Religion and Biblical Studies at George Fox University in Newberg, Oregon. Though he teaches mostly in the discipline of Old Testament studies, he also regularly offers courses about both spiritual formation and Quakers. In addition to his service in university teaching, Howard engages in several other forms of public ministry. He is a recorded Friends minister and has served as a pastor and Christian education worker. He often speaks in local churches and in varieties of workshops, retreats, and church conferences. As an active writer, Howard contributes articles for magazines and journals and has authored three books, *Rhythms of the Inner Life, Laughing Pilgrims: Humor and the*

Spiritual Journey, and *Stepping in the Light: Life in Joy and Power*. Beyond these activities, Howard enjoys photography, playing trumpet in a brass ensemble, and exploring the great outdoors, especially in Oregon.

CURT NICCUM has served in various capacities among Churches of Christ the past twenty-five years, primarily in Texas, Indiana, and Oklahoma. He obtained a doctorate in Christianity and Judaism in Antiquity from the University of Notre Dame. His research has focused on textual criticism, which has included work with international collaborations such as the Dead Sea Scrolls Project and the International Project on the Text of Acts. For the past twelve years he has taught theology and Greek at schools associated with the Restoration Movement, first at Oklahoma Christian University and now at Abilene Christian University. He also sits on the board of *Restoration Quarterly*, a scholarly journal within the Stone-Campbell tradition.

REVD. PROF. HIEROMONK IRENAEUS M.C. STEENBERG is a priest-monk of the Orthodox Church and scholar of patristics and Eastern Christianity. Formerly a don in theology at the University of Oxford and Chair of Theology in Leeds, he is currently Visiting Professor in Orthodox Studies at Santa Clara University, Professorial Research Fellow at Leeds Trinity University College, UK, and Principal of the St. John of San Francisco Orthodox Academy in San Francisco, California. His recent works include *Of God and Man: Theology as Anthropology from Irenaeus to Athanasius* (T. & T. Clark, 2009), and *Irenaeus on Creation: The Cosmic Christ and the Saga of Redemption* (Brill, 2008), as well as numerous articles and chapters on the history and doctrine of the early church.

STEVEN M. STUDEBAKER, PhD (Marquette University) holds the Howard and Shirley Bentall Chair in Evangelical Thought and is Assistant Professor of Systematic and Historical Theology at McMaster Divinity College, Hamilton, Ontario. He is an active member in the Society for Pentecostal Studies and the editor of *Defining Issues in Pentecostalism: Classical and Emergent*, author of *Jonathan Edwards' Social Augustinian Trinitarianism in Historical and Contemporary Perspectives* and several articles on Pentecostal theology. He is ordained with the Assemblies of God.

JOHN VISSERS has served as Principal of the Presbyterian College, Montreal, and Adjunct Professor of Christian Theology at McGill University since 1999. Previously, he was the Senior Minister at Knox Presbyterian Church, Toronto, and Professor of Systematic Theology at Tyndale Seminary. He is a graduate of the University of Toronto, Knox College, and Princeton Theological Seminary. He is the author of *The Neo-Orthodox Theology of W. W. Bryden* (Pickwick, 2006) and has published numerous articles both scholarly and popular on the Reformed tradition. Vissers is an ordained minister of The Presbyterian Church in Canada and lives in Montreal, Quebec.

Introduction

GORDON L. HEATH *and* JAMES D. DVORAK

BAPTISM HAS BEEN IDENTIFIED with Christianity since the church's inception on Pentecost in Jerusalem almost 2,000 years ago. However, in the centuries that followed its birth, the seemingly simple command of Jesus in Matthew 28 to make disciples and baptize them has been understood and practiced in a variety of ways. Sadly, such differences of opinion regarding baptism have, at times, divided the church, sometimes in shamefully and scandalously violent ways.

However, despite contemporary differences among Christians, the toxicity level of interaction has lessened. In fact, differences in polity and practice of baptism are, at least among some traditions, increasingly less of an issue. The willingness of some Baptist churches to accept into membership those baptized as infants (without being re-baptized the "right" way as adult believers) is just one example of a growing willingness to make baptismal differences less of a barrier among Christians. Critics of such elastic boundaries say such practices reveal a vacuous theology among leaders and laity, a loss of denominational identity, or a misguided postmodern perspective that is unable to say that anything is the only way. Those in favor of such openness see the shift as a positive sign that Christians are more concerned with the kingdom of God and the work of the Spirit than with old denominational boundaries and doctrinal peculiarities.

Some of the most remarkable changes in attitudes have taken place since the 1960s. The ecumenical movement was active before the sixties through organizations such as the World Council of Churches (WCC), but what provided a significant impetus to the ecumenical enterprise was the Second Vatican Council (1962–1965). The Roman Catholic Church had never actively engaged the ecumenical movement before Pope John XXIII and the Second Vatican Council. In its *Decree on Ecumenism*, the council moved the Catholic Church away from the harsh attitudes of the past, attitudes especially enshrined in the anathemas of the Council of Trent in the sixteenth century. The council witnessed a dramatic demonstration of this new attitude towards other Christian communions when Pope Paul VI and the Orthodox Patriarch Athenagoras I formally expressed their regret for the mutual excommunications of their predecessors back in 1054. The importance of such decisions and actions was not that everything had been solved, but that the church was placed on a trajectory towards dialogue. And that dialogue has often focused on baptism.

A brief glimpse at ecumenical events and statements since the 1960s provides a sense of how significant baptism is to the wider movement. The WCC's various statements, messages, liturgies, and studies derived from its Commission on Faith and Order indicate how important baptism is to the ecumenical movement. For instance, the following list gives a representative sample of the types of WCC work related in whole or in part to baptism.

- *Ecclesiology and Ethics* (1969), Report
- *The Eucharistic Liturgy of Lima* (1982), Liturgical Text
- *Baptism, Eucharist and Ministry (Faith and Order Paper, no. 111)* (1982), Study Document
- *Message from the Fifth World Conference on Faith and Order* (1993), Message
- *Becoming a Christian: The Ecumenical Implications of Our Common Baptism* (1997), Report
- *Message from the Plenary Commission Meeting, Kuala Lumpur* (2004), Message
- *One Baptism: Towards Mutual Recognition* (2006), Study Document
- *Study Guide on Baptism, Eucharist and Ministry* (2009), Background and Context

For the most comprehensive summary of the WCC ecumenical attempts related to baptism, see its recent publication, edited by Thomas F. Best, *Baptism Today: Understanding, Practice, Ecumenical Implications* (2008).

Scholars not necessarily within the more formal ecumenical movement have also begun to direct their attention to baptism. For a helpful summary of academic interest in baptism, see the introductory chapters of Stanley E. Porter's and Anthony R. Cross's edited volumes on baptism.[1] Two very recent works written for two very different audiences provide examples of the current high quality of work related to baptism. Everett Ferguson's *Baptism in the Early Church: History, Theology, and Liturgy in the First Five Centuries* (2009) is a mammoth work that explores the antecedents to Christian baptism, as well as baptism in the New Testament, Church Fathers, and church history into the fifth century. No serious scholar of baptism can ignore this work. Martin Marty's *Baptism: A User's Guide* (2008) is an example of writing for the other end of the spectrum. This easy-to-read guide from an iconic scholar in the discipline of Christian history is accessible and ecumenical. It is meant to deepen one's baptismal faith and understanding, no matter where one is on the spectrum of baptismal theology. In both cases, the works are fresh attempts to understand a practice that (almost) all Christian communions perform.

So why another publication on baptism? In this book we have sought to bring together three Christian traditions that have not usually been brought together under one roof: Catholic, Protestant, and Orthodox.[2] Even now books still focus on the differences just between the varieties of Protestant views.[3] Our vision is much larger, for we desire to see the widest possible dialogue regarding this vital practice. Consequently, we have invited authors from a number of Protestant traditions, as well as one from Roman Catholicism and one from Orthodoxy. This broader perspective will, we hope, provide a grander vision of the diversity of the church, as well as a deeper sense of the differences that divide (and the similarities that unite). The inclusion of Orthodoxy is especially important due to the growing presence of Orthodox churches in the West. The Western (Catholic and Protestant) ignorance of this ancient church, and the Orthodox ignorance of the Western traditions, requires a move towards genuine understanding rather than blanket denunciations or characterizations of the "other."

---

1. Porter and Cross, "Recent Debate," 33–39; Porter and Cross, "Ongoing Debate," 1–6.

2. A recent book sponsored by the World Council of Churches does bring these three together. See Best, *Baptism Today*.

3. For instance, see Wright, *Baptism*; Armstrong, *Four Views*. To be fair to Wright, we must note that his book focuses on the most common options among evangelical Protestants.

The emphasis on historical development is a distinct contribution of this volume, for often denominations state their position without any context (as if theological positions were timeless and arrived directly from heaven). Consequently, we wanted to make sure that each position that was articulated provided the context for its contemporary doctrinal statements.

This book has also been written with the changing times in mind. As countless commentators have noted, the church in the West is experiencing dramatic paradigm shifts related to attendance and establishment. What does infant baptism mean in an increasingly post-Christian culture? How does the demise of Christendom impact baptismal theology and practices?[4] What does it mean when increasing numbers of Christians declare that denominational identity (including views of baptism) does not impact their choice of what church to attend? How do seminaries train ministers when they no longer have a fairly homogenous student body training for a particular denomination? This book will not cut through this Gordian Knot of problems, but it will, we believe, provide a helpful forum for a variety of Christian positions to be presented and defended so that Christians can at least operate out of understanding rather than ignorance.

All contributors in this volume write about their own traditions, and a number write not just as academics but as ordained leaders in their churches. We believe that this is an important component of the project, for we wanted people to be both passionate and knowledgeable about their position—not something easily attained when writing about someone else's tradition. The insider's perspective that each author brings allows a passionate presentation of each perspective, but also a committed defense of the same.

The goal of this ecumenical enterprise is not to pretend that differences do not exist, nor to force an anemic "lowest common denominator" unity. Nor do we expect an easy or quick resolution to the problem of differences (as if just more education would solve all problems in the church). As the following chapters indicate, the differences appear impossibly intractable (e.g., infant or adult? immersion or affusion? necessary or not? sign? symbol? sacrament?).[5] What we hope for as educators and

---

4. Wright, "Recovering Baptism," 51–66.

5. As David Wright notes, such differences raise troubling questions about the perspicuity of Scripture. See Wright, "Evangelical Diversity."

church leaders is that readers will at least begin to understand the differences that so divide the church. We also hope that such understanding will nudge us just a bit closer together as baptized followers of Jesus Christ. The gracious spirit of each contributor to this volume indicates that it is possible.

As editors we would like to thank the contributors for their willingness to engage in a project that has taken far too long to complete. Their patience, expertise, and passion for the subject has been greatly appreciated. Lois Dow at McMaster Divinity College Press and the various editors at Wipf and Stock need to be commended for their assistance and professionalism. Jamie Robertson's assistance in the process has also been appreciated. Finally, our families need to be thanked, for they are the ones who often suffered through our distraction and fascination with this project.

1

Baptism in Orthodox Christianity

IRENAEUS M. C. STEENBERG

F ROM THE EARLIEST DAYS of the church, something unique has been understood to take place in the mystery of baptism. While in its form it is clearly a thing "outward"—submerging the body beneath water, speaking certain words—it has been understood from the very first to effect an inner mystery. It is here that a person is "born again," and comes, in St. Paul's words, to "put on Christ." There is an exterior washing, yet an interior forgiveness of sins (Acts 2:38; 22:16). The human creature is drawn up into the life of the Trinity, born to new life and a fullness of grace. As the priest prays in the Orthodox baptismal rite, the Lord "grants forgiveness of sins to this Thy servant, bestowing on him a life of regeneration."[1]

In the Orthodox Church, baptism ranks among those sacraments—known in Orthodoxy as Mysteries—in which all the faithful participate. While not all will marry, not all will be ordained, all Orthodox Christians are baptized. The Christian life is a baptized life: the sacrament stands right at its heart, both its beginning and its constant center. So infants, even babies, are baptized; so converts are baptized or have baptism perfected and completed by "economy" on their reception; so baptism forms an ongoing part of the spiritual life of every Orthodox person.

How is this so? What is bound up in the Orthodox understanding of baptism that gives it this centrality and significance? The present chapter will explore the question from a series of perspectives on

---

1. From the priest's prayer at the ablution.

baptism itself, and on its place in Orthodox life, keeping in mind throughout a certain pastoral emphasis, rather than engaging in a purely academic discussion.

First, we must look at the historical testimony to the practice of baptism, and the relevance of that history to its understanding and practice today. Second, the theological perception of baptism in Orthodoxy must be examined; namely, its vision of baptism as entry, as well as the joining of the human person to the life, suffering, death, and resurrection of the Lord, and thus its connection to the Orthodox vision of deification. Finally, we will turn to a series of directly pastoral issues involved in Orthodox baptism today, emerging from its theological and ecclesiological conceptions of the sacrament's nature and place in the church.

BAPTISM IN HISTORY: ANCIENT TESTIMONY AND ITS RELEVANCE

When it comes to a pastoral consideration of the historical testimony of baptismal practice, a few elements are of critical importance. There are, of course, myriad others relevant to liturgical historians and theologians—the advent of the rites of baptism with their shape and development, baptismal creeds, the relationship to other sacraments—but the historical testimony of baptismal practice has practical, pastoral relevance for our purposes in primarily three areas.

First is the centrality of baptism to the Christian life. That baptism is a critical foundation of the Christian faith, right at its heart and not a peripheral or secondary concern, is evidenced for Orthodox by the overwhelming weight of historical testimony. The first that the Judean public sees of the incarnate Son is his baptism in the Jordan (Matt 3:13–17; Mark 1:9–13; Luke 3:21–22; John 1:29–34); the charge he gives his apostles at his ascension is to baptize all nations (Matt 28:18–20); the evangelical mission of those apostles is clearly of conversion through baptism (Acts 2:40, 41). From its earliest days, the acts of becoming and being Christian are demarcated by this baptismal experience, which the apostles themselves link both to Christ's baptism and exhortation, as well as to the indwelling of the Holy Spirit (Acts 10:44–48). As such, this historical documentation also provides a picture of precisely what baptism is: the immersion of the person in water, three times, tied together with the reception of the Spirit (in the Acts, the coming of the Spirit at times precedes the baptism in water, at times follows it; more to say on this in due course).

The testimony of the first-generation church is followed by that of the post-apostolic era, where numerous witnesses to the central role of baptism in Christian life, thought, and practice are encountered. It is emphasized in Irenaeus, Hippolytus, Tertullian, and others in the second century; and there are documents showing its role as so central that they accommodate circumstances in which full immersion in water (taken as the norm in all early documents) is not possible—specifying that if "living" water (i.e., running water, as in a river or stream) is not available, other water may be used; and where no water sufficient for immersion is available, baptism by pouring water over the body may serve as an irregular, yet acceptable, solution.[2] By the mid-second and third centuries there were dedicated tracts on the nature of baptism, and by the fourth, full pre- and post-baptismal catechetical programs, which are still extant, demonstrating a rich culture surrounding this cardinal sacrament of initiation.[3]

The purpose here cannot be to trace out the full testimony to baptismal practice in the early church or in later phases of its life; rather, it is to demonstrate and become aware—as is key for Orthodox Christian self-understanding—that baptism as a foundational act of Christian life, practiced as three-fold immersion tied in to the receipt of the Holy Spirit, is integral to Christianity from the very first. The voice of history places baptism at the heart of Christianity. To be Christian is to be baptized—to have a portion in the baptismal life of the Father's only Son; to be a partaker of his Spirit. This is history with a practical message, for Christianity in our day, if it is to remain the Christianity of the apostles and the church founded by the incarnate Lord (and Orthodox ecclesiology is marked out by its conscious continuity with the life and practice of the church from all ages), must retain this centrality foundational from the first.

Second, the practice is the baptism of people of all ages. Tied to the observation of the centrality of baptism in various historical contexts is the testimony to precisely *who* is baptized, and when. It is clear from the Scriptures that all ages were baptized—the old as well as the young—and this is a pattern that is also seen across the historical witness. The apostles baptized whole families, which would clearly include children (Acts 11:14; 16:15, 31; 1 Cor 1:16), and there are other witnesses to the baptism

---

2. This is spelled out clearly in the *Didache* 7.
3. Such as that of Cyril of Jerusalem, which we shall discuss at length below.

of children and infants in the early, as well as later, church.[4] In the great baptismal instructions of the fourth and fifth centuries, it is clear that there are a great number of adult converts who will be baptized; but it is equally clear that they will bear children with them into the baptismal waters. Similarly, there exist various conciliar statements from local and broader church councils that take as a given the fact of infant baptism and offer direction on its implementation.[5]

For Orthodox, such historical testimony is the precedent for the ongoing practice of baptism of all ages—including newborn infants. While debates in other historical and ecclesiastical contexts might question the legitimacy of the practice of infant baptism, at least partially on grounds that baptism might be taken as an intellectual assent of will and thus cannot apply to infants, Orthodoxy has always maintained the practice of baptizing infants and children. This is first and foremost for theological reasons (which we shall address below); but, as the historical testimony of the earliest church clearly shows, is also the retained practice of apostolic and early Christianity.

Third, there is the interconnectedness of baptism to the full liturgical worship of the church. A final area in which the historical testimony to baptism and the development of the rite within the church has practical, pastoral significance today is in the interconnectedness of the baptismal sacrament to the fuller liturgical life of the church—and in particular, to the eucharistic mystery of liturgical communion. Extant testimonies to baptismal practice in various historical periods speak with a fairly common voice on one point: baptism and Eucharist are intertwined. In

---

4. See Hippolytus, *The Apostolic Tradition* 21.16: "Baptize first the children, and if they can speak for themselves let them do so; otherwise let their parents or other relatives speak for them"; Cyprian of Carthage, *Letter* 64.2: "As to what pertains to the case of infants: you said that they ought not be baptized within the second or third day after their birth . . . in our council it seemed to us far otherwise, and no one agrees to the course you think should be taken"; John Chrysostom, *Baptismal Catecheses* 1.6.21: "You see how many are the benefits of baptism! . . . For this reason we baptize even infants, though they are not defiled by sins, so that there may be given to them holiness, righteousness, adoption, inheritance, brotherhood with Christ, and that they may be His members"; and many others.

5. See the Council of Carthage V (401), canon 72: "It seemed good that whenever there were not found reliable witnesses who could testify that without any doubt that they [abandoned children] were baptized, and when the children themselves were not, on account of their tender age, able to answer concerning the giving of the sacraments to them, all such children should be baptized without scruple, lest a hesitation should deprive them of the cleansing of the sacraments."

the great baptismal catechetical writings, it is the preamble for receipt of Holy Communion, and even today baptism remains that sacrament by which one enters into the full liturgical life of the church in which the other sacraments may also be partaken of, first and foremost among these (normally received immediately after baptism), the Eucharist. In theological debates throughout history, questions arose over whether un- or improperly-baptized clerics could administer the authentic Eucharist (this was at the heart of the Donatist schism); even the architecture of early Christian temples and places of worship emphasized the interconnectedness of baptism and Eucharist—so the earliest known example of deliberately Christian architecture, the Christian house at Dura-Europos (early third century), demonstrates a processional order of worship that linked baptism, catechesis, and Eucharist inextricably in the very shape of the building itself.[6] There is thus a significant emphasis, not simply on baptism proper, but on its liturgical nature (i.e., it is a rite; it has clear shape, form, ritual), as well as its deliberate, emphatic interconnectedness to other liturgical mysteries within the Christian community.

This, together with the other historical examples discussed above, paints—in Orthodox understanding—a clear portrait of the ecclesial, sacramental, liturgical nature of baptism as an integral part of church life from the first days of Christianity. The practice of baptism today is thus understood as an act of continuity with Christians of every generation, from Christ himself. Neither its centrality, nor its shape and form, are understood to be innovations or matters of any legitimate variance. Baptism, both in the *fact* of its practice and in the *manner* of its practice, is seen in terms of continuity with the church's apostolic foundations.

MOVING INTO THEOLOGY: BAPTISM AS ENTRY

Thus far the historical precedent has been established. Yet one does not baptize, much less get baptized, for reasons of history. What history offers is testimony to the fact that, in baptism, one *enters into the Christian life* in the manner that Christians have always done so. It is the entry itself that is the mystery grounding the Mystery.

What does it mean to call baptism an "entry"? To answer this, one must first recognize a central ecclesiastical vision of Orthodoxy:

---

6. For a helpful, brief overview of the Christian house at Dura-Europos and its importance in revealing early liturgical form, see Doig, *Liturgy*, 10–17.

Christianity is fundamentally what St. John of Kronstadt (1829–1908) called "the life in Christ." That is, Christianity is not, at its heart, a collection of dogmas, of practices, of ideas or confessions: it is a *life*, and more particularly it is *Christ's life*, into which the faithful are joined and have their share. Christians are those who live their lives "in Christ," as participants in his life of self-sacrificial glory.

To "enter" Christianity is, therefore, to take up a part in this life of the true and risen Lord; to cast off the "old man" and be grafted into the new (Eph 2:14–16). The "entry" is into the life, death, and resurrection of the Son. The context *out of which* the person moves is the fallen, broken world of transgression and sin; and one moves from this, not simply into something good or better, but *into the very life of the obedient and loving Redeemer*.

Baptism, as entry, is the mystery by which this movement into the life of Christ is made a reality in the human creature. We see this exposed in the moving testimony of St. Nicholas Cabasilas, a fourteenth-century layman who penned some of the church's most important documents of liturgical reflection:

> In the sacred Mysteries, then, we depict His burial and proclaim His death. By them we are begotten and formed and wondrously united to the Savior, for they are the means by which, as St Paul says, "in Him we live, and move, and have our being" (Acts 17:28). Baptism confers being and, in short, existence according to Christ. It receives us when we are dead and corrupted and first leads us into life. The anointing with chrism perfects him who has received [new] birth by infusing into him the energy that befits such a life. The holy Eucharist preserves and continues this life and health, since the Bread of Life enables us to preserve that which has been acquired and to continue in life. It is therefore by this Bread that we live and by the chrism that we are moved, once we have received being from the baptismal washing. *In this way we live in God.*[7]

Nicholas here refers to chrismation as well as baptism: the rite of anointing with holy oil (*chrism*) as the seal of the Holy Spirit, which the Orthodox Church—again in continuity with ancient historical precedent[8]—practices together with baptism itself. In baptism and chris-

---

7. Cabasilas, *Life in Christ* 1.6 (emphasis mine).

8. On the gift of the Spirit connected with baptism, see Acts 19:5, 6; cf. 1 John 2:20. On chrismation more clearly defined as the rite of anointing for the sealing

mation, the human person is united to Christ's life by the Spirit. The creature is "wondrously united to the Savior" and the sacrament "leads us into life." It is significant to note Nicholas's emphasis on the change in life that thus occurs: the Christian "receives being" from the baptismal washing. Clearly, he has already had a kind of being prior to the baptismal rite (he was born, he has a body, etc.); but Christian life is *being in Christ*, and so one's true being, one's true life, begins in this divine entry into the life of the Lord.

This is the new life that comes from the new birth, or regeneration, of baptism. We see it emphasized in the prayer offered by the priest at the ablution (the wiping away of the holy chrism at the end of the joint baptism-chrismation rite):

> Thou that through holy baptism hast granted forgiveness of sins to this Thy servant, bestowing on him (her) a life of regeneration: do Thou Thyself, Sovereign Master and Lord, be pleased that the Light of Thy countenance evermore shine in his (her) heart; maintain the shield of his (her) faith against the plotting of enemies; preserve in him (her) the garment of incorruption, which he (she) has put on undefiled and unstained; preserve in him (her) the seal of Thy grace, being gracious unto us, and unto him (her) according to the multitude of Thy compassions, for glorified and blessed is Thine all-honorable and majestic Name: of Father, and of Son, and of Holy Spirit, both now and ever, and to the ages of ages.[9]

The newly-baptized have been granted "a life of regeneration"; they have received new light in their hearts (for their hearts have been drawn into Christ, "the Giver of Light"), and they have been clothed in "the garment of incorruption." In short, they have been taken up into Christ's life, and so receive the blessings of his person. This is why baptism is understood as so foundational a sacrament to Christianity, and why (as we have seen) it has been practiced as such from the apostolic period onward. In the words of St. Gregory of Nyssa (ca. 335–ca. 394), "baptism, then, is a purification from sins, a remission of trespasses, *a cause of renovation and regeneration*."[10] It is this mystery that affects the entry

---

with this Spirit, celebrated together with baptism, see Cyril of Jerusalem, *Mystagogic Catecheses* 3.

9. Priest's prayer at the ablution.
10. Gregory of Nyssa, *Oration*, 519 (Emphasis mine).

of the creature into the life of its Creator. All of Christian life is, in clear terms, the ongoing manifestation of this baptismal life; and so baptism is the foundation of all Christian acts—of love, of sacrifice, of prayer—for in baptism one is raised to participate in *Christ's* love, *Christ's* sacrifice, *Christ's* prayer, since in baptism the Lord "sanctifies the first-fruits of every action."[11]

This is not to say that baptism causes a kind of "magical" transformation into a fully Christ-like being. Baptism is an entry, not a conclusion. Human freedom is not lost in baptism; rather, it is perfected and healed, so that it has the power not simply to choose sin, but also to choose the right. This is stressed by the tenth/eleventh-century monk, St. Symeon the New Theologian:

> Baptism does not take away our free will or freedom of choice, but gives us the freedom no longer to be tyrannized by the devil unless we choose to be. After baptism it is in our power either to persist willingly in the practice of the commandments of Christ, into whom we were baptized, and to advance in the path of His ordinances, or to deviate from this straight way and to fall again into the hands of our enemy, the devil.[12]

What is experienced in baptism, then, is the entry into the full life of Christ—a life that brings the freedom "no longer to be tyrannized by the devil," but that offers this freedom precisely as a new possibility, not a forced or foregone conclusion. In baptism, the life in Christ is made available to humanity. People are called into the Son's life by the Spirit, with the aim of drawing them to the Father,[13] and have the doors to this new life fully opened to them. They are drawn up, drawn in, to the life of God. Again in the words of St. Gregory, reflecting on Jesus' baptism by John as a paradigm of all baptismal life: "Today He is baptized by John that He might cleanse him who was defiled, that He might bring the

---

11. Ibid.

12. Palmer, *Philokalia*, 48.

13. One is reminded of this intently Trinitarian emphasis in numerous ways: the three-fold plunging in the waters; baptism in the threefold Name; baptism itself as an imitation of Christ's baptism in Jordan, in which the Father's voice was heard and the Spirit seen. As Augustine of Hippo remarked in his second sermon on the New Testament (§1): "We behold and see as it were in a divine spectacle exhibited to us, the notice of our God in Trinity, conveyed to us at the river Jordan."

Spirit from above and exalt man to heaven, that he who had fallen might be raised up and he who had cast him down might be put to shame."[14]

BAPTISM, DEATH, AND DEIFICATION—
BEING JOINED TO THE SUFFERING CHRIST

If baptism is thus an entry into the life in Christ, which is the very substance of Christian existence and the full experience of the church, one must ask just what this life truly is. To what is a person joined, in being drawn into the life of the Lord?

First, the Orthodox understand baptism to effect the sacramental participation by the human person in the *death* of the Lord. This is manifest in the words of St. Paul: "Know you not, that so many of us as were baptized into Jesus Christ were baptized into His death? Therefore we are buried with Him by baptism into death: that like as Christ was raised up from the dead by the glory of the Father, even so we also should walk in newness of life" (Rom 6:3, 4). The very core of baptism is the plunging beneath the waters—an act symbolic of death, of burial, and hence its attractiveness to various groups and individuals in the ancient world (such as St. John the Forerunner) as an icon of repentance. One must die to the old self, the self of sin and transgression, in order to be born anew; and the death-bearing symbol of the plunging is interconnected precisely with the resurrectional symbol of being taken up from beneath the water, brought out of death into life (this rich symbolism is, together with historical precedent, part of the reason why Orthodox retain the practice of baptism by full immersion, rather than sprinkling: sprinkling is rather more an icon of anointing, and one might question how far it serves as a vivid symbol of death and resurrection).

It is in the mystical identity of symbol and reality, above all as regards this vision of death and re-birth in the resurrectional Christ, that the true depth of baptism as understood in an Orthodox context begins to be seen. It was as plain to the Church Fathers as it is to us today that one does not truly die in baptism, nor is one truly resurrected. One is drawn into a sacramental participation with the acts of the passion and resurrection, but one is not physically there. Yet, the nature of baptism as a divine mystery in which the Holy Spirit *draws one into a reality beyond the physical experience of the moment*, causes each baptism to be a true

---

14. Gregory of Nyssa, *Oration*, 518.

miracle: one dies "in symbol," yet by the Spirit one "truly" dies. One is drawn out of death "in an image," yet because the Spirit affects the heart even as water affects the flesh, one is "truly" joined to Christ's resurrection. Thus there is a genuine, mystical death and re-birth in baptism—one truly dies with the Lord, and truly rises with him.

For a vivid picture of this symbolism as reality, we need look no further than the mid-fourth-century catechetical lectures of St. Cyril of Jerusalem (ca. 313–386), which constitute one of our only complete sets of extant pre- and post-baptismal orations from the early church. Cyril conveys to his hearers the full reality of what they experience in baptism, and draws particular attention to all the symbolic connections with the sacrificial Christ. So, for example, he notes to those who have recently been baptized:

> As soon, then, as you entered [the baptismal waters], you put off your tunic; and this was an image of putting off the old man with his deeds (cf. Colossians 3:9). Having stripped yourselves, you were naked—in this also imitating Christ, who was stripped naked on the Cross, and by His nakedness put off from Himself the principalities and powers, and openly triumphed over them on the tree.... O wondrous thing! Ye were naked in the sight of all, and were not ashamed; for truly ye bore the likeness of the first-formed Adam, who was naked in the garden, and was not ashamed.[15]

Note Cyril's emphasis on "imitating Christ." Here he refers not simply to the actual act of baptism itself (that is, the threefold plunging beneath the waters, followed by chrismation with oil, which is an imitation of the Trinitarian encounter and descent of the Spirit at the Jordan), but even to the comport of the whole rite: the apparel and removal of apparel, etc. Every motion of the baptized is part of the symbolic life of the Son, which is joined into the symbolism of all humanity (hence the connection to Adam in Paradise).

The symbolism reaches its zenith at the moment of baptism proper. Continuing his discourse to the newly-baptized, Cyril remarks:

> After these things, you were led to the holy pool of divine baptism, as Christ was carried from the Cross to the sepulcher which is before our eyes. And each of you was asked whether he believed in the name of the Father, and of the Son, and of the Holy

---

15. Cyril of Jerusalem, *Mystagogic Catechesis* 20.2.

> Spirit, and you made that saving confession, and descended three times into the water, and ascended again; here also hinting by a symbol at the three-day burial of Christ. For as our Savior passed three days and three nights in the heart of the earth, so you also in your first ascent out of the water, represented the first day of Christ in the earth, and by your descent, the night.... And at the selfsame moment ye were both dying and being born; and that water of salvation was at once your grave and your mother. And what Solomon spoke of others will suit you also; for he said, in that case, "There is a time to bear and a time to die" (Eccl 3:2); but to you, in the reverse order, there was a time to die and a time to be born; and one and the same time effected both of these, and your birth went hand in hand with your death.[16]

The symbolism is here remarkably robust. One does not simply walk to the pool of baptism: one is led there by the clergy, as Christ was led to the Cross and carried to the sepulcher (Cyril mentions this sepulcher being "before our eyes" since he is preaching in Jerusalem at the site of Golgotha). One confesses thrice, is plunged in the waters thrice, as a symbol of the three-day burial of the Lord. But Cyril is also speaking beyond symbolism merely as representation or re-enactment: symbol here is truly participatory, mystical. "At the selfsame moment ye were both dying and being born"—the language here is not representational, but participatory. The death and resurrection of Christ are symbolized, but in that symbol, one *authentically dies*, is *authentically born anew*. This is summarized in Cyril's exclamation that follows:

> O strange and inconceivable thing! We did not really die, we were not really buried, we were not really crucified and raised again; *but our imitation was in a figure, and our salvation in reality*. Christ was actually crucified, and actually buried, and truly rose again; and all these things He has freely bestowed upon us, that we, sharing His sufferings by imitation, might gain *salvation in reality*. O surpassing loving-kindness! Christ received nails in His undefiled hands and feet, and suffered anguish; while on me without pain or toil by the fellowship of His suffering He freely bestows salvation.[17]

---

16. Ibid., 2.4.

17. Ibid., 2.5 (emphasis added). Cf. Gregory of Nyssa, *Oration*, 520: "And we, in receiving baptism in imitation of our Lord and Teacher and Guide, are not indeed buried in the earth (for this is the shelter of the body that is entirely dead, covering the infirmity and decay of our nature), but coming to the element akin to the earth, namely, to water, we conceal ourselves in that as the Savior did in the earth."

Here we see an expression of the very heart of baptism: in the sacramental rite, one is truly united to the sacrificial life of the Lord—that life met in His death and perfected in His rising from the grave. While the baptismal act may be a symbol, the ancient Christian expression (and the view retained in Orthodoxy) is that symbol and reality are united in sacramental experience. One dies and is resurrected "in figure," but this death and resurrection is made, in the sacrament, "salvation in reality."

This perception of the participatory mystery of baptism is a key dimension of Orthodox thought. St. Gregory the Theologian, bishop of Nazianzus (330–ca. 389), reflected on it in simple yet powerful statements: "Christ is baptized . . . ; let us then be buried with Christ by baptism, that we may also rise with Him; let us descend with Him, that we may also be exalted with Him; let us ascend with Him that we may also be glorified together."[18] And we see it more fully drawn out in one of the great baptismal homilies of St. John Chrysostom (ca. 347–407):

> Are we only dying with the Master and are we only sharing in His sadness? Most of all, let me say that sharing the Master's death is no sadness. Only wait a little and you shall see yourself sharing in His benefits. "For if we have died with Him," says St Paul, "we believe that we shall also live together with Him" (Rom 6:8). For in baptism there are both burial and resurrection together at the same time. He who is baptized puts off the old man, takes the new and rises up, "just as Christ has arisen through the glory of the Father" (Rom 6:4). Do you see how, again, St Paul calls baptism a resurrection?[19]

In all these examples (and they are but a few of what could be cited), we see a consistent theme common to the Orthodox understanding of baptism: the human person, entering into the life of Christ, is mystically joined to his life, death, resurrection and, ultimately, his glory. This is, of course, always to be seen in the context of the preservation of human freedom we have already identified above; but there is, in the baptized life, the genuine possibility of participation in the Lord's incarnate self-sacrifice and offering of love. This understanding supports, again, the practice of baptizing not only assenting adults, but even children and infants; for baptism is not seen primarily in terms of intellectual affirmation or confession (though, when one *is* of adequate age, it cannot be

---

18. Gregory of Nazianzus, *Baptism*, 9.
19. John Chrysostom, *Instructions* 10.11.

separated from such confession), but in terms of this union of life in the sacrificial Christ. This life is offered freely to all, of every age, by the church, in imitation of Christ who offered his salvation to even the little children.[20]

The same confession of such union and participation in Christ, connects baptism to—or rather, sets it as the foundation of—the Orthodox doctrine of "deification," or "becoming divine." The goal of human life, of Christian life, is to be joined fully to the life of God in the eternal kingdom. This life has been offered, in Christ, into the very fabric of humanity: Christ took flesh, uniting human and divine within the living person. In the famous words of St. Athanasius of Alexandria (ca. 293–373), God "assumed humanity that we might become God"[21]—not "God" in the sense of any deity proper (there is only one God, and none other like him; Deut 4:35), but in the sense of genuine adoption into Christ, becoming sons and daughters of the Father and thus recipients of his divine love and being. Deification is, otherwise described, the process of becoming conformed to Christ, of *living Christ's life*, such that one can proclaim authentically with St. Paul, "It is no longer I who live, but Christ lives in me" (Gal 2:20).

In this, one is conformed to Christ chiefly by being united to his death and resurrection—the very things symbolized and made real in baptism. One cannot be "Christ-like" simply by being kind, by being loving, by being pious; genuine Christianity must involve imitating Christ *in his suffering*, his *self-offering*, his obedience "even unto death" (Phil 2:8). Only then can one be said truly to have followed Christ into the grave as co-sufferer, that, lying there, one may also be raised by him into new and abiding life. Thus baptism offers to the Christian a challenging hope: *it presents him or her with the opportunity to suffer and to die*. It does not merely offer the forgiveness of sins, nor is it simply an image of renewal. More than this, it offers the possibility to be united to Christ in his Passion; to join him at the Cross, and so at the empty tomb.

St. Cyril concludes his discussion of baptism in the following words:

> Let no one then suppose that baptism is merely the grace of remission of sins, or further, that of adoption, as John's was a baptism conferring only remission of sins. For we know full well

20. Matt 18:3; 19:14; Luke 18:16.
21. Athanasius, *Incarnation*, 54.

that, even as it purges our sins and ministers to us the gift of the Holy Spirit, so also it is *the counterpart of the sufferings of Christ*. For this cause Paul just now cried aloud and said, "Or are you ignorant that all we who were baptized into Christ Jesus, were baptized into His death?" (Rom 6:3). We were buried therefore with Him by *baptism into His death*. These words he spoke to some who were disposed to think that baptism ministers to us the remission of sins and adoption, but has not further the fellowship also, by representation, of Christ's true sufferings.[22]

In Orthodoxy, baptism is this generous self-offering of the Lord, who calls his creature into his own life of death and resurrection. One is symbolically, mystically, united to death, "buried" in the water as Christ was buried in the earth. A life united to his sacrifice is begun: this will not be the only time the Christian person is overwhelmed by his or her sin; it will not, by far, be her longest or hardest struggle. But as the person's body is lifted up from the waters, the salvific message of this baptismal death is physically, visibly proclaimed: it is only those who have died, who are able to rise.

PASTORAL ISSUES

Thus far this chapter has traced out the key historical and theological perspectives on baptism that are central to its place in Orthodox Christianity. What remains are the pastoral issues bound up in so significant a sacrament. If indeed baptism is understood to be both among the most ancient and abiding practices of the church, and if it is understood to effect so powerful a transformation and potential for new life in the one who is baptized, then its application is a critical dimension of Orthodox ecclesiastical and pastoral life.

Three key pastoral areas need to be addressed in this context. First, there is the Orthodox insistence upon a certain understanding of there being *one* baptism, and what this means in a modern ecclesiastical context. Second, and related to this, there is the question of baptism and re-baptism, and the whole issue of how baptism relates to conversion from other traditions. Third, there is the question of how baptism ought to relate to catechesis amongst those who are received into the Church of an adult age, either from another tradition or religion, or from none at all.

---

22. Cyril of Jerusalem, *Mystagogic Catechesis* 2.6 (Emphasis mine).

The Creed of Nicaea-Constantinople, the cardinal symbol of faith in the Orthodox Church, states clearly and unequivocally: "I believe in *one baptism* for the remission of sins." When this Creed was formulated, debated, and re-formulated in the fourth century, this was already a loaded statement. Even in that early period of Christian history, there were already groups offering "another baptism," baptizing in different ways, with different formulae and aims, to different ends. The Creed's insistent language therefore has always had a certain practical focus (i.e., it spells out one baptism for one church), but it is also theological. If baptism is truly the joining of the person to the life of the Holy Trinity, and if there is truly one God, Father, Son and Spirit, then there can be only one baptism as there is only one life to which the human creature is joined—that of the one Son. "Other" baptisms would be either demonstrative memorials (i.e., acts that memorialize this true Son) but do not in fact effect true union and participation in this same Son (else they would be identical to the "one baptism" and not something "other"); or, if they intended a genuine participation, entry, and union, would, as "other" to the one baptism into the one Son, ultimately be uniting the person to another confession of God.

The confession that there is "one baptism" is thus part of the church's confession of who God is, and how the human person is to be related to him (which is, after all, why mention of baptism finds its way into the Creed in the first place: it is part-and-parcel of the confession of God, of theology). In the early history of the church, when people were by and large more ready to see variation in the faith as error and heresy, this confession was deliberately exclusive. *This* is the one baptism; others are no baptism at all. However, this was in a period when divisions *within* the church were principally accepted in terms of local practice and varying expressions. The idea that conflicting *theologies* could be embraced by varying groups who are altogether called Christians was a concept that simply did not fit. Thus even while there was variation in the ancient church across the Empire and world, the "one baptism" confessed in the Creed was understood to be the uniform theological act of the undivided, indivisible one church (also confessed in that Creed).

While it may be the case that in the multi-religious world of today, some would accept a change here—namely, that "church" is to be understood not as one group or another with the right theology and all others as deviant from this and in error, but instead as the overarching confession of Christ exemplified in various different groups and theologies—the Orthodox Church does not. Its ongoing confession of "one baptism" is linked to its ongoing confession of "one church," and, rather like those who debated and crafted the Creed, still sees deviation from the teachings of this one church (and thus, deviations from its one baptism) as errors, rather than alternatives. As in the early days, there are practical aspects to this ongoing insistence; but at its heart the matter remains theological. Insistence that there can be but *one* church and hence *one* baptism remains bound up in the theological confession of *one* Christ whose body the church is, and into whose life baptism unites the human creature. Deviation from the core of "one church, one baptism" is not perceived as problematic principally in terms of the rightness or wrongness of other groups *per se*, much less in terms of validity of sacramental practices in various bodies or attempts to define who and what is with grace and who is without it. Rather, it is perceived as problematic because it is understood as a direct challenge to the true unity of the one Christ.

Despite that qualification of perception, this has, of course, ramifications for the pastoral approach to Orthodox baptism in a religious world that often does not share this view. While Orthodox scholars and pastors do and long will debate the specific manners in which this position is to be explained and understood, the basic position of the Church has always been that *her baptism* is that "one baptism" of the Creed, the one baptism that authentically joins the human person to the self-sacrificing Christ. Needless to say, this hardly fits with what is the common ecumenical mindset of many in the twentieth and now twenty-first century; but for Orthodoxy, this confession is part-and-parcel with the authentic confession of God as Trinity, given that baptism is a theological mystery of participation rather than simply a "rite of initiation."

What are the pastoral ramifications of this insistence on "one baptism"? In the first instance, it sets the contours by which Orthodoxy will and must engage in the broader religious and Christian milieu of the modern world. The question of the Orthodox Church's relationship to the ecumenical discussions of the present age is hotly contested within the Orthodox community itself, and is not an issue that I wish to broach at any length in this study. It is sufficient to note that the very debate has its core here, in the ancient confession of "one baptism," perceived not simply as the territorial claims of one community over another, but as intimately, inextricably bound up in the theological vision of the church.

Orthodox theologians and scholars, if they are to be authentic to the tradition of their Church in broader-ranging discussions on such matters, must retain this theological grounding and trace out its implications for those discussions. At the more practical level of pastoral discussions, however, this confession needs to be the bedrock for understanding and conveying the Church's vision of baptism to those who seek it as catechumens. This, then, ties the issue of confessing "one baptism" with another pastoral issue that is its direct outgrowth; namely, the question of how one is to receive into the Orthodox Church those who convert from another Christian tradition.

Were all conversions into the Orthodox Church made by those who came from non-Christian backgrounds, the ancient practice of reception by baptism would hardly be controversial at all. However, such is not the case. Christianity is fragmented; and while Orthodox confess that the church is never divided, it is a sad reality of human sin that the "one church" hardly covers all those who call themselves Christians, and there are thousands of groups that bear the Christian name. What is one to do, then, when a person seeks to be received into the Orthodox Church, not from a non-Christian or non-religious background, but from another Christian tradition, and more particularly, from a tradition that practices baptism and in which the person has in fact been baptized? This is a pastoral issue of tremendous importance, as it is a situation that occurs with such regularity.

It is, first of all, important to note that this is not a new concern or question. Internal Christian divisions may be the result of human sin, but the antiquity of such sin meant that these arose even in the early church. Thus St. Basil the Great (330–379) writes in a letter concerning a group known as the Cathari:

> As to your enquiry about the Cathari, a statement has already been made, and you have properly reminded me that it is right to follow the custom obtaining in each region, because those, who at the time gave decision on these points, held different opinions concerning their baptism.... Thus they used the names of *heresies*, of *schisms*, and of *unlawful congregations*. By heresies they meant men who were altogether broken off and alienated in matters relating to the actual faith; by schisms men who had separated for some ecclesiastical reasons and questions capable of mutual solution; by unlawful congregations gatherings held by disorderly presbyters or bishops or by uninstructed laymen.

> As, for instance, if a man be convicted of crime, and prohibited from discharging ministerial functions, and then refuses to submit to the canons, but arrogates to himself episcopal and ministerial rights, and persons leave the Catholic Church and join him, this is unlawful assembly. To disagree with members of the Church about repentance, is schism. Instances of heresy are those of the Manicheans, of the Valentinians, of the Marcionites, and of these Pepuzenes; for with them there comes in at once their disagreement concerning the actual faith in God. *So it seemed good to the ancient authorities to reject the baptism of heretics altogether, but to admit that of schismatics, on the ground that they still belonged to the Church.*[23]

What is evident here is an awareness, not simply that there are different *kinds of divisions* within the Christian community—heresies, schisms, unlawful assemblies—but also that the differing nature of these divisions meant that the response to them, when their members came to the church seeking entry, was also to be different. Much as the black-and-white categories might appeal, St. Basil at least did not regard the matter as simply "one is in or one is out." Human sin fractures communion in more nuanced ways than that resulting in "heresy," which is a deliberate deviation from the one faith of the one church; "schism" which is a fracture of its concord and unity in love; and "unlawful assembly," which is the maintenance of its theological and unitive realities, but promulgation of discord and disorder in chiefly practical measures. When a person comes to the church from a fractured group, then, St. Basil insists that how he or she is to be received into the church must be grounded in the nature of the fracture. If it is a matter of coming from a group that has been marred by unlawful assembly, he suggests that the manner of reception is simply by confession of sin and repentance. The baptism received in such a group is still the one baptism of the one church, confessing the one Trinity, and so the person is disjoined from the fullness of the church only by the inappropriate nature of the assembly.

The case of clear-cut heresy is also straightforward for St. Basil: where it is clear that the group in question is heretical, that it denies the true faith and practices belief in a God differently understood, conceived, and known, then it cannot be conceived as the true church, and hence the baptism it has practiced is understood as no baptism. This is

---

23. Basil, *Epistle*, 188.1 (emphasis added).

how he sees the group called Pepuzeni (Montanists), and so writes, later in the same letter:

> What ground is there, then, for the acceptance of the baptism of men who baptize into the Father and the Son and Montanus or Priscilla? For those who have not been baptized into the names delivered to us have not been baptized at all.[24]

Such persons, when they come to the church for reception, are to be baptized. This, however, is not understood as a re-baptism (confession of "one baptism" inherently disallows the possibility of multiple baptisms), but as a *first* baptism, for—as St. Basil explicitly states—the rite practiced in heresy is no baptism at all.

The more challenging category is that in the middle, between simple unlawful assembly and the extreme of utter heresy: namely, schism. St. Basil acknowledges that certain groups have fallen into error, which goes beyond issues of administrative discipline and touches on matters of the faith, but which is not yet so extreme as the deliberate rejection of right belief and acceptance of false (heresy). This is, even for St. Basil, a grey area. Such error is found in degrees: it can become so extreme that, even if still not quite heresy, it nonetheless is divisive enough to warrant treatment of the same type (i.e., that those coming from such groups should be received by baptism); or it can be slight enough that such strictures ought not apply, and those who come to the church should be received, not by baptism, but in the following manner: "On every ground let it be enjoined that those who come to us from their baptism be anointed in the presence of the faithful, and only on these terms approach the mysteries [i.e., sacraments]."[25]

Here St. Basil affirms that, despite their schism, the baptism received by those in such schismatic groups remains the one baptism of the church; yet for the error that has been introduced, must be perfected through anointing (more on this in a moment). He is cautious throughout his discussion (and the letter from which we have been quoting, namely St. Basil's *Epistle* 188, is, in its entirety, essential reading on this issue): he would clearly prefer to receive some of these schismatics by baptism, and acknowledges that the line between schism and heresy is at times extremely hard to discern. Yet he retains the practice of reception

24. Ibid.
25. Ibid.

by other means where it may so be appropriate via *economia* (that is, a pastoral softening of the strictures of the canons where one in episcopal authority recognizes it is for the benefit and salvation of the faithful).

The "anointing in the presence of the faithful" to which St Basil refers, is understood by Orthodox as the mystery of chrismation. As we have already mentioned above, this rite is normally performed together with baptism as a single liturgical action when an infant is brought into the church, and indeed baptism-chrismation is largely conceived of as a single rite in the current liturgical forms used (as well as the ancient). Yet they remain two distinct sacraments: the entry into the life, death, and resurrection of Christ—and thus the church which is his body—in the waters of baptism; and the sealing with the Holy Spirit—the perfection and conclusion of union in the church—in chrismation. What is indicated in St. Basil, as elsewhere in the church's tradition, is that in the case of baptism in schism (but not heresy), the baptism itself is accepted and understood as the one true baptism of the one church, for the fracture of schism is made perfect and united fully into the undivided life of the church (the realm of the Spirit) through such chrismation. Therefore, a person received into the church from this category of division is received by chrismation, perfecting and completing the baptism received already through the church's one mystical body, but in a state of division through schism.

The practical, pastoral dimensions to this discussion and this history of practice are many, and there are ongoing debates within Orthodoxy on how such categories are to be conceived and applied in the modern world, which sees Christendom more divided than at any other point in its history. As ever, the line between schism and heresy remains hard to discern. Just how far does another tradition's confession have to differ from Orthodoxy's before it moves from schism to heresy, and thus reception is more appropriately effected by baptism than chrismation? Are these categories still applicable in the modern world?

Despite the complexities and confusions, there are some basic points that are worth raising and re-iterating in every age. First, the Orthodox Church maintains, as we have seen, a pastoral approach to the question of reception, which acknowledges degrees of division and separation and how they are to be responded to in the rapprochement of reception in conversion. If the categories may have shifted since St. Basil's day, the underlying theme of approach has not. Second, the Orthodox Church does not conceive of the variations in terms of validity and invalidity, but rather as part of the theological confession of the unity of the one church in the one Christ. Third, and perhaps most important in terms of pastoral practice, the tradition of the church has been one of *personal pastoral discernment*, rather than establishment of global norms for reception. For his part, St. Basil never says that everyone must be received by baptism or everyone by chrismation: the means of reception is based on discernment of one's state of union or division from the church. In modern-day Orthodoxy, various jurisdictions have attempted to make one form of reception or another the universal norm (either by, for example, insisting that all converts be baptized; or, conversely, that chrismation be the norm for all converts, unless one has never been baptized in another Trinitarian Christian tradition)—but such globalizing approaches can never reflect the authentic history of Orthodox practice.

A final pastoral issue relating to baptism is the manner in which it is to be related and connected to catechesis, or instruction in the faith. As already mentioned, the normal practice in Orthodoxy is to baptize infants some eight days after birth, so in such cases catechesis is hardly an issue (at least of the baptized; the parents and God-parents could often benefit from a period of renewed catechesis at this stage in their lives). Yet Christianity has always been a religion of mission, and thus a religion that invites conversion. When dealing with mature, adult persons coming into the Church, the interconnection of catechesis and baptism is a critical pastoral issue that ought to be considered carefully.

In the modern day, it is all too common to see the relationship in this manner: those desiring reception into the Church (whether by the full rite of baptism and chrismation, or by *economia* through chrismation alone, as determined by the bishop) are given a long period of education and instruction in the doctrines of the faith, its practices and life; and then, at the conclusion of this long period, are received through the sacrament. The catechesis often takes the form of parish classes for catechumens, inquirer's discussion groups, personal instruction by the priest, and particularly in the modern era, the reading of a great many books.

In the more antique tradition of the church, however, catechesis followed an almost exactly inverted practice. Full discussion about the details of the faith—of Eucharist, of dogma, of spirituality, etc.—was reserved until *after* the illumination of baptism, not before it. Catechesis was conceived as primarily an experiential practice: being exposed to the church in worship in gradual phases, in which instruction was offered as the explanation of observed experience. At the beginning of the catechumenate, only the opening moments of the services were experienced. Later, a fuller experience of the Liturgy was provided, up until the period of the expulsion of the catechumens prior to the Creed (since the Creed was not taught to catechumens until quite late in the catechumenate). Through this exposure, accompanied by pastoral guidance and direction, entrance into the church was first and foremost through encounter with the mystery of her worship. This worship would have baffled most non-Christians of the earlier period, feeling far more foreign than ever it possibly could to people today who convert from other Christian traditions; yet this remained the "way in." It is the mystery of worship that converts a heart; over-intellectualization most often proves a barrier and a hindrance. For this reason, the specifically educational phase of the catechumenate in the ancient church came rather late—often times just in the weeks of Great Lent, prior to baptism on Holy Saturday; or even in just the last weeks of Lent. The experiential practice of being exposed to worship was paramount; and that experience was crafted deliberately. It gradually moved toward, but did not include, experience of the Eucharistic celebration itself, since exposure to this prior to baptismal illumination risked transforming it into an intellectual observer-act.

When it did come, the educational aspect of catechesis was the capstone of exposure and experience, reserved until the final pre-baptismal stages; and then, it was succinct and brief, and did not include great detail about the interior mysteries (i.e., the sacramental doctrines of Eucharist, etc.). The only complete example of a full catechetical program from the early church that remains is that of St. Cyril of Jerusalem, which we have examined already above; and the eighteen orations that comprise it are often misread as constituting a lengthy catechetical program. In point of fact, these were delivered together, in fairly rapid succession, at the very end of Great Lent. They would have come after a long period of increasing exposure to the church through her worship (perhaps a year), and through increasing participation in her ascetical life (fasting, almsgiving, provided rules of prayer and reading); but the proper educational element was the *final stage* of preparation for baptism.[26] This educational

---

26. Cyril was, of course, aware that this normative pattern could be and was abused, and he has somewhat scolding words to offer those who appear for his catechetical talks

segment provided a brief overview of the central doctrines of the faith. There was brief summary of the central theological doctrines of God, humanity, sin, redemption, the incarnation; and a tremendous lot said about baptism itself, and the cleansing to be received in the Spirit. Rather little was said of the Eucharist. The Creed was provided: and at least officially, this would have been the first time that catechumens would have been given or heard the creed. It was understood not primarily as a dogmatic text, but an ascetical tool to prepare one for the Eucharist—still how the Nicaea-Constantinopolitan Creed is used liturgically to this day (which is why it comes after the dismissal of the catechumens, leading into the anaphora).[27] It was not understood chiefly as a teaching text, nor even a confessional text, but a mysterious entering into the faith found fully in the chalice. It was forbidden for the catechumens to write it down: it was to be committed to the heart, borne into their very souls as they moved to the waters of baptism, and from those waters to the chalice of Christ.

Finally, baptism formed the central point, not the endpoint, of catechesis. It was only *after* baptism that the central mysteries of the faith—Eucharist, fuller doctrine, Christology, asceticism, sanctification, deification—were taught, in post-baptismal lectures that often bore a title celebrating this aspect: *Mystagogics*. St. Cyril's example includes five lengthy post-baptismal mystagogic catechetical orations. It was at this stage, and not earlier, that the deep mysteries of the church were expounded: the Eucharist, since now it is a thing experienced rather than pondered, and that experience can be elucidated and reflected upon rather than speculated about in anticipation; sanctification, since now it is a thing of actual happenstance in the sacraments, and that mode of life can be considered from the inside rather than wondered at from the outside.

If too often today enquirers after the faith falter in their approach, it is at least in part because something of this right approach to catechesis has been lost. Efforts today regularly tend, as already noted, to go about things in precisely the opposite manner, to begin almost at the outset by teaching the great mysteries of the faith. Modern catechesis is a dramatically, profoundly, *educational/intellectual* experience. How different this

---

off the street, sometimes for reasons other than the desire borne of increasing liturgical familiarity; see *Procatechesis* 5.

27. Cyril's was another creed, the so-called "Jerusalem Creed."

is from the practice of the church's own history. Should one be at all surprised that so many find stumbling blocks in speculative problems with the faith and its practices? How could it be otherwise, given that the life in Christ is taught as if it is an educational field of study? The divine services, rather than being apportioned out in a manner that gradually draws one in and converts the heart, are laid bare from the outset. Catechumens are forced to witness the most sacred mysteries of the church, feeding on a sense of openness and welcoming that pervades the modern mindset, but which is in fact terribly unfair to the catechumen. What is there to do, when confronted suddenly, unpreparedly, with the full wonder and mystery of the Eucharist, except speculate wildly about its nature? What is there to do, when forced unpreparedly into the full expression of the church's liturgical faith and practice, except to ponder at its strangeness, worry over its foreignness, contemplate its oddities? Ought the church to consider those in the past who were given the great gift of a gradual exposure: encountering the services piece by piece, so that they might gradually sink into and convert the heart and mind, rather than overwhelm and challenge it?

CONCLUSION

As long as Christians have been following their Lord, they have been baptizing as he was baptized, and as he commanded them in love to do. What was, in the time of St. Paul, the mysterious, wonderful means by which one "puts on Christ" (Gal 3:27), remains so today, and in Orthodox Christianity baptism remains at the very heart of the life in Christ. In this mystery, life is transformed. The heart is illumined. The human creature is drawn up into the very life of its Creator. It is only appropriate to conclude with the words of St. John Chrysostom:

> In baptism are completed the articles of our covenant with God; burial and death, resurrection and life; and these take place all at once. For when we plunge our heads down in the water, the old man is buried in a tomb below, and wholly sunk for ever; then, as we raise them again, the new man rises in his place. As it is easy for us to dip and to lift our heads again, so it is easy for God to bury the old man, and to show forth the new. And this is done thrice, that you may learn that the power of the Father, and the Son, and the Holy Spirit fulfils all this. To show that what we say is no conjecture, hear Paul saying, "We were buried with Him

by baptism into death" (Rom 6:4); and again, "Our old man was crucified with Him" (Rom 6:6); and again, "We have been planted together in the likeness of His death" (Rom 6:5). And not only is baptism called a "cross," but the Cross is called baptism. "With the baptism," says Christ, "with which I am baptized, shall ye be baptized" (Mark 10:39); and "I have a baptism to be baptized with, which ye know not" (cf. Luke 12:50). For as we easily dip and lift our heads again, so He also easily died and rose again when He willed; or rather, much more easily, though He tarried the three days for the dispensation of a certain mystery.[28]

FURTHER READING

Basil the Great, *Epistle* 188.1.

Cyril of Jerusalem, *Mystagogic Catecheses* 2.2 (*Oration* 20.2).

Gregory of Nazianzus, *Homily 40, On Holy Baptism* 9.

John Chrysostom, *Baptismal Instructions* 10.11.

---

28. John Chrysostom, *Homily* 2.

2

Baptism in the Roman Catholic Church

Gerard Kelly

The practice of baptism in the Roman Catholic Church will be properly understood from a consideration of the liturgical texts and rites by which it is celebrated. Today Roman Catholics follow two rites of baptism, one for children and one for adults. Both rites were developed in the years immediately after the Second Vatican Council. Prior to this there was a single rite of baptism, which remained largely unchanged since the reforms after the Council of Trent and the publication of the *Rituale Romanum* in 1614. Each of the post-Second Vatican Council rites begins with a *Decree* that formally promulgates the new rite, authorizes its use throughout the world, and explains the rationale for its development. At the beginning of each rite is the General Introduction to Christian Initiation, which is followed by an Introduction proper to each rite. This is followed by the rite itself, consisting of the prayers, invitations, addresses, and declarations that form part of the rite, as well as details about the actions that complete the rite. Taken as a whole, these books provide the theological foundations for baptism in the Catholic Church and guide pastoral practice.

The revised rites mark a return to a more ancient practice of allowing the theology and ritual to inform each other and to develop in tandem. One feature of the period from the thirteenth century through to the seventeenth century (and thus to the practice until the mid-twentieth century) is that theology and liturgy became separated and developed independently of each other.¹ It will be central to the methodology of this essay that I follow the methodology of the current rites, and allow the rite itself to present the theology of baptism.

This study will begin with a description of the two revised rites. These documents lay the theological and the pastoral foundations for baptism in the Roman Catholic Church. Taking our lead from them we will then explore baptism under four headings: baptized into the Christian mystery, baptism and faith, baptized in the church, and living baptismally.

THE BAPTISMAL RITES

The Rite of Baptism for Children

The "Rite of Baptism for Children" (RBC) was published in Latin in 1969.² Translations into other languages were made on the basis of this "typical" edition.³ The "Decree" authorizing RBC indicated that the revision was made in order to comply with five requirements set out by the Second Vatican Council. The first two set out the guiding principle for revision and its major focus. First, the rite should be better adapted to the actual condition of children; second, and consequently, the role and responsibilities of parents and godparents should be more clearly expressed. The remaining three requirements addressed specific situations: where a large number were to be baptized; where baptism was to be administered by a catechist in mission areas; and where a child had already been baptized in an emergency rite and was now being brought to the church.⁴

The ritual has been developed accordingly, with three chapters presenting respectively the rite of baptism for several children, for one child, and for a large number of children. This is followed by two chapters

---

1. See Spinks, *Early and Medieval Rituals*, 156.

2. *Ordo Baptismi Parvulorum*. A second edition with minor changes was published in 1973. For the Declaration from the Sacred Congregation for Divine Worship regarding the second edition see International Commission on English in the Liturgy, *Documents*, 719 (DOL293).

3. Translations were made into local languages and approved for use in each country. The English translation, based on the second typical edition, is contained in *Rites*, 359–458. I will follow the usual method of referring to each of the rites by citing paragraph number.

4. See *Rites*, §365.

presenting the rite to be used when no priest or deacon is present and baptism is administered by a catechist, and a rite for children in danger of death when no priest or deacon is available. The penultimate chapter gives the rite for bringing a baptized child to church, and the final chapter gives a number of optional texts for use during the ceremony. These different rites are in fact a single rite, but with adaptations appropriate to the circumstances.

The General Introduction to RBC begins with three paragraphs on the importance of baptizing children.[5] It understands children to be those who are not yet able to profess personal faith. The reason for baptizing children is because the church does not wish to deprive them of the means of salvation. In following this ancient practice the Roman Catholic Church does not wish to convey that baptism is not connected to faith. On the contrary, it states that children are "baptized in the faith of the church, a faith proclaimed for them by their parents and godparents who represent both the local church and the whole society of saints and believers."[6] Faith, then, is not considered in isolation as a subjective response, but first and foremost as that gift of God that conveys salvation. This is not to suggest that the personal faith of the child is not important. RBC places great emphasis on the on-going faith formation of the child. "The foundation of this formation will be the sacrament itself that they have already received."[7]

The Rite of Baptism for Children is structured around five elements, which are described in the Introduction.[8] The first is the reception of the child. This is a relatively brief action where the parents and godparents indicate their desire that the child be baptized. It also indicates the church's intention to welcome the child into the family of Christ the Savior. These intentions are expressed by a series of questions put to the parents and godparents, by a declaration about the church's intention, and by the parents, godparents and minister tracing the sign of the cross on the child's forehead. This first part of the rite may take place at the door of the church, and at its conclusion there is a procession into the body of the church.

5. RBC, §§1–3.
6. Ibid., §2.
7. Ibid., §3.
8. Ibid., §§15–19.

The second stage of the rite is the Liturgy of the Word. Here Scripture is read; in the homily it is explained and related to this child's baptism; and those present pray prayers of intercession for the child, its parents, and all present. This prayer usually concludes with a Litany of the Saints, which both acknowledges that the child is to be baptized into a community that extends across time, and seeks intercession for the child. The final action at this second stage is an anointing with the Oil of Catechumens, accompanied by a prayer, called a Prayer of Exorcism.

At the third stage of the rite the water to be used for the baptism is blessed, "by invoking God and recalling his plan of salvation."[9] The parents and godparents proclaim their own faith by means of the Renunciation of Sin and Profession of Faith. They do this by responding to a series of questions put to them by the priest. These formulations follow the classic pattern found in the ancient liturgies, with the profession of faith taking the Trinitarian form, expressing belief in Father, Son, and Holy Spirit. The Introduction notes that the celebrant and the community add their assent to this profession of faith. It should be noted here that the parents and godparents make this profession of faith in their own right and are not speaking on behalf of their child.

The fourth stage begins with a question: "Is it your will that N. should be baptized in the faith of the church that we have all professed with you?" This question emphasizes that baptism is linked to Christian faith, and that this faith is safeguarded and professed in and by the church. The baptism follows immediately. There are two essential aspects of this: the baptism is with water, and it is by invocation of the Holy Trinity. The usual action with water is either immersion or pouring. The action is threefold and accompanies the threefold invocation of the Trinity.

The final stage consists of a series of brief rites that complete the sacrament. There is an anointing of the crown of the head with the Oil of Sacred Chrism, recalling the anointing of Christ and the new state of the baptized child as a member of the body of Christ. After the anointing there are three brief ceremonies: clothing with a white garment, presentation of a lighted candle, and the prayer over the ears and mouth (Ephphetha). Each of these ceremonies highlights the christological focus of baptism. The candle, lit from the Paschal Candle, is presented to the parents and godparents, with the admonition that it is entrusted to them to be kept burning brightly.

---

9. Ibid., §18.

The rite concludes by looking forward to the next stages in the child's initiation, namely Confirmation and first Eucharist. The whole community then joins in the Lord's Prayer followed by a blessing pronounced by the priest.

The Rite of Christian Initiation of Adults

The "Rite of Christian Initiation of Adults" (RCIA) was published in Latin in 1972.[10] Once again, translations into other languages were made on the basis of this "typical" edition, with an English translation appearing in 1987.[11] As with the earlier rite, the "Decree" indicated the requirements set by the Council. The fundamental requirement was that the rite of baptism of adults be revised such that it include a catechumenate for adults divided into several steps, following the ancient practice. Thus a major element of the Christian initiation of adults would be "a period of well-suited instruction," which would be accompanied by appropriate liturgical rites celebrated at successive intervals of time.[12]

The Introduction to RCIA notes two principles that underlie the rite and its reform: that it be endorsed by the ancient practice of the church, and it be suited to contemporary missionary activity.[13] Like ancient Christian initiation rites, RCIA takes place over a long period of time, indicating that initiation is a gradual process, a "spiritual journey."[14] The rite notes that this journey varies according to the many forms of God's grace, the free cooperation of individuals, the action of the church, and the circumstances of time and place. This variety is brought out in the structure of the rite, which consists of three steps of varying length and intensity. At each stage on the journey, the catechumens are accompanied by the local Christian community, which reflects with them on the central mysteries of Christ, provides an example of the Christian life, and recalls and renews its own conversion.

---

10. *Ordo Initiationis Christianae Adultorum*.

11. See *Rites*, 15–340. This translation notes that the English text is arranged in a slightly different way from the Latin "in the interest of pastoral utility and convenience" (§30). However, the equivalent paragraph numbers of the Latin text are noted in the margin of the English text. When referring to RCIA I will use the paragraph numbers in the English translation.

12. *Rites*, 34.

13. RCIA, §2.

14. Ibid., §5.

The first step on the journey of Christian initiation comes at the end of a period of inquiry on the part of a potential candidate.[15] Such a person will have reached a point in their initial conversion where they now wish to become a Christian, and want to be accepted as a catechumen by the church. During this period the church's task is to evangelize the person, helping them to listen to the call of God, which may have manifested itself in a variety of ways, and to open their hearts to the Holy Spirit. The emphasis is on responding to God's help, hearing a call to a new way of life, and being drawn into the mystery of God's love. The person's initial experience is deepened by means of a suitable explanation of the gospel and by meeting families and other groups of Christians. The aim of this period is that the candidates demonstrate the beginnings of the spiritual life, and that basic Christian teaching take root in their lives. RCIA expresses it in these words: "There must be evidence of the first faith that was conceived during the period of evangelization and precatechumenate and of an initial conversion and intention to change their lives and to enter into a relationship with God in Christ."[16] This period concludes with the first formal rite in the RCIA, the acceptance into the Order of Catechumens. This rite is simple and begins with a declaration by the candidates that they are prepared to begin this spiritual journey and an affirmation by their sponsors that they are willing to help the candidates follow Christ. This is followed by a signing of the cross on the forehead of the candidates and a presentation of a cross and Bible. The rite also provides options that could be used in particular circumstances, especially in mission contexts. Examples of these are an exorcism and renunciation of false worship, and the giving of a new name in accordance with the local culture.

The second period on the journey of Christian initiation is the Catechumenate. This period may last for several years, depending on the circumstances of the catechumen. The purpose is to give the candidates "suitable pastoral formation and guidance, aimed at training them in the Christian life."[17] This is a period where the spiritual gifts that they have already manifested can be brought to maturity. The rite outlines four ways in which this is achieved. First, a suitable catechesis will help them not only to have an appropriate knowledge of Christian dogmas and

---

15. This period is described in ibid., §§36–40.
16. Ibid., §42.
17. Ibid., §75.

precepts, but also to develop a profound sense of the mystery of salvation. In other words, the catechesis is about deepening their knowledge of the faith as well as their lived experience of it. Second, the catechumens learn to live the Christian life, especially by prayer, public witness, and self-renunciation. Third, there are suitable liturgical rites that help the catechumens on this spiritual journey. Particular importance is placed on celebrations of the Word of God, which are linked with the liturgical seasons and contribute to the instruction of the candidates. Catechumens will normally participate with the whole community at the Sunday liturgy, but be dismissed at the conclusion of the Liturgy of the Word, before the Eucharist. Fourth, the catechumens are introduced into the apostolic life of the church. The liturgical focus of this period, namely that the liturgy itself is the place of formation in Christian faith, ensures that there is always interaction between Christian doctrine, the Christian community, and the lived experience of catechumens.[18] RCIA describes it thus: "The instruction that the catechumens receive during this period should be of a kind that while presenting Catholic teaching in its entirety also enlightens faith, directs the heart towards God, fosters participation in the liturgy, inspires apostolic activity, and nurtures a life completely in accord with the spirit of Christ."[19]

The long period of the catechumenate concludes with what RCIA refers to as the second step, the Rite of Election or enrollment of names. This usually takes place at the beginning of Lent and marks the beginning of an intense period of preparation for the sacraments of initiation, which will be received at Easter. The Introduction to RCIA describes this step in these terms: "This step is called election because the acceptance made by the church is founded on the election by God, in whose name the church acts. The step is also called enrollment of names because as a pledge of fidelity the candidates inscribe their names in the book that

---

18. This connection was expressed clearly by Pope Benedict XVI in his question and answer session with priests of Rome at the beginning of Lent (Feb 26) 2009: "With the Word, we must open places of experience of the faith for those who seek God. That's what the ancient church did with the catechumenate, which was not simply a kind of catechesis, a doctrinal thing, but a place of progressive experience in the life of the faith, in which the Word was also revealed, which became comprehensible only if it was interpreted by life and realized in life. Thus alongside the Word, it seems important to me to have a place of hospitality in the faith, a place where one can have a progressive experience of the faith," National Catholic Reporter (http://ncronline.org/node/12551). See Fox, "Pope Benedict Answers."

19. RCIA, §78.

lists those who have been chosen for initiation."[20] This quote brings out clearly that election is the business of God. In connection with this it points to the indispensable role of the church, which acts in God's name. This intimate connection between Christian initiation and the church is signified by the fact that the rite of election is presided over by the bishop or his delegate, and usually takes place in the cathedral church on the First Sunday of Lent.

The candidates—the elect as they are henceforth called—now begin the third period, that of purification and enlightenment. This period customarily coincides with Lent. Its purpose is to prepare the elect for the sacraments of initiation by offering a "more intense spiritual preparation, consisting more in interior reflection than in catechetical instruction."[21] There are a number of rites that accompany this period and they are celebrated on the Sundays of Lent. In the first place there are the Scrutinies, which take place on the Third, Fourth, and Fifth Sundays of Lent. Their purpose is twofold: to uncover and heal what is weak, defective, or sinful in the hearts of the elect; and to shine a light on and strengthen what is upright, strong, and good in the elect.[22] Each Scrutiny also includes a rite of exorcism, which recalls the mystery of salvation whereby a person is delivered from sin by Christ, is freed from the effects of sin, and receives new strength for their spiritual journey. The Sunday Gospel readings, particularly in Year A, develop the theme of each Scrutiny. The Introduction to RCIA expresses it this way:

> [the] spirit [of the elect] is filled with Christ the Redeemer, who is the living water (Gospel reading of the Samaritan woman in the first scrutiny), the light of the world (Gospel reading of the man born blind in the second scrutiny), the resurrection and the life (Gospel reading of Lazarus in the third scrutiny). From the first to the final scrutiny the elect should progress in their perception of sin and their desire for salvation.[23]

A second important rite is the Presentations, where the elect are presented with the Creed during the week after the first scrutiny, and the Lord's Prayer during the week after the third scrutiny. These are "the ancient texts that have always been regarded as expressing the heart of the

20. Ibid., §119.
21. Ibid., §139.
22. Ibid., §141.
23. Ibid., §143.

Church's faith and prayer."[24] The elect who receive them are to take them into their lives and "give them back" by reciting them on Holy Saturday some time before the Easter Vigil. Other rites also take place on Holy Saturday: the Ephphetha rite and the choosing of a baptismal name.

This third period leads into the third step of Christian initiation, the celebration of the sacraments of initiation, during the Easter Vigil on Holy Saturday night. The setting is significant, because it is taking place in the midst of a vigil during which the church remembers the history of salvation and celebrates the resurrection of the Lord. The high point is the baptismal washing with water and the invocation of the Trinity. This is preceded by the blessing of the Easter water, which will be used in baptism, by an anointing with the Oil of Catechumens, and by the renunciation of sin and profession of faith. After the baptismal washing, additional brief rites bring out the meaning of baptism: the anointing with chrism, the clothing with a white garment, and the presentation of the lighted candle. The sacrament of Confirmation will also be celebrated with the newly baptized immediately after this. When this happens the anointing with chrism immediately after baptism is omitted. The newly baptized then share in the celebration of the Eucharist for the first time.

The celebration of baptism, confirmation, and Eucharist as a single ceremony during the Easter Vigil is a return to the ancient practice of the church. One of the clearest examples of this, and one which was formative in the evolution of RCIA, is the *Apostolic Tradition* of Hippolytus.[25] This ancient practice makes clear the unity of Christian Initiation. This is also the intention of the new rite: "The conjunction of the two celebrations [of baptism and confirmation] signifies the unity of the paschal mystery, the close link between the mission of the Son and the outpouring of the Holy Spirit, and the connection between the two sacraments through which the Son and the Holy Spirit come with the Father to those who are baptized."[26] Participation in the Eucharist is described as the "culminating point of their Christian initiation."[27]

---

24. Ibid., §147.

25. See the text in Whitaker, *Documents*, 4–8. For a discussion of *Apostolic Tradition* and the rites of Christian initiation, see Johnson, *The Rites*, 72–85. For a study of the instruction given to candidates for baptism in the ancient church, see Yarnold, *Awe-Inspiring Rites*.

26. RCIA, §215.

27. Ibid., §217.

The final period in Christian initiation, which takes place after the celebration of the sacraments, is the period of postbaptismal catechesis or mystagogy. This is a period when the newly baptized deepen their understanding of and participation in the paschal mystery, and are helped to live fully the new life they have received. The main liturgical focus during this period is the Sundays of the Easter season. Just as the final stages of preparation for baptism took shape around the Sundays of Lent, so the Sundays of Easter, particularly the Gospel readings, offer the source for a catechesis that not only helps the newly baptized to better appreciate the Christian mystery, but also to face the practical consequences of living the life of one of the baptized.

INITIATION AS THE THEOLOGICAL MATRIX

Both RBC and RCIA are rites of initiation. In order to appreciate the full significance of initiation as a framework for understanding the theology of baptism, it will be helpful to look more generally at rites of initiation from an anthropological point of view. Rites of initiation exist in traditional societies as a means of bringing someone fully into the life of that society (usually a person moving from childhood to adulthood). The purpose of the rites is to mediate the history, culture, and ways of expression of a community to the person being initiated. This takes place at a symbolic level, with effects that are tangible and real: through these symbolic acts a person acquires the identity of this people. Initiation involves symbolic exchange, which allows the person being initiated not just to know the way of life of this people, but also to take on an identity as one of them and to embrace their way of life.[28]

There are three basic moments in the act of initiation. The first involves the telling of the stories that belong to this people. These are the stories of their origins, their location, their relationships, and life both inside and outside their community. These are also the stories that distinguish them from other peoples. Often these stories are a secret and can only be known by the initiated. Therefore, the telling of these foundational stories marks a special moment in the maturation of a young member of that people, and may involve a separation from the rest of the people before they are fully re-introduced back into the people, now as full, adult members. But more is needed than knowledge of the identity-

---

28. I am relying here on the basic insights of Chauvet, *Symbol*.

stories. The second step in the initiation process involves rituals whereby the person being initiated makes a transition from simply hearing the stories and knowing about them, to actually becoming part of them. In many societies this involves a physical marking of the body or the letting of blood. Here is the basic symbolic act that communicates the changed situation of the people being initiated. The story is, as it were, engrafted onto the people being initiated, so that they now own the story and are owned by it. The third phase requires that the initiated people learn to live concretely as one of this people. More than simply knowing the mores of the society and its ethical foundation, they are expected to make decisions that show them to be true members of this people. In other words, identity as a member of this society demands an ethical life. The initiated person assumes the (ethical) task of living in such a way as to promote the well-being of this people and to have a care for its future.

This same threefold pattern is discernible in the earliest examples of Christian baptism. Consider, for example, the baptism of the Ethiopian eunuch in Acts 8:26–40. The first element—which I have called story—occurs in vv. 30–35. The eunuch is already reading the Scriptures and trying to make sense of what he is reading. He invites Philip to join him in the chariot and to explain the text. Philip interprets it as speaking about Jesus and all that has happened to him. The second element—which I have called ritual—occurs in vv. 36–38, when the eunuch calls on the chariot-driver to stop, and the eunuch goes down into the water and is baptized by Philip. This ritual action takes place as the way for the eunuch to own the story and to become part of it. He wants to become a disciple of Jesus and to be part of the gospel that Jesus preached. The final element—which I have called ethics—occurs at v. 39, where the eunuch goes on his way rejoicing. It is as if the author of Acts is describing the sort of life that from now on this eunuch will live. Following hints in other parts of Luke–Acts (but also in other New Testament books), it is reasonable to assume that this "rejoicing" involved such things as telling other people about Jesus and the gospel of God that he preached (i.e., mission), turning aside from despair and alienation and living in the confidence that the kingdom has come, living in fellowship with the disciples of Jesus, and caring for the poor (cf. Acts 2:42–45).[29]

---

29. These are all typical themes in Luke–Acts. This same pattern in evident in the account of the disciples on the road to Emmaus (Luke 24:13–35). See Chauvet, *Symbol*, 167–70.

This same threefold pattern, derived from anthropological insights and evident in Acts 8, is also present in Christian baptism. The first of the elements, story, connects the catechumens/elect to the past, to the story of what God has done. As we saw above, they become hearers of the Word of God and come to know the revelation of God's mighty works. They receive instruction based on the Word of God. This word, however, is never just an account of the past; it is also a summons in the present. Hence, by means of the second element, ritual, the Word of God inserts the elect into the story of God's mighty works in their existential situation. The central ritual is the action with water, and other rituals help bring out the depths of meaning of the ritual action with water. The third element in the Catholic rites, after the water ritual, is mystagogy. This period marks the time when the newly baptized are shaping a Christian life in the midst of the community and the world. Their life is now oriented to a future that has been promised by God and is made concrete through the ethical choices they make.

A further common element in this pattern is that it gives an identity to a person. As in traditional societies, it is right to speak of the baptism of the Ethiopian eunuch as bestowing on him the particular identity of a follower of Jesus. This identity is clarified by means of the reading and interpretation of the Scriptures; it is appropriated when he enters into the water to be baptized; and it is lived as he goes off rejoicing. Similarly, the rites of baptism in the Catholic Church make people Christians and bestow a particular identity on them. The General Introduction to Christian Initiation expresses this in its opening paragraph:

> Through the sacraments of Christian initiation we are freed from the power of darkness and joined to Christ's death, burial and resurrection. We receive the Spirit of filial adoption and are part of the entire people of God in the celebration of the memorial of the Lord's death and resurrection.[30]

Two brief comments are in order at this point: first, the identity bestowed in baptism means that the baptized are "in Christ"; second, they become members of the community of the followers of Jesus. These ideas will be explored in more detail in the following sections.

---

30. "General Introduction to Christian Initiation," n. 1 (hereafter GICI). Text and translation in *Rites*, 3.

FOUR ASPECTS OF BAPTISM

Baptized into the Mystery of Christ

There is a basic question that will concern us in this section, namely, what is the foundation story concerning baptism? There is also a related question: what is the foundation story concerning Christian identity? The answer is given in a concise way in the General Introduction to Christian Initiation. One paragraph in particular gives the story in a nutshell:

> Far superior to the purifications of the Old Law, baptism produces these effects by the power of the mystery of the Lord's passion and resurrection. Those who are baptized are united to Christ in a death like his (cf. Rom 6:4–5); buried with him in death, they are given life again with him, and with him they rise again (cf. Eph 2:5–6). For baptism recalls and makes present the paschal mystery itself, because in baptism we pass from the death of sin into life. The celebration of baptism should therefore reflect the joy of the resurrection, especially when the celebration takes place during the Easter Vigil or on a Sunday.[31]

This paragraph relies on two biblical texts. That from Romans is the classic text concerning baptism. This is not the place to enter into a detailed exegesis of the text, but a few comments are in order. In Romans 6, Paul is primarily concerned with the practical life of the Christian, who has been freed from sin. In the preceding chapters he has been constructing the doctrinal foundation, which he relies on in chapter 6. In brief, it is the doctrine of salvation in Christ. He began by contrasting sin and righteousness. Sin is universal: "all have sinned and fall short of the glory of God" (Rom 3:23). Yet sin has been overcome, and God has acted to bring justification through the redemption that is in Jesus: "they are now justified by his grace as a gift, through the redemption that is in Christ Jesus" (Rom 3:24). Paul is giving a teaching about Christ, and to develop his argument he sets up a comparison between Christ and Adam: "Therefore, just as one man's trespass led to condemnation for all, so one man's act of righteousness leads to justification and life for all. For just as by one man's disobedience the many were made sinners, so by one man's obedience the many will be made righteous" (Rom 5:18-19). This teaching about Adam and Christ has consequences for human beings:

---

31. GICI, §6.

"For if the many died through the one man's trespass, much more surely have the grace of God and the free gift in the grace of the one man, Jesus Christ, abounded for the many" (Rom 5:15). As he had said earlier, "the righteousness of God has been disclosed ... through faith in Jesus Christ for all who believe" (Rom 3:21–22).

In Romans 6, Paul appears to take for granted that believers have died to sin through their baptism. He goes on to explain what happened to them in baptism: they were baptized "into Christ Jesus" and baptized "into his death" (Rom 6:3). Brendan Byrne comments:

> As in the parallel references to baptism in Gal 3:27–28 and 1 Cor 12:12–13, behind the expression here lies the characteristic Pauline idea of the risen Lord as personally constituting a sphere of influence or milieu of salvation "into" which believers are drawn through faith and baptism, henceforth to live "in Christ" (cf. v. 11). Christ does not lose his personal identity but, nonetheless, as risen Lord and "life-giving Spirit" (1 Cor 15:45), he somehow "contains" within his person, in a communal sense, the messianic community destined for salvation. The present allusion to this truth goes beyond earlier presentations (Gal 3:27–28 and 1 Cor 12:12–13) in its suggestion that baptism involves not simply a being joined in a static "spatial" sense but also a dynamic insertion into what might be called his overall "career"—death, burial and risen life.[32]

The baptized person has thus ended an old way of life and begun a new life in Christ: "so that we might walk in newness of life" (Rom 6:4). Byrne argues that there is an eschatological aspect here in Paul's thought. Walking in newness of life "flows from the risen life of Jesus and belongs essentially to the new age," but is something that is already lived here and now.[33] Byrne comments further:

> Though not yet wholly removed from the conditions of the present, passing age (suffering, temptation, death), believers are summoned and empowered to live out the righteousness appropriate for the new. For Paul, it is precisely the hope of one day sharing fully the risen life of the Lord that sheds worth and dignity upon present life in the body (cf. 1 Cor 6:13–14) and motivates the desire to live out God's gift of righteousness.[34]

32. Byrne, *Romans*, 190.
33. Ibid.
34. Ibid.

Baptism is thus a central ritual in the Christian life. Through it a person participates in the mystery of Christ—in his life, death, and resurrection—and thereby enters into the realm of salvation. Salvation is God's mighty work and the fulfillment of God's act of creation. In Christ, salvation has definitively entered into the world. Through baptism a person now participates in this "end-time," and is empowered to live here and now in the faith received as God's gift.

These themes are brought out more explicitly in the second text referred to in the GICI, quoted above, namely Eph 2:5–6. Once again, it is important to consider the larger context of the letter, which, according to some commentators, is a commentary on baptism and the baptismal life.[35] In the opening chapter the author celebrates God's plan for the world—a plan that has existed since before the creation of the world and that reaches its fulfillment in Christ Jesus and the shedding of his blood. It is God's plan of salvation, which has been gradually unfolding through the ages and is now definitively revealed in Christ Jesus. The author of Ephesians uses this doctrine to ground the practical life of the Christian: "a plan for the fullness of time, to gather up all things in [Christ], things in heaven and things on earth" (Eph 1:10). Theology will speak of this "gathering up" using the language of communion. Salvation is about communion: the communion believers have with God and also the communion they share with each other. This image is made even more explicit and related to the concrete life of the community at Ephesus a little later in the letter:

> But now in Christ Jesus you who were once far off have been brought near by the blood of Christ. For he is our peace; in his flesh he has made both groups into one and has broken down the dividing wall, that is the hostility between us. He abolished the law with its commandments and ordinances, that he might create in himself one new humanity in place of the two, thus making peace, and might reconcile both groups to God in one body through the cross, thus putting to death that hostility through it. (Eph 2:13–16)

---

35. See MacDonald, *Colossians and Ephesians*, 213. MacDonald uses a social-scientific approach to the biblical text, and argues that the reference to being sealed with the Holy Spirit (1:13) is probably a direct reference to baptism. See also Boismard, *L'Énigme*, 54–55. Boismard argues for a primitive version of this letter written by Paul and later edited and expanded by a redactor. The primitive text, he says, was a commentary on the baptismal ceremony that had been practiced since the very beginnings of Christianity and of which Paul had already spoken in the Letter to the Romans (16).

Those who participate in the salvation won by the blood of Christ are thus made into a new people, a people reconciled with God, who live in peace with God and each other.

By linking Christ's saving death to God's plan from before the foundation of the world, the author brings out the universal scope of God's saving action in Christ Jesus. It is offered to all as a free gift. The author reminds his readers how they were drawn into this action of God: they heard the word of truth, the gospel of salvation; they believed in Christ; and they were sealed with the Holy Spirit (cf. Eph 1:13). The effect is that they were "raised up" with Christ and "seated with him in the heavenly places" (Eph 2:6). It is true that as a description of baptism, Ephesians is less explicit than Romans; nevertheless, Ephesians offers us a dense theology of baptism similar to that in Romans.

The theology of these two letters became the basis for the development of the understanding and practice of baptism. To focus on the western church, we can cite the earliest treatise on baptism, that of Tertullian, written at the turn of the third century, which begins: "The present work treats our sacrament of water that washes away the sins contracted at the time of our original blindness and releases us into eternal life.... But we little fish, like our great Fish, Jesus Christ, are born in water, nor can we be saved in any other way than by remaining permanently in the water."[36] For Tertullian, sin equates with death, and baptism is the remedy for sin and gives eternal life. Later in the treatise he will explain that the water of baptism saves (brings forth life) because it is water sanctified by the Holy Spirit.[37] The image of the fish becomes a metaphor for Christian identity: the baptized person shares in the life of Christ, who forgives sin, saves from death, and releases into eternal life. Equally important, the baptized person should remain immersed, as it were, in the saving grace of Christ.

The other towering influence on the theology of baptism in the west is Augustine of Hippo. There is an underlying tension in his writing because, following Paul, he is constantly contrasting the grace of God and human sinfulness. It is Augustine who is credited with embedding the teaching about baptism in a theology of original sin. The pastoral consequences of this have been significant, and in some cases, have led to an over-emphasis on the "washing of original sin" at the expense of being

---

36. Tertullian, *On Baptism*, 1.
37. Ibid., 4.

re-created in the image of God. However, this was not Augustine's focus.[38] Following the line from Paul, Tertullian, and others, he did indeed speak about baptism as the forgiveness of sins.[39] On one occasion, when referring to the baptism of infants, he was clearly arguing that the effect of baptism for them was the same as for adults. "Infants die to original sin only; adults, to all those sins which they have added, through their evil living, to the burden they brought with them from birth."[40] Writing a little later in the same work he spoke of baptism as a rebirth through the anointing of the Holy Spirit, just as Christ was born by the anointing of the Holy Spirit.[41] This is an important insight because it points to a theme that has been more common in the eastern church, namely the "deification" of the believer through the Holy Spirit. Moreover, it is a theme that is already present in Paul (cf. Rom 8:14–17), namely, the baptized as the adopted children of God and heirs with Christ. Baptism restores in us the image of God that was lost at the Fall. To understand properly the place of original sin in Augustine's teaching about baptism it must be recognized that original sin brings into sharper focus the marvelous work of God in Christ Jesus whereby the sinful human being is reborn in the image of God, as a son or daughter of God.[42] The General Introduction to Christian Initiation brings this out clearly:

> Baptism, the cleansing with water by the power of the living word (cf. Eph 5:26), washes away every stain of sin, original and personal, and makes us sharers in God's own life (cf. 2 Pet 1:4) and his adopted children (cf. Rom 8:15; Gal 4:5).[43]

---

38. For an illuminating treatment of Augustine's teaching and preaching directed to those preparing for baptism, see Harmless, *Augustine*.

39. For example, writing in *Enchiridion* 8.42, Augustine stated: "This is the meaning of the great sacrament of baptism, which is celebrated among us. All who attain to this grace die thereby to sin—as [Christ] himself is said to have died to sin because he died in the flesh, that is, 'in the likeness of sin'—and they are thereby alive by being reborn in the baptismal font, just as he rose again from the sepulcher." In Finn, *Early Christian Baptism*, 152.

40. Augustine, *Enchiridion*, 8.43. In Finn, *Early Christian Baptism*, 152. Johnson, *The Rites*, 213, notes: "in the context of the Pelagian controversy, Augustine himself had developed his theology of original sin largely based on the already existing practice of infant baptism within the north African churches of the fourth and fifth centuries."

41. See Augustine, *Enchiridion* 8.49, in Finn, *Early Christian Baptism*, 153.

42. It is important to remember that Augustine's idea of original sin developed in response to the Pelagian crisis. The point was always to stress the necessity of the grace of God.

43. GICI, §5.

The celebration of baptism in the Roman Catholic Church tells this story of the mystery of God's plan, which has been realized in Christ, in terms of the renunciation of sin and the bestowal of grace, and draws the candidates into this mystery.

Baptism and Faith

Immediately before their baptism, the candidates are asked to renounce Satan and to make the profession of faith. The unity between the profession and the renunciation is best understood in terms of the relationship between the forgiveness of (original) sin and the saving grace of Christ. Just as the forgiveness of sin brings the saving grace of Christ into sharper relief, as we saw above, so the renunciation of sin is properly understood in the light of the profession of faith. The General Introduction to Christian Initiation calls baptism "the sacrament of that faith by which, enlightened by the grace of the Holy Spirit, we respond to the Gospel of Christ."[44] Faith is at the core of baptism; faith is a gift of God, in the Holy Spirit.

It is important not to separate the act of making a profession of faith from the content of the faith. The profession of faith, in its trinitarian form, has traditionally been called the "symbol"; it is a concise statement of the saving work of God. For this reason the trinitarian form accompanies the water ritual in the act of baptism. Cardinal Walter Kasper comments:

> The *trinitarian confession* is in fact the sum and substance of the entire Christian faith. Therefore baptism in the name of the triune God is also more than one formula, interchangeable with others for administering baptism; it is rather a confession of the historical and theological basis and inner content of baptism. In addition it is the epiclesis and promise of salvation, not as a mere ritual, and certainly not as a ritual working by "magic"; but in the power of this authoritative promise, baptism obtains its power to effect salvation.[45]

For this reason Roman Catholics understand faith and baptism to be necessary for salvation. They appeal to a number of biblical texts,[46] but especially John 3:5, "no one can enter the kingdom of God without being

---

44. Ibid., §3.
45. Kasper, "Implications," 528.
46. For instance, 1 Cor 6:11; 1 Pet 3:21; Mark 16:16; Matt 28:19.

born of water and the Spirit," and Mark 16:16, "The one who believes and is baptized will be saved; but the one who does not believe will be condemned."[47] So when Roman Catholics speak of the necessity of baptism for salvation, they understand this in the context of the necessity of faith for salvation and hence also of the proclamation of the gospel. For this reason the General Introduction to Christian Initiation adds this comment:

> That is why the Church believes that it is its most basic and necessary duty to inspire all, catechumens, parents of children still to be baptized, and godparents to that true and living faith by which they hold fast to Christ and enter into or confirm their commitment to the New Covenant. In order to enliven such faith, the Church prescribes the pastoral instruction of catechumens, the preparation of the children's parents, the celebration of God's word, and the profession of faith at the celebration of baptism.[48]

Roman Catholics have always understood baptism in an ecclesial context, so in order to understand it more fully we need to consider the connection between baptism and the church.

Baptized in the Church

There is a basic question that will concern us in this section: what role does the church have in baptism? There is also a related question: what do Roman Catholics mean when they speak of baptism as a sacrament? Once again, we can turn to the General Introduction to Christian Initiation for a concise answer to these questions:

> baptism is the sacrament by which its recipients are incorporated into the Church and are built up together in the Spirit into a house where God lives (cf. Eph 2:22), into a holy nation and a royal priesthood (cf. 1 Pet 2:9). Baptism is a sacramental bond

---

47. The question of who can be saved remains an important pastoral question. At the Second Vatican Council the Roman Catholic Church's teaching office responded to this pastoral concern when the Dogmatic Constitution on the Church, *Lumen gentium* 16, taught: "There are those who without any fault do not know anything about Christ or his church, yet who search for God with a sincere heart and, under the influence of grace, try to put into effect the will of God as known to them through the dictate of conscience; these too can obtain eternal salvation." Text and translation in Tanner, ed., *Decrees*, II: 861. See also Vatican II's Decree on Missionary Activity, *Ad gentes*, 7 (in Tanner, *Decrees*, II:1017).

48. GICI, §3.

of unity linking all who have been signed by it. Because of that unchangeable effect (given expression in the Latin liturgy by the anointing of the baptized person with chrism in the presence of God's people), the rite of baptism is held in the highest honor by all Christians. Once it has been validly celebrated, even if by Christians with whom we are not in full communion, it may never lawfully be repeated.[49]

This paragraph makes reference to the Letter to the Ephesians, which I discussed earlier. The later verses of Ephesians 2 speak of the effects of baptism, namely that the baptized are "members of the household of God" and "a dwelling place for God." Throughout the letter this is developed in the language of the body, the body of Christ. In Ephesians 4, the baptized are challenged to live in such a way that the unity and peace of the body are maintained, because this is the salvation given by God in Christ. Recall the opening verses:

> I therefore, the prisoner in the Lord, beg you to lead a life worthy of the calling to which you have been called, with all humility and gentleness, with patience, bearing with one another in love, making every effort to maintain the unity of the Spirit in the bond of peace. There is one body and one Spirit, just as you were called to the one hope of your calling, one Lord, one faith, one baptism, one God and Father of all, who is above all and through all and in all. (Eph 4:1–6)

Body of Christ language is important for a Roman Catholic understanding of baptism and its relationship to the church. When Roman Catholics speak of baptism as initiation they clearly mean that it is initiation into Christ, as demonstrated earlier in this essay, but they also mean initiation into the church. For them, initiation into the church *is* initiation into Christ. Walter Kasper makes a subtle distinction when he writes: "The church is not brought into being by people gathering together to form a church. Thus, in my view, we do not enter the church through baptism; rather we are accepted into the church as a pre-existing reality of salvation."[50] Clearly, for Kasper, the church is not a human creation, but has come into existence by God's action and makes visible the saving work of God. Baptism and the church are inextricably connected. Baptism is a rite of the church; it is an action in the church. To under-

---

49 Ibid., §4.
50. Kasper, "Implications," 530.

stand this properly we need to understand a basic principle in Roman Catholic theology, namely "sacrament."

"Sacrament" refers to the way people encounter Christ and thereby become participants in God's saving plan. However, before explaining in what sense baptism is a sacrament we must first understand sacrament as an ecclesial reality. In other words, we need to explain the relationship between the church and the action of God. Let me invoke a recent exposition of this relationship, that of the French theologian Louis-Marie Chauvet.[51] His starting point is the resurrection of Jesus and the new situation this brings about for encounter with Jesus. After the resurrection, immediate encounter with the earthly Jesus is no longer possible, as he is absent, having ascended to be "seated at the right hand of the Father." Nor do we have access to his heavenly presence, because in heaven he is still absent to us on earth. Thus we live in an in-between time. Nevertheless, as we learn from the resurrection appearances of Jesus, he is still present to people and encounter is still possible. This happens in a way that is both similar and different to the way the disciples had previously encountered him. Luke, in his Gospel and the Acts of the Apostles, shows that the saving encounter with the risen Lord is mediated through the interpretation of the Scriptures in the light of Jesus' death and resurrection, and through the symbolic rituals that draw people into the word of God and fellowship with the risen Jesus.[52] I have already drawn attention to this pattern in speaking of the baptism of the Ethiopian eunuch in Acts 8. This pattern of mediation, which is already visible in the apostolic community, continues in successive generations. In recognizing this we are at the core of the church's identity; the Christian community becomes the place where saving encounter with Jesus is mediated. Chauvet expresses it starkly: "The passage to faith requires an acceptance of the church, for it is in it that the Lord Jesus allows himself to be encountered."[53]

This is how the Roman Catholic Church understands the church, and why it can speak of the church as "sacrament." The church is the place of saving encounter with the risen Jesus; it mediates the saving grace of Christ. The opening paragraph of the Second Vatican Council's Dogmatic Constitution on the Church, *Lumen gentium*, states it succinctly: "the

---

51. See Chauvet, *Symbol*, 161–89.

52. Perhaps the clearest example of this is the encounter of the disciples on the road to Emmaus.

53. Chauvet, *Symbol*, 171.

church is in Christ as a sacrament or instrumental sign of intimate union with God and of the unity of all humanity."[54] The reader will notice here echoes of the mystery of God's plan, spoken of in the letter to the Ephesians. We can thus speak of a sacramental structure for the church: it is an instrumental sign, an effective sign of salvation in Christ.

Baptism, as an action of the church, is also understood as an effective sign of salvation in Christ. Kasper calls it "a symbol that bestows what it describes through the action of the Spirit of God."[55] Thus, for Roman Catholics, baptism is more than a promise or pledge of salvation. Equally, it entails more than a commitment being made by the person being baptized. Rather, something objective happens in baptism: a person receives new life from God. Moreover, the church is the body through which God works.

I mentioned above that the saving encounter with the risen Jesus was both similar and dissimilar to the way that the disciples had encountered him during his earthly life. This needs further explanation. It is similar in that it happens by means of the stuff of creation; it is dissimilar in that it is not an immediate encounter, but a mediated encounter. This, of course, takes account of the fact that God has chosen to communicate with us human beings through the Incarnation of his Son. God continues to use the stuff of creation as the vehicle for divine encounter. In the case of baptism, we recognize that water is that vehicle. The early Christian writers made much of this, but always demonstrated that something was "added" to the water. That something was the Word and the Spirit. Augustine of Hippo emphasized that the water is effective because of the power of the word of God. That word is Christ himself, the Incarnate Word, and it is also the word of faith handed on by the apostles and professed by the church. The word comes to expression in the prayer of the church. Augustine explained this in his commentary on the Gospel of John:

> "Now you are clean through the word that I have spoken to you." Why does he not say, "you are clean by reason of the baptism by which you were washed," but says, "by reason of the word that I have spoken to you," except that in the water also the word cleansed? Take away the word, and what is the water except water? The word is added to the elemental

---

54. *Lumen gentium*, 1. Text and translation, Tanner, *Decrees*, II: 849.
55. Kasper, "Implications," 537.

substance, and it becomes a sacrament, also itself, as it were, a visible word.[56]

Ambrose of Milan, another witness to the theology that developed in the western church, emphasized that the water is effective because of the power of the Holy Spirit, filling the water with the grace of Christ. As with Augustine, the stuff of creation becomes a vehicle for God's saving action, because God acts in it and uses it for this purpose. Ambrose instructed the newly baptized in these words:

> You saw the water, but not all water has a curative power: only that water has it which has the grace of Christ. There is a difference between the matter and the consecration, between the action and its effect. The action belongs to the water, its effect to the Holy Spirit. The water does not heal unless the Spirit descends and consecrates the water.[57]

For both Ambrose and Augustine—and for the tradition of the church that follows them—baptism involves both a sign and a reality. The sign (i.e., water that has now been sanctified and empowered by God) becomes the vehicle to convey the reality (i.e., salvation in Christ). This happens in the church and presupposes the faith of the church. In the ritual of baptism the church acts in faith, which is not only trust in God, but also invocation of God to remember and act today on behalf of God's people.

Living Baptismally

We have seen how baptism brings about a radical change in those who have been baptized, making them new persons in Christ. As a consequence, the baptized are in a new relationship with God as well as a new relationship with their fellow human beings. This raises an important question about the consequences of baptism for the on-going life of the baptized. While some people may be accustomed to thinking of baptism principally in terms of an event that happens once in a person's life, the reformed liturgy of the Roman Catholic Church emphasizes that the gift received in baptism is lived out and bears fruit throughout the whole of a person's life. Both RBC and RCIA refer to the new responsibilities faced by the Christian as a result of baptism. RBC looks forward to the

---

56. Augustine, *Tractates on the Gospel of John*, 117.
57. Ambrose, *The Sacraments*, 105.

on-going formation of the child and to the completion of their sacramental initiation through Confirmation and first Eucharist.[58] Referring to the completion of initiation, the General Introduction to Christian Initiation notes: "Thus the three sacraments of Christian initiation closely combine to bring us, the faithful of Christ, to his full stature and to enable us to carry out the mission of the entire people of God in the Church and in the world."[59] This focus on mission, and on a relationship with the church and the world, is also emphasized in the instruction on mystagogy in RCIA: "Out of this experience [of the sacraments they have received], which belongs to Christians and increases as it is lived, they derive a new perception of the faith, of the church, and of the world."[60] The ritual presumes that the newly baptized will continue to grow in the Christian life.

In this sense baptism has existential consequences. What has happened in baptism, namely that a person has become a son or daughter of God and brother or sister to all the baptized, should become visible in the concrete situation and circumstances of that person's life. For all the baptized there is a tension between the reality of what has happened to them in baptism and their existential situation. Through their baptism they have been drawn into that "new humanity" (Eph 2:15), which is the fulfillment of God's plan. In other words, they participate in the life, death, and resurrection of Jesus and have thereby been initiated into the final future promised by God. At the same time, however, they still live in the world, which falls well short of revealing the glory of God. This tension brings us to a further element in our theological understanding of baptism, namely the eschatological context of baptism. It is important for understanding how the baptized live.

In Roman Catholic theology the eschatological dimension of baptism is linked to our understanding of it as a sacrament. In a sermon to the newly baptized, one week after their baptism, Augustine takes up the question of the new responsibility they have to live the Christian life and addresses the existential tension they experience. He reminds them of the power of the sacrament to bring about what it proclaims: "This is the inherent power of the sacrament. It is the sacrament of new life, which

---

58. Of course, in the RCIA these latter two sacraments are celebrated at the same time as baptism.

59. GICI, §2.

60. RCIA, §245.

begins now with the remission of all past sins, and will be brought to perfection at the resurrection of the dead."[61] Sacramentally, they already live in that future life promised by God; existentially, they participate in its gradual unfolding in the world.

This theological tension was already identified in key biblical texts about baptism and the paschal life. It is present in Rom 6:11, where Paul reminds those who have been baptized that they are alive to God and should look towards God. In other words, baptism has opened up the future for them, and they must look to that future to guide them in shaping a life in their present concrete situation. This is expressed even more explicitly in Col 3:2–4: "set your minds on the things above, not the things here on earth, for you have died and your life is hidden with Christ in God. When Christ who is your life is revealed, then you also will be revealed with him in glory." The tension is between the present and the future, earth and heaven. The point is not that baptism has removed them from the world, but rather that it has oriented the way they live in the world and are engaged with it. In fact, they become witnesses to a future that will be perfected at the resurrection of the dead. Their participation already in the promised future in Christ, through the sacrament of baptism, will henceforth shape the way they live. In this way, to live baptismally is to construct a life on the basis of faith in Christ, who is the fulfillment of God's plan for the whole of creation. One can agree with Chauvet who argued, "because [baptism] is eschatological, it has to be realized in ethical practice."[62] The baptismal life is thus an ethical life. It involves making decisions on the basis of the mystery that is celebrated in baptism and into which a person enters through baptism.

In considering this, however, we must be careful not to fall into a perspective that focuses solely on the individual believer. As mentioned earlier, baptism is always ecclesial. There are two sides to this that I want to consider. The first is that the community of the baptized, the church, has a concern for all its members. In other words, the baptized person is assisted by the community to shape a genuinely human and Christian life. In this sense, baptism places great responsibilities on the church that baptizes. The church has a responsibility of pastoral care for its members, and will provide a variety of means to nurture them. Among these means is the quality of the corporate life of its members, especially

---

61. Augustine, *Sermon 8*, 331–32.
62. Chauvet, *Symbol*, 440.

in their internal relations. The theological basis for this is the church's understanding of itself as a communion. The church nurtures communion with God and communion among the church's members. Another important means of nurture is participation in a sacramental life. The celebration of the sacraments draws the baptized into an experience of God's grace, and a re-affirmation of what has happened in baptism.

The second side of the ecclesial focus of baptism concerns the responsibility of the individual Christian within the mission of the church. For most people this happens through a life lived as a witness to a promise that is already realized in baptism. In a very real way, the day-to-day lives of ordinary believers become a declaration that the gospel proclaimed by Jesus is not some utopian ideal, but a real possibility for people today. For some people, participation in the church's mission is also realized concretely through some form of ministry or public service in the church. In the years since the Second Vatican Council the Roman Catholic Church has seen a flourishing of lay ministries. Theologically, these are understood as ultimately emerging from the grace and call received at baptism.

We can further explore the link between the theology of baptism and its pastoral consequences by looking once again to the rite itself, specifically to the anointing of the newly baptized. This post-baptismal anointing with chrism reinforces that the baptized are anointed with the Spirit. It signifies that the baptized, anointed with the same Spirit with which Jesus was anointed at his baptism, take Jesus and the gospel he preached as their model. They are anointed with the Spirit in order to live in the Spirit. The words that accompany the anointing refer to Christ being anointed priest, prophet, and king and proclaim that the baptized have become members of a priestly people. This designation helps us understand something more about baptismal living.

The primary biblical text, already referred to in the General Introduction, is 1 Pet 2:5, 9, which exhorts the readers to be built into a spiritual house and to be a holy priesthood, offering "spiritual sacrifices acceptable to God through Jesus Christ." This biblical language of priesthood and sacrifice refers to worship of God. The same sentiment is found in Rom 12:1–2, where Paul exhorts his readers to offer their bodies as a living sacrifice, which is spiritual worship. Such worship is doing God's will, knowing what is good and acceptable. Hence, rather than the language and imagery of priesthood and sacrifice being a reference to cultic activity, it is much more akin to the understanding of sacrifice found in the Prophets, namely a life lived in integrity and justice. To return to a point made earlier, this in effect describes the life of the baptized as a life marked by communion with God and with our fellow human beings.

CONCLUSION

The Roman Catholic Church has been using the revised rites of baptism for over thirty years. During that time we have seen how these rites have shaped the life of dioceses and local parish communities and led to a renewal of church life and practice. Baptism is now understood as a central moment in the life of the church, affecting the whole community and not just the person being baptized. Local parishes find themselves face-to-face with the very core of Christian faith, namely the saving mystery of Christ. As they prepare people for baptism and support them on their faith journey, local parishioners are reminded of their own baptism and the commitment they made. Many people are using baptism as a lens through which to interpret the whole of Christian existence. Hence, rather than seeing baptism primarily as a one-off event, it is more and more understood as an event that continues to have ramifications not only in a person's life, but also within the life of the community. The challenge of baptism is always before us.

These developments in the understanding and practice of baptism indicate that the aims of the Second Vatican Council are being realized. The return to the ancient sources, on which the liturgical renewal has been based, is resulting in a breath of fresh air blowing through the church. The practice of baptism is leading to a renewal of Christian life.

FURTHER READING

International Commission on English in the Liturgy. *Documents on the Liturgy 1963–1979: Conciliar, Papal, and Curial Texts.* Collegeville: Liturgical, 1982.

The Rites of the Catholic Church. Vol. 1. New York: Pueblo, 1990.

Whitaker, E. C. *Documents of the Baptismal Liturgy.* Revised and expanded by Maxwell E. Johnson. Collegeville: Liturgical, 2003.

3

The Lutheran Theology of Baptism

Robert Kolb

> Blessed be God and the Father of our Lord Jesus Christ, who according to the riches of his mercy has preserved in his church at least this sacrament [of baptism], untouched and untainted by human ordinances, and has made it free for all nations and classes of human kind and has not permitted it to be oppressed by filthy, godless monsters of greed and superstition. For he desired that by it little children, who were incapable of greed and superstition, might be initiated and sanctified in the simple faith of his Word.[1]

When Martin Luther introduced baptism in his *Babylonian Captivity of the Church* (1520), his understanding of how God works through this sacrament had not yet matured, but this treatise, as a programmatic writing for his mode of reform, did lay down foundations for his treatment of the Word of God in sacramental form that shaped his maturing view and that of his followers.

MARTIN LUTHER ON BAPTISM

Luther's earliest lectures on the Psalms (1513–1515) seldom mentioned baptism. That reflects his view at this time that God's Word in its "mediated" or concrete form mattered little in comparison to an "inner" or "spiritual" connection that God forged with his faithful. Jonathan Trigg

---

1. Luther, *Werke*, 6:526,35–527,2; Luther, *Works*, 36:57. Grönvik, *Taufe*, provides an overview of Luther's view of baptism.

reviews explanations offered by scholars for his reticence on the subject.[2] Most likely is that, as he himself observed, his university training and the preaching of his contemporaries had diminished the on-going significance of this sacrament for daily life and ignored what he came to see as its critical function in God's economy of salvation.[3] In his Romans lectures (1515–1516), Luther's interpretation of what would later become his key baptismal passage, Rom 6:3–11, remained heavily dependent on Augustine and without any sense that baptism functions as God's active Word that buries sinful identity and raises up a new identity in Christ. Instead, Luther applied the motif of death and resurrection quite independently of the sacrament itself to the spiritual need to reject sin and receive life from God.[4] His *Sermon on Baptism* (1519) marked the beginning of a new emphasis in his thinking, although it showed no indication of his view of the power of God's Word in sacramental form, which later became the center of his baptismal proclamation.[5]

That focus, along with other critical elements in his mature view, developed on the basis of two different agendas. The first was his critique of medieval Christianity as a religion of ritual, which reflected much of ancient Germanic traditional religious practice and thus regarded performance of ritual as the chief means of establishing the human relationship with God. This form of religious observance presumed that God is pleased with human beings when they fulfill outward forms, regardless of the faith that motivated these ritual good works. Like all other Protestant reformers, Luther interpreted the defense of sacramental validity in medieval theology, which held that the sacraments work *ex opere operato* (accomplished by performance of the work), as belief that their external use produced a guaranteed magical, automatic bestowal of God's grace. Luther always maintained that the validity of the sacraments depended on God's Word alone, but regarded medieval attitudes as promoting disregard for the necessity of faith as the maturing Christian's reaction to what God says in the sacraments. He believed that popular belief had turned the sacraments into the most widespread form of dependence on outward human action rather than God's grace received by the believer's trust.

2. Trigg, *Baptism*, 116–34.
3. Luther, "Babylonian Captivity," in *Werke*, 6:527,9–528,19; *Works*, 36:57–59.
4. Luther, *Werke*, 56:321,23–330,12; Luther, *Works*, 25:308–17.
5. Luther, *Werke*, 2:727–37; Luther, *Works*, 35:29–43.

Second, Luther attacked those who, in reaction against this belief, held that the sacraments are merely signs of God's grace, not instruments through which he actually bestows his mercy and forgiveness, thereby creating new life in sinners. A long-standing medieval tradition of reform advocated rejection of any notion of God's acting through the sacrament. This way of thinking was biblicistic, depending on the authority of Scripture rather than ecclesiastical traditions and teachers. It was also moralistic, defining the Christian life as moral obedience to God's commands rather than ritual practices. This led these reformers to be anti-clerical and anti-sacramental. They often believed that Christ would soon introduce his millennial kingdom.[6]

Against these views, Luther formulated his understanding that God works through his Word in oral, written, and sacramental forms to re-create sinners as children of God. He presumed that these forms of the gospel effectively accomplished a new birth or a new creation by addressing sinners and creating in them a "recognition of God's glory in the face of Jesus Christ," parallel to God's speaking in Genesis 1, as Paul stated in 2 Cor 4:6.[7] In applying this concept of God's Word to its baptismal form, he depended especially on descriptions of baptism as new birth (John 3:3–12, Titus 3:3–8) and as death or burial of the sinner and resurrection to new life in Christ (Rom 6:3–11, Col 2:11–15).[8] Infrequently, he reaffirmed that baptism is God's action by citing 1 Cor 1:12–14. Galatians 3:28 served him in reinforcing the proclamation of a new identity through putting on Christ in baptism. Matthew 28:19 served Luther as the dominical "words of institution" of this sacrament, although he also grounded its use in Jesus' baptism, without drawing precise parallels to God's saving work in baptizing sinners. In interpreting these passages he consistently stressed God's action and the reality of baptismal death and resurrection or rebirth for sinners in God's sight through this sacramental form of his Word. Luther used the image of

---

6. Cohn, *Pursuit*.

7. Luther, "Genesis Lectures," in *Werke*, 42:13,31–14,22; Luther, *Works*, 1:16–17. See Oyer, *Lutheran Reformers*, 114–39. Luther generally held that Anabaptists should not be executed for their belief, contending that only "the sword of the Spirit, the Word of God," can defeat heresy, although he briefly retreated from that view in the early 1530s (ibid., 135–39).

8. His use of Colossians 2, however, was almost always about the comparison to circumcision to justify infant baptism. He seldom substituted the passage for Rom 6:3–11 to posit baptismal death and resurrection of sinners.

cleansing less often (Eph 5:25–27) and only occasionally cited 1 Pet 3:21 as a general reference to justification through God's cleansing of the conscience in baptism. John Oyer noted contradictions in Luther's picture of Anabaptism, for instance in his *On Rebaptism* (1528);[9] these may have reflected the varying, sometimes contradictory, beliefs of groups that fell into that kind of reform movement.[10] He grouped Thomas Müntzer, a spiritualist, together with Anabaptists, for instance. He did encounter genuine defenders of the necessity of rebaptism as believer's baptism in Saxony from 1526 on.[11]

His catechisms (1529) stand at a critical juncture in the development of his mature view of baptism. The *Small Catechism*'s sections on baptism and the Lord's Supper follow a similar structure, to facilitate the children's learning. Written in the context of his first major engagement with Saxon Anabaptists in 1527–1528, the first question asked what baptism is: "baptism is not simply plain water. Instead, it is water enclosed in God's command and connected with God's Word." Fundamental to Luther's understanding of baptism was its nature as one form of God's Word, linked by God's gracious accommodation to the whole human creature, to the external element of water. Christ had instituted this sacrament with his command and promise in Matt 28:19, the children learned. Second, Luther asked what gifts or benefits baptism grants. "It brings about forgiveness of sins, redeems from death and the devil, and gives eternal salvation to all who believe it, as the words and promise of God declare." The example of Mark 16:16 follows. Luther then met the question posed by the Anabaptists: "How can water do such great things?" The reply affirmed, "Clearly, the water does not do it, but the Word of God, which is with and alongside the water, and faith, which trusts this Word of God in the water." Paul had said so in Titus 3:5–8. Luther's fourth question laid the foundation for the continuing use of God's initial baptismal action in the believer's life. The "significance" of baptism is that "the old creature in us with all sins and evil desires is to be drowned and die through daily contrition and repentance, and . . . daily a new person is to come forth and rise up to live before God in righteousness and purity forever," the application of Rom 6:4 to the believer's entire life, placing the Christian life in the context of the eschatological

---

9. Luther, *Werke*, 26:144–74.

10. Oyer, *Lutheran Reformers*, 123. Cf. Williams, *Radical Reformation*, passim.

11. Oyer, *Lutheran Reformers*, 6–113.

conflict with Satan and the on-going struggle against sin.[12] Luther followed this question with instructions on personal confession of sins and absolution, which he defined as the daily repetition of God's baptismal act, putting sinful identity to death through the law's condemnation and renewing the believer's identity as child of God through the gift of forgiveness and life.[13]

The *Large Catechism* expanded this instruction, for parents and pastors. In it Luther stressed that God has commanded and instituted baptism as a means by which he conveys his promise of salvation: "Although performed by human hands, it is nevertheless truly God's own act."[14] God promises and delivers "victory over death and the devil, forgiveness of sin, God's grace, all of Christ, and the Holy Spirit with his gifts."[15] He acts through his creative Word to save; indeed, faith saves, as the God-given human reaction to God's promise, but that does not alter the power of God's Word in baptismal form as the instrument of his giving. Satan undermines what God does in baptism by diverting faith from God's giving in the sacrament, either by preventing recognition of its true nature or by turning the rite into a magical happening.[16]

His confrontations with Anabaptists in 1526–1528 caused Luther to defend infant baptism in the *Large Catechism*. He argued that baptism had brought countless people into the church; God would not have given them the Holy Spirit, Luther reasoned, if he did not recognize baptism as establishing his relationship with them. More substantially, he also grounded his belief in baptizing infants on baptism's nature as God at work through this form of his Word. God's promise remains certain, even when individual recipients, in the mystery of the continuation of sin and evil in the lives of the baptized, receive it in bad faith as adults or abandon their faith and the relationship it established some time later. This argument rests on the distinction between baptism's validity as God's act and the necessity of faith for enjoying the benefits of the promise.[17] Implicit in his argument is his belief that original sin separates all

---

12. Kolb and Wengert, *Book of Concord*, 359–60. See Arand, *That I May Be*, 167–70; Peters, *Kommentar*, 4:71–126.

13. Kolb and Wengert, *Book of Concord*, 360–62. See Peters, *Kommentar*, 4:11–67.

14. Kolb and Wengert, *Book of Concord*, 457.

15. Ibid., 461.

16. Ibid., 458–62.

17. Ibid., 62–65. See Brinkel, "Die Lehre Luthers."

mortals from God; since infants can die, they exhibit the presence of that alienation that strikes to the heart and root of sinful human existence. Therefore, he defended continued use of baptism by midwives when newborns seemed about to die.[18]

Luther believed that baptism actually changes the identity of the baptized into that of God's child. Therefore, in view of the continuation of the eschatological struggle against Satan, the world, and one's own sinful desires even after baptism, the "Christian life is nothing else than a daily baptism . . . For we must keep at it without ceasing, always purging whatever pertains to the old Adam so that whatever belongs to the new creature may come forth." That means that the old creature's sinful habits must be reduced and set aside while gentleness, patience, and other virtues grow. "This is the right use of baptism . . . Where this does not take place but rather the old creature is given free rein and continually grows stronger, baptism is not being used but resisted." Without faith it remains "a mere unfruitful sign," but as the program of daily repentance for the entire Christian life, as God's promise that remains forever, it continues to "snatch us from the jaws of the devil and makes us God's own, overcomes and takes away sin and daily strengthens the new person." It is "the daily garment" (Gal 3:27) that Christians wear continually as they produce the fruits of faith.[19] It provides both comfort that God's promise stands when believers fall into sin and the motivation and power for putting sinful desires to death and serving others through new obedience to God.

Luther never treated the mode of baptism, but a casual observation in the *Large Catechism*, "this act or ceremony consists of being dipped into the water, which covers us completely, and being drawn out again," indicates that his focus on Romans 6 led him to continue the frequent, though not universal, medieval custom of immersion of infants when the font was large enough.[20]

Luther's lectures on Galatians (1531) and Genesis (1535–1545) reflect the further development of his baptismal thought. Particularly his use of Rom 6:3–11 in 1531 confirms Trigg's judgment that Luther's "doctrine of justification by faith is intimately related to—indeed even

---

18. Luther, "Sermons on Baptism, 1534, 1539," *Werke*, 37:27–261,2; Luther, *Werke*, 47:657,4–659,10.

19. Kolb and Wengert, *Book of Concord*, 465–67.

20. Ibid., 464–65.

predicated upon—[his] understanding of the abiding covenant of baptism."[21] For his Galatians lectures frequently describe God's justifying act as the burial of sinners and the resurrection of his children to walk in Christ's footsteps.[22] In his Genesis lectures he frequently directed students to "seeking God where he wants to be found," in the concrete forms of his Word, particularly preaching, absolution, baptism, the Lord's Supper, conversation that conveys the gospel, and Scripture. By 1535 he had largely abandoned describing the sacraments with Augustine's designation of "sign." God's presence and power assert themselves through the various forms of his Word. Through them God is at work among his people, calling them to repentance and bestowing forgiveness, life, and salvation. God veils or hides himself, Luther asserted, in common, ordinary language and elements, to reveal himself in his choice of seemingly "weak" and "foolish" words that deliver his power and wisdom in the midst of a sinful world (1 Cor 1–2).[23] God not only forgives sins through his baptismal promise, he also establishes his covenant relationship by initiating new life in reclaiming sinners in their baptisms. Thus, parallel to circumcision, baptism has become by God's design the "entry gate" to his kingdom.[24] Thus, it is his means of gathering people into his church. In contrast to the Anabaptists, he paid "far more attention to the focus or centre about which the Church is gathered than to the boundary which defines it and delineates its precise membership and extent."[25] Indeed, baptism marks all those whom God wants to bring to himself, but in God's eschatological battle with Satan, some of the baptized live falsely, in a "church" opposed in some way or other to God and his truth. Nonetheless, the Holy Spirit continues to fight to recall them to true faith in the promise God gave them in their baptism.[26]

Luther did continue his polemic against magical, ritualistic views of baptism and other, scholastic errors in medieval theology. In preparing for discussion with Roman Catholics at the papally-called council, Luther composed his *Smalcald Articles* (1537) and objected specifically to the view of "Thomas [Aquinas] and the Dominicans" that attributed

21. Trigg, *Baptism*, 2.
22. Kolb, "God Kills to Make Alive."
23. Trigg, *Baptism*, 20–39.
24. Ibid., 39–45.
25. Ibid., 47, 46–53.
26. Ibid., 48–53, 56–60.

spiritual power to the water as water, apart from the Word, and to Duns Scotus and the Franciscans, whom, he wrote, emphasized the divine will, again apart from water and Word, in baptism's saving action.[27]

From the mid-1520s on, Luther's preaching reflected his deep pastoral concerns that informed his use of baptism.[28] Several times he devoted a series of sermons to catechetical treatment of the sacrament. These sermons especially aimed at the comfort of those who might doubt their status in God's sight, by reaffirming that God's Word is certain: believers can count on his baptismal promise, which will not fail. Reacting against medieval Ockhamism's use of the concept of "covenant" as affirming human participation in salvation, Luther seldom used the term, but he did in preaching on baptism. His belief in infant baptism permitted him to affirm that this covenant involved only God's action, his unshakable commitment to save his chosen people. The certainty of the promise becomes concrete in God's use of external means, Luther argued, urging his hearers to turn to their own experience of God's Word in this form.[29] Yet his realism caused him to warn parishioners that baptism has brought them into the continuing eschatological conflict between God and Satan. They must expect to have to fight temptation from the devil, the world, and their own sinful desires. Baptism dare not be used as a license to sin, he admonished, insisting that hearers live lives of daily repentance, fleeing from disobedience to trust in the Savior who had claimed them in baptism.[30]

Luther not only preached on baptism; he was sensitive to its liturgical presentation in the congregation. In 1523 he published a German baptismal liturgy. He advised those who used the service that this act of God formed a vital part of the eschatological conflict with Satan. "It is no joke to take sides against the devil and not only to drive him away from the little child but to burden the child with such a mighty and lifelong enemy."[31] Luther retained a number of medieval customs surrounding

---

27. Smalcald Articles, III:v, 2–3; see Kolb and Wengert, *Book of Concord*, 320.
28. Kolb, "Benefit"; Ferel, *Gepredigte Taufe*.
29. Kolb, "Benefit," 355–58.
30. Ibid., 358–60.
31. Luther, *Werke*, 12:47,11–20; Luther, *Works*, 53:102; the order is found in Luther, *Werke*, 12:42–48; Luther, *Works*, 53:96–103; the 1526 revision, Luther, *Werke*, 19:537–41, 53:107–9. It was republished in many versions. See Kolb and Wengert, *Book of Concord*, 371–75.

the baptismal words, including the minor exorcism, which later in the sixteenth century became an important mark of Lutheran baptism as opposed to Calvinist baptisms.[32] He also retained immersion of infants, reflecting Paul's teaching that God acts to restore his relationship with mortals from the beginning of their mortal life through this form of his promise. Luther's order contained a long prayer which featured comparisons of baptism with the deliverance of Noah and his family from the flood, Israel through the Red Sea, and Christ's baptism.

Kent Burreson's investigation of possible medieval sources for Luther's rite of 1523 and this "flood prayer" demonstrates extensive dependence on the *Agenda communis* of 1505 (four editions extant, 1505–1520) or a similar work. As in many other instances, Luther used what was at hand, in this case the diocesan usage as practiced in Wittenberg. However, already in 1523 he was adding his own "Wittenberg" touch.[33] Burreson concludes that, in the absence of direct medieval models of this form of baptismal prayer, it is safest to conclude that Luther is the redactor who brought its elements together in this particular form, combining its second half from one late medieval source, with the typology present in its first half, which he may well have found in Saxon usage of the time or constructed himself.[34]

Luther's 1526 revision of the baptismal liturgy simplified it but also strengthened his central theological concerns, focusing on God's promise that conveys his gift of forgiveness of sin, which meant "life and salvation." He did not alter the essential shape of the older liturgical form, but highlighted its nature as the regenerative washing and drowning that brings new life to God's chosen people.[35]

LUTHER'S COLLEAGUES AND FOLLOWERS ON BAPTISM

The continuation of this liturgical tradition began with Luther's close associate at Wittenberg, Philip Melanchthon (1497–1560), who composed an *Instruction for Visitors* when the Wittenberg faculty became involved in the visitation of Saxon parishes organized by Elector John in 1527–1528. This work encouraged baptisms in the presence of the

---

32. Nischan, "Exorcism Controversy."
33. Burreson, "Saving Flood," 120–72.
34. Ibid., 173–259.
35. Ibid., 260–98.

congregation, and it did not specify one ritual for all of Saxony, permitting continuation of the use of older ritual forms.[36] As Luther's plans for reform spread across German-speaking lands, a number of his followers, above all his Wittenberg colleague Johannes Bugenhagen (1485–1558), authored ecclesiastical constitutions that always set down forms for baptism. Luther's influence emerges in almost all of them as they reflect his concern to emphasize that God promises and thus effects a saving relationship with his people through this sacramental form of his Word. Retention of a number of ceremonies in the liturgy—exorcism, the sign of the cross, the laying of hands, the renunciation, and the post-baptismal robing and blessing—were "thought to communicate the essence of God's regenerative activity in baptism."[37] The second generation of Wittenberg students continued to revamp liturgical usage in the second half of the sixteenth century, but its core remained, reiterating Luther's fundamental message that God acts in baptism to give his saving promise to infants. Perhaps the chief alteration in the baptismal form in that period is found in the addition of catechetical admonitions, which "nearly made some of the baptismal rites into mini-catechisms."[38]

Melanchthon did not fully capture or reproduce Luther's baptismal teaching. In 1521 Melanchthon wrote his first edition of the *Loci communes* or *Commonplaces* (*Topics*) of theology, which in its later editions (1535, 1543) became the dominant pattern and form for Lutheran doctrinal instruction. In 1521, as Luther was edging toward his concept of the Word of God as God's dynamic instrument, Melanchthon tended to favor the description of baptism as a "sign," to be sure, one which "signifies God's work" and favor, a sign that "lifts up, strengthens, and encourages" faith.[39] Thus, he did not come to equate it with God's justifying action in his re-creative Word. In later editions of his *Loci* he contended that baptism reassures believers but did not state that it actually effects what God does to them when he forgives them.[40] He echoed Luther's view that it signified the transition from death to life, deliverance from

---

36. Ibid., 304–5.

37. Ibid., 411, see 305–412.

38. Ibid., 460, see 413–61. Cf. Tranvik, "Other Sacrament," 201–4. On twentieth-century Lutheran baptismal liturgical practice and its historical background, see Pfatteicher, *Commentary*, 28–109; Nagel, "Holy Baptism."

39. Melancthon, *Werke*, 2,1:144–45.

40. Ibid., 2,1:508–9.

death's clutches, and that its significance remains for the Christian's entire life. It calls believers to mortify the flesh and at the same time gives those who trust in Christ hope for overcoming mortality. In this way Melanchthon substituted the remembering of one's baptism for the medieval practice of the sacrament of penance.[41] In his presentation of Wittenberg teaching to Emperor Charles V in 1530, the *Augsburg Confession*, Melanchthon simply confessed that baptism is necessary, offers grace, and that through it children are entrusted to God and become pleasing to him.[42] His opponents took no exception to this brief statement, and so his *Apology* [*Defense*] of the Confession (1531) only expanded on its rejection of rebaptism, arguing that God offers salvation through this sacrament.[43] By the end of his life, Mark Tranvik argues, Melanchthon had strayed from Luther's emphasis on baptism, making it one topic among many, and diminished its practical use in everyday Christian living, not according it the key place in God's way of justifying sinners and governing their lives that it occupied in Luther's thinking.[44]

Luther and his Wittenberg colleagues were not the only theologians who shaped Lutheran thinking in the sixteenth century. In south Germany none of his disciples exercised such widespread, profound influence as Johannes Brenz (1499–1570), reformer of the town of Schwäbisch Hall and later superintendent of the churches in the duchy of Württemberg. Brenz reduplicated much of Luther's thought, but developed somewhat independently his expression of evangelical teaching. He wrote the second-most popular Lutheran catechism in 1535. Instead of following Luther's pattern of law (the ten commandments), gospel (the creed), and the Christian life (the Lord's Prayer, the use of the sacraments, a program for daily devotional life, and a table of Christian callings of service to neighbor), Brenz began with baptism, preceding the Creed, Lord's Prayer, Decalogue, and Lord's Supper, in "a chronological replication of the Christian life."[45] Baptism provides the foundation for the entire Christian faith and life in his catechism. He regarded baptism as God's Word and sign of his grace and the forgiveness he offers. In

---

41. Ibid., 2,1:145–46. Cf. Tranvik, "Other Sacrament," 42–48.

42. Kolb and Wengert, *Book of Concord*, 42–43.

43. Kolb and Wengert, *Book of Concord*, 183–84. Cf. Oyer, *Lutheran Reformers*, 140–78.

44. Tranvik, "Other Sacrament," 61–62, 85–87.

45. Ibid., 81, see 77–85.

addition, Brenz anchored salvation in God's election and regarded baptism as a ratification of God's choosing his own elect in eternity. Like a wedding ceremony, it is a public confirmation of a relationship God has already established.[46]

As with many aspects of his thought, Luther's own students reproduced his understanding of baptism in varying degrees and repeated elements of it with different accents. On the one hand, Johannes Mathesius (1504–1565), pastor in Joachimsthal in Bohemia, could proclaim that baptism is God's act of re-creation that sets the entire Christian life in motion, establishing the identity of God's chosen as his children and impelling them to new obedience.[47] On the other hand, Tranvik notes that as vociferous a defender of Luther's legacy as Tilemann Heshusius (1527–1588), pastor and professor in several places, oft exiled because of his bold defense of Luther's views as he understood them, mentions baptism as the source of rebirth and new life only once in his extensive comments on the baptismal passage in John 3.[48] Among the most influential students of Luther's and Melanchthon's followers were the authors of the Formula of Concord of 1577, a document that addressed twelve areas of conflict that beset their adherents who tried to sort out their legacy in the third quarter of the sixteenth century.

SEVENTEENTH-CENTURY LUTHERANS ON BAPTISM

The tradition was delivered to secondary and university students in the next generation by, among other textbooks, the *Compendium of Theological Topics* of Leonhard Hütter (1563–1616). He repeated the basic definitions of baptism and its action from Luther's *Small Catechism* and expanded that material with a defense of infant baptism on the basis of Christ's institution of the sacrament for all nations (Matt 28:19) and Christ's expression of love for infants (Matt 18:14; 19:14; Mark 10:13–14). He argued that baptism should not be repeated because God's covenant and promise is sufficient when made once. That one baptism recalls Christians to daily repentance, but need not be repeated.[49]

---

46. Brenz, *Catechismus* (1535; Wittenberg: Schwenck, 1563), A7b–A8a, D6a.
47. Mathesius, *Postilla*, L1b.
48. Tranvik, "Other Sacrament," 165.
49. Hütter, *Compendium*, 428–43.

Johann Gerhard (1582–1637), perhaps the foremost seventeenth-century representative of Lutheran teaching, reinforced and extended Hütter's treatment and similar discussion by his predecessors in his *Theological Topics* (1610–1622).[50] He also dedicated one of the "sacred meditations" of his widely-used devotional text of that title to the sacrament. He affirmed baptism as rebirth, a washing of regeneration (John 3:3–8; Titus 3:3–8), and compared its re-creation to the act of God in creating the worlds in Genesis 1. Gerhard loved medical metaphors and applied this image in mentioning baptism's healing of sinners. Piling up biblical images, including Old Testament water images (deliverance from the Egyptians at the Red Sea, Ezekiel's picture of life-giving, healing water in the temple, Ezek 47:1–12), Gerhard confessed the sacrament to be a covenant, God's sure promise of life, the delivery of Christ's death and resurrection in the crucifixion, the putting on of Christ, the blotting out of sin, and delivery from the devil's payment of death for sin.[51]

Lutheran theology can always be sung. Luther's hymn, "To Jordan When Our Lord Had Gone," focused on the baptism of believers, reminding those who sung that baptism apart from faith brings no benefit, but that it establishes the baptized as new-born, an heir of God's kingdom.[52] It is perhaps a sign of the relative diminution of baptism in the period after Luther that, when compared with the Lord's Supper or other major aspects of ecclesiastical teaching and life, few Lutheran hymns of the late sixteenth and seventeenth centuries treated the first sacrament. Those that did emphasized the need of all sinners, infants included, for forgiveness of sins because of original sin, and the comfort that God's baptismal promise gives as it delivers the benefits of Christ's death and resurrection. They also left no doubt that baptism produces faith and new obedience in the life of repentance.[53] In the seventeenth century, Paul Gerhardt (1607–1676) also rehearsed the sinful state from which baptism delivers in his twelve strophes on baptism, echoing Titus 3 as he rejoiced in its liberation from Satan's prison, the curse of sinful nature, and death itself. In baptism we put on Christ, become holy, pious,

50. Gerhard, *Loci theologici*, 4:256–398.
51. Gerhard *Meditationes*, Latin original, 2:99–103, German translation, 1:426–30.
52. Luther, *Werke*, 35:468–70; Luther, *Works*, 53:300–301.
53. For instance, Selnecker, "Das Sacrament," 4:255; Ringwald, "Von Stiftung," 924; Philipp der Jüngere, "Vom heiligen Tauff," 5:34–35; Ulm, "Gesang vom H. Tauff," 5:352–53.

and good through God's pronouncement in the sacrament.[54] Erdmann Neumeister (1671–1756) celebrated becoming God's own child in baptism, emphasizing the necessity of Christ's rescue from sin, and comfort receiving the benefits of his sacrifice that the baptismal cleansing of conscience effects. His hymn defies death since baptism has given life and the inheritance of paradise.[55] Neumeister's contemporary Emilie Juliane von Schwarzburg-Rudolstadt (1637–1706) wrote of putting on Christ and being numbered with God's family through baptism (Gal 3:27), also as preparation for death.[56] At the same time the Danish bishop Thomas Hansen Kingo (1634–1703) versified Mark 16:16 and affirmed the continuing impact of baptism on daily life and its hope of life everlasting.[57]

Baptism was present in song and catechesis, preaching and praxis, in Lutheran churches throughout the eighteenth and nineteenth centuries, but it served as a sacrament of initiation. Repentance was preached without much use of Luther's connection to the sacrament. For differing reasons, clergy and laity alike who were influenced by Pietism and the Enlightenment passed lightly over baptism, although the revival of interest in the theology of Luther and the sixteenth-century Lutheran confessional documents in the nineteenth century took baptism seriously as God's act, necessary to establish a relationship also with infants, who from birth fell under the curse or original sin. They did not emphasize its use in daily Christian living.

LUTHERAN BAPTISMAL THEOLOGY IN THE TWENTIETH CENTURY

Fresh interest in Luther's theology of the Word and a revival of liturgical interests by the mid-twentieth century has resulted in a new emphasis on Luther's insights into this sacrament and its use in congregational and individual Christian life. The rise of Baptist groups in traditional Lutheran lands, particularly in Nordic countries, the necessity felt by immigrant Lutherans of dealing with the English-speaking Baptist tradition, especially in North America, and the formidable challenge of Karl

---

54. Nelle, *Gerhardts Lieder*, 101–3.
55. *Lutheran Service Book*, 594.
56. Ibid., 598.
57. Ibid., 601.

Barth to infant baptism[58] also shaped some Lutheran writing on baptism in the twentieth century. Heidelberg theologian Edmund Schlink (1903–1984) and others, including authors of surveys of dogmatic theology, focused above all on baptismal regeneration as God's act of salvation through this form of his saving Word and, in that connection, on infant baptism. The four chapters of Schlink's book-length treatment provide an overview of the major topics treated by twentieth-century Lutheran theologians in their presentations on baptism: its institution by Christ, "the saving activity of God through baptism," its administration, reception, and use in parish life, and its mode or form.

Lutherans generally began discussions of baptism with Christ's institution of the sacrament in Matt 28:19 and Mark 16:16.[59] Schlink presented baptism against the background of Old Testament use of water to proclaim God's cleansing acts of reconciliation, of John's baptism, and of Jesus being baptized and his references to his death as a baptism. He noted that Paul's epistles presumed baptismal practice, not urging readers to be baptized but reminding them of its power and effects in their lives. These included the bestowal of forgiveness, the presence of the Holy Spirit, and its association with trust in Jesus as Savior.[60]

Lutherans cannot think of baptism apart from Jesus Christ as its foundation and goal: his death and resurrection bestow their benefits upon God's people through baptism (Rom 6:3–11; Col 2:11–15). They cannot think of baptism apart from the Holy Spirit, who delivers those benefits in this form of his re-creative Word (2 Cor 1:21–22).[61] Robert Jenson states simply, "The identification of baptism with forgiveness is so close in Acts that the mere phrase 'forgiveness of sins' seems normally to denote baptism (Acts 5:31; 10:43; 13:38; 26:18)."[62] Baptism gives God's enduring promise of forgiveness and regeneration, restoration to humanity through incorporation into Christ's death and resurrection, through new birth.[63] Particularly, Schlink strove to explicate the delicate balance that holds together Luther's

---

58. Barth, *Teaching of the Church*.

59. Scaer, *Baptism*, 24–29.

60. Schlink, *Doctrine of Baptism*, 9–41; Schlink, *Dogmatik*, 479–83; cf. Scaer, *Baptism*, 30–67.

61. Schlink, *Dogmatik*, 483–85.

62. Jenson, "Baptism," 319.

63. Ibid., 319–26.

understanding of God's re-creative action in his Word of forgiveness and life, the water as external sign, and the faith that the Holy Spirit creates through this sacramental Word as the constitutive element of the human creature's relationship to the Creator. God's Word in its baptismal form delivers salvation (1 Pet 3:21), but it saves by creating the relationship that provides cognitive recognition of God as Lord and Savior and the trust in him that constitutes faith in maturing human beings. God's gospel of new life in Christ creates and awakens faith; faith clings to God through Christ and claims the person's new identity through his death to sin and his resurrection to true human life. If this balance disappears, false views of baptism quickly appear, Schlink warned: a magical view that makes it no more than a ritual that works automatically without claiming the trust of the sinner; or a symbol, no more than a representation of what God does apart from sacramental means; or a command to human obedience to pledge oneself to God; or a poor alternative to baptism in the Spirit largely separated from God's Word.[64]

In baptism God assigns the baptized to Christ, Schlink states. God enters deeply into human life by bringing the baptized into Christ's name, as his possession, and that bestows freedom and hope. For Christ shares his death and resurrection with the baptized, giving them new life, which gives them a new personhood in Christ and sets them on a new way of conducting life (Rom 6:3-11). Baptism dare never be conceived apart from Christ and apart from the baptized's personal reception of his death and resurrection. For the Holy Spirit, according to the New Testament, is at work in bringing the re-creative Word of Christ to the baptized, and he continues to work in their lives, preserving their faith, moving and guiding them to "walk in the Spirit," in Christ's footsteps.[65] Dietrich Bonhoeffer (1906-1945) was speaking of baptismal death in the life of daily repentance when he wrote his famous words, "When Christ calls a man, he bids him come and die," (literally, "every call of Christ leads into death"); he explained, "The call to follow Jesus, baptism in the name of Jesus Christ, is death and life. The call of Christ and baptism leads Christians into a daily struggle against sin and Satan."[66] Norwegian

---

64. Schlink, *Doctrine of Baptism*, 88-105, 120-26.

65. Ibid., 42-72. Cf. Elert, "Anchoring," 221; Jenson, "Baptism," 330-33.

66. Bonhoeffer, *Discipleship*, 87-88. Cf. his chapter treating baptismal death as God's act of justification of sinners and thus, for them, a decisive break from sin, 205-12.

theologian Ole Hallesby (1879–1961) summarized the same material by concluding that in baptism God bestows forgiveness of sins, joins the baptized to the Holy Spirit, and unites them with Christ.[67]

The Holy Spirit also creates the church through baptism, incorporating those baptized into God's people, Christ's body (1 Cor 12:13), and himself as he comes to dwell in them as his temple.[68] "The proclamation of the gospel was from its beginning not only a call to repentance and to faith but also to baptism."[69] The baptized therefore live in service to God through service in the world as those who worship him together and move into every area of human life with his love. Incorporation into the church dare never be understood as merely external membership in an institution; it bestows a new identity, a new family relationship, a new way of life.[70] Schlink stressed the ecumenical significance of baptism, pointing out the almost universal recognition of other church's baptisms (Baptists being the exception, he stated), believing that this fact should invite all to Eucharistic fellowship,[71] a conclusion not shared by all Lutherans.

Lutherans in the twentieth century have insisted that baptism is, like natural birth, a one-time only event as God gives new birth to sinners (John 3:3–5).[72] The Holy Spirit works through his Word in baptizing, but he has entrusted baptism to his church. In those instances where the words of baptism are used properly apart from a congregational context, baptism may be valid, but its nature as an act of God's people for incorporation into their assembly strongly encourages restricting its use to the context of the church.[73]

In addressing the dispute over infant baptism, most Lutherans concede that specific evidence for infant baptism is lacking before 200 AD, but point to its almost universal status as an aspect of ecclesiastical life that was taken for granted in the earliest mention of it.[74]

---

67. Hallesby, *Infant Baptism*, 12–13.
68. Schlink, *Dogmatik*, 485–86.
69. Ibid., 479.
70. Schlink, *Doctrine of Baptism*, 72–85.
71. Ibid., 206–10.
72. Ibid., 109–14.
73. Ibid., 114–20.
74. Hallesby, *Infant Baptism*, 16–20; Schlink, *Doctrine of Baptism*, 130–36. Cf. Jeremias, *Infant Baptism*.

Their dogmatic arguments rest upon the presupposition that God is acting through his Word as an instrument of forgiveness and salvation in baptism and upon the need of all human beings from birth for deliverance from sin, which manifests its presence in the lives of all through mortality, the wages of sin (Rom 6:23a).[75] Bonhoeffer placed infant baptism within the context of the community that "carries" the baptized child into conscious faith within the eschatological context of the individual's entire life.[76] He wrote,

> Baptism is the call to the human being into childhood, a call that can be understood only eschatologically . . . The child is near to what is of the future—the eschata. This too is conceivable only to the faith that suspends itself before revelation. Faith is able to fix upon baptism as the unbreakable Word of God, the eschatological foundation of its life. Because baptism lies temporally in the past and is, nonetheless, an eschatological occurrence, the whole of my past life acquires seriousness and temporal continuity.[77]

Finnish theologian Uuras Saarnivaara (1908–1998), who also taught in the United States, attempted to bridge the gap between "Baptist" thought and a Lutheran understanding of the sacrament with his semi-popular but sophisticated *Scriptural Baptism*, which he subtitled *A Dialog between John Bapstead and Martin Childfont*. In it he endeavored to explore the biblical basis of infant baptism and address the issues of baptism as an act of God or human beings, of baptismal regeneration and mode of baptism, of its use in the ancient church, and of the validity of its promise. He hoped that the form of dialog would give both views full voice although Baptists would probably think John could have presented a better defense of their position. In their initial conversation, John, who left his and Martin's church when he became convinced that his own baptism as an infant was against Scripture, agrees with Martin on the critical role that presuppositions and cultural prejudice play in deciding how to interpret Scripture. This is Saarnivaara's recognition of the epistemological underpinnings of the debate.[78] As Martin lays the foundation for his argument, he turns to the parallel Paul drew (Col

---

75. Hallesby, *Infant Baptism*, 20–26; Schlink, *Doctrine of Baptism*, 142–60; Scaer, *Baptism*, 5–23, 124–46.

76. Bonhoeffer, *Sanctorum Communio*, 240–42.

77. Bonhoeffer, *Act and Being*, 159–60. See Jenson, "Baptism," 319–20.

78. Saarnivaara, *Baptism*, ix–xiii.

2:11–15) between circumcision and baptism, and to Jewish proselyte baptisms that involved infants. He emphasizes the definition of the Greek *brephos* (fetus, infant) in Luke 18:15 as an indication that Christ wants the youngest children to be in relationship with him. Saarnivaara rejected any concept of infant faith as untenable in the light of modern psychology, but argued that God determines the relationship that human creatures have with him and therefore can and does create relationships with *brephois*. If adults must receive the kingdom of God in the manner of these infants, then the infants themselves must receive, obviously passively, this gift of God.[79]

Saarnivaara's Martin argues chiefly on the basis of his understanding of baptism as God's action: "baptism is an act of God and of His Church upon you. It must find a correspondence on your part by faith and surrender to Christ. Baptism is God's act upon you, faith and surrender is your act toward God."[80] In explaining 1 Pet 3:21 and Rom 6:3–11 Martin uses the analogy of rescuing a drowning person. The rescuer saves the person, the rope that is the instrument by which rescue is conveyed saves the person, as does that person's grasping the rope—analogous to Jesus, the baptismal Word, and faith. All are necessary, and baptism truly can be said to save, to bury sinful identity and create the new identity in Christ. Examining other passages strengthens Martin's position that God acts through his Word joined to baptismal water, creating a relationship that must blossom into faith—when the receiver of God's promise is able to believe, in the case of infants.[81] For faith completes the relationship created by God's initial approach to sinners.

Hallesby anticipated Saarnivaara's arguments in his 1923 treatment of the relationship between infant baptism and adult conversion. He ended his volume,

> Baptism is *individualized grace*. Baptism is the most distinct expression of the love of God for the individual . . . When I was baptized, God performed the act upon me and it concerned no one else but me. In order to be of greater help to the sinner, God has met him not only with *words* spoken to him as an individual, but in an act. And this act is to stand at the beginning of our life

---

79. Ibid., 1–22.
80. Ibid., 32.
81. Ibid., 36–52.

and tell us more forcefully than any word, that God has once for all granted us His grace. And He never takes it back.[82]

Most Lutheran theologians in the twentieth century have not advocated a concept of infant faith in a psychologically explainable form.[83] Werner Elert suggested that "the question concerning the faith of children loses importance" because baptism's validity dare not be made conditional upon faith but rather on God's promise, and because baptism must be active throughout the believer's life, not simply as an initial starting point.[84] Indeed, all Lutheran thinkers insist that as baptized children grow, faith is necessary in the working out of God's promise on the human side. Lecturing in the early days of modern psychological theory, Hallesby stressed the possibilities of the Word of God, as used in the community surrounding the child, having an effect on its subconscious and growing consciousness as well as the obligation of parents and congregation to give instruction in the faith at an early age. In so doing he was addressing the problem of lapsed members of establishment Lutheran churches, who grew up without such instruction.[85] This topic commanded the attention of many church leaders, who recognized the dangers associated with automatic baptism of children whose parents show little or no commitment to Christ or the church.[86]

Twentieth-century Lutheran thinkers have accentuated the importance of baptism as a basis for the Christian community and its entire life together. The saving Word in the sacrament of rebirth introduces God's children to their life of receiving the Word in its other, teaching or nourishing, forms, and to the life of praise and of service to the household of faith and the entire world. The participation in Christ's death and resurrection effected by baptism (Rom 6:3–11) brings people together in his body as a community of praise and service (Rom 12).[87]

Overshadowing much European comment on the baptismal community is the frustration Saarnivaara reflected with the establishment Lutheranism of northern Europe. He wrote that, "a great majority of

---

82. Hallesby, *Infant Baptism*, 96.

83. One exception is Scaer, *Baptism*, 147–56.

84. Elert, *Structure*, 298–300.

85. Hallesby, *Infant Baptism*, 28–83.

86. E.g., Schlink, *Doctrine of Baptism*, 126–30, 116–66; Schlink, *Dogmatik*, 486; Wingren, *Gospel*, 137–46; Jenson, "Baptism," 326–28.

87. Wingren, *Gospel*, 137–53.

people who have been baptized in their infancy are unbelievers and travel the broad way which leads to destruction. But that is not the fault of baptism . . . In our time, infant baptism is used too indiscriminately." But his solution was to urge that this problem be addressed by faithful parenting and stricter discipline of its use in the establishment church setting, not by abolishing infant baptism. He disagreed with John's position that a true believer cannot fall from grace, operating with Luther's law/gospel distinction though not mentioning it explicitly. He admitted not being able to understand those verses that speak of some branches being cut off by God (Rom 9:19–22; John 15:6; Matt 10:22; 24:13; Mark 13:13; 1 Tim 4:1; Heb 6:4–6).[88]

Particularly, Hallesby addressed the necessity of calling the baptized who have lapsed to repentance, and the place of baptism in that task. Using the analogy of the electrical wiring of a building, he wrote,

> In the hour of Baptism God laid the wire into the little child's soul. From that moment "the power is on." It accomplishes in the child all that the child has "contacts" enough to receive. The Word will see to it that there are more and more contacts in the child's soul to receive and to utilize all the power to which it has received access through Baptism. Now when a baptized person falls away from God, nothing is changed in the "wiring." The power is on as before. It is only the contact in the soul which has been destroyed . . . When a fallen person is awakened and brought to repentance, no change takes place in the wiring or in the amount of power . . . The change which occurs at repentance takes place only within the person. The contact is put in order again. The living connection with Christ is re-established.[89]

Lutherans have also attempted to demonstrate the place of baptism in witnessing to those outside the faith.[90] The missionary imperative in making disciples according to Christ's command (Matt 28:19) through baptism has won Lutheran treatment.[91] Furthermore, the gift of new identity in Christ has been presented as a significant appeal to many in

---

88. Ibid., 61–78
89. Hallesby, *Infant Baptism*, 91.
90. Anderson, *Baptism*.
91. Wingren, *Gospel*, 137–38; Jenson, "Baptism," 315–16.

Western cultures who are dissatisfied with, or even despairing over, their way of life and defining themselves.[92]

Twentieth-century Lutheran theologians uniformly agreed that the mode of baptism was an adiaphoron. Saarnivaara's Martin states, "We have no argument against the correctness of immersion as a form of baptism. But we are in disagreement concerning the necessity of this form."[93] Lutherans probably would have ignored this topic for the most part had not the challenge of those who insist on immersion become so prominent in the modern ecumenical exchange. However, some have argued against a recent Lutheran tendency to avoid immersion, pointing out precedent for the practice in the early church and the Reformation without insisting on its necessity.[94] Schlink's simple statement, "the New Testament gives no instruction on how to baptize—and it certainly does not offer a formula for Baptism," was taken for granted apart from the objections of others. Because God is acting in connection with baptismal water through his Word, Word and water are necessary, but beyond that no mode is prescribed. Schlink requires only that "the form of Baptism must demonstrate the connection that exists between Baptism, faith, and church."[95] He is open to liturgical forms traditionally associated with Lutheran baptisms, including the laying on of hands, anointing, signing the baptized with the cross, exorcism, forms for consecrating the water, and other ritual actions, so long as it is clear that they have "no constitutive significance for the validity and effect of Baptism" and do not obscure what is happening in baptism as God acts to establish a saving relationship with the sinner in this form of his Word.[96]

CONCLUSION

In some regards baptism is receiving a stronger accent in Lutheran theology at the beginning of the twenty-first century than it has since Luther's own time. Its nature as a form of God's re-creative Word and thus as his saving action, which bestows his promise of life and salvation at the beginning of the Christian life and which accompanies believers

---

92. Kolb, *Make Disciples*.
93. Saarnivaara, *Baptism*, 98 (94–98).
94. E.g., Scaer, *Baptism*, 91–101; Jenson, "Baptism," 317.
95. Schlink, *Doctrine of Baptism*, 172, 179 (172–94).
96. Ibid., 194–205.

throughout the struggles of their lives with sin and evil, and the mystery of their continuation in their lives, has won new appreciation in contemporary contexts. The use of baptism in pastoral care has won particular emphasis as it gives assurance of God's faithfulness to his promise in the baptismal form of his Word and reminds believers of their calling to live out the baptismal life in repentance and faith, walking in Christ's footsteps.

FURTHER READING

Luther, Martin. "Baptism." In Luther's *Large Catechism*: *The Book of Concord, The Confessions of the Evangelical Lutheran Church*, edited by Robert Kolb and Timothy J. Wengert, 456–67. Minneapolis: Fortress, 2000.

Chemnitz, Martin. "Concerning Baptism." In Chemnitz's *Examination of the Council of Trent Part II*, trans. Fred Kramer, 119–77. Saint Louis: Concordia, 1978.

Hütter, Leonhart. "Of Baptism." In Hütter's *Compendium locorum theologicorum . . . englisch*, edited by Johann Anselm Steiger, 1045–52. Stuttgart-Bad-Cannstatt: Frommann-Holzboog, 2006.

4

Baptism in the Reformed Tradition

JOHN VISSERS

THE EASTERN ORTHODOX GREEK spiritual theologian Nicolas Cabasilas (d.1371) wrote that "the water of baptism destroys one life and reveals another; it drowns the old man and raises up the new."[1] To be baptized is to be born according to Christ; it is to receive existence, to come into being out of nothing. It might seem odd to begin an article on baptism in the Reformed tradition with a quote from a fourteenth-century Greek mystical writer. But Cabasilas nicely articulates an issue that is, I want to argue, central to our understanding and practice of baptism in the church today: Christian identity and existence.

BAPTISM AND IDENTITY

It would be difficult to overstate just how foundational baptismal identity is for Christian life. In the words of James Torrance, through baptism we "participate in *all* that (Christ) has done and is doing for us, that we might receive him with *all* his blessings . . . He baptizes us into that life of communion for which we were created in the image of the triune God."[2] To be baptized, then, is to receive a new existence in Christ, to become a new creation in union with God's crucified Messiah (cf. 2 Cor 5:17); it is to be made in the image for which we were originally created; it is, as the Eastern theologians remind us, to become a person. Baptismal identity creates the basis for Christian

---

1. Cabasilas, *Life*, 66, 73.
2. Torrance, *Worship*, 79 (Italics mine).

worship, discipleship, ethics, spirituality, and mission. It embodies our justification, sanctification, and vocation. The waters of baptism are the wellspring for a life of faith, hope, and love.

The question of Christian identity, and therefore of baptism, is of vital importance for the church today. Our time in the Western world, it is said, is a post-Christian, postmodern, secular, and religiously pluralistic time. The church, it is argued, is in exile; people of faith are described as "resident aliens."[3] As a consequence, the Christian community is going through a kind of "identity crisis." In his recent book, Canadian philosopher Charles Taylor describes our time as "A Secular Age." Western culture, he says, is not simply characterized by a decline of certain beliefs and institutions; it is characterized by a total change in our experience of the world. We have moved, he argues, "from a society where belief in God is unchallenged and indeed, unproblematic, to one in which it is understood to be one option among others, and frequently not the easiest to embrace." Faith is now one option among many, and an embattled one at that.[4] If Taylor is correct, and I think he is, at least in part, things are not the way they used to be. Our situation, therefore, ought to elicit questions about where we are, who we are, whose we are, and what we ought to be and become and do; questions about identity and existence, and questions about the meaning and practice of baptism.

In his book *Exclusion and Embrace*, Yale theologian Miroslav Volf argues that we do not find our identity by retreating inward, but by participating in God's identity as God's people. When we see ourselves as having been incorporated into the self-giving love of the triune God, as having been embraced by the outstretched arms of Christ on the cross, and as having been welcomed by the open arms of a parent receiving a prodigal, then we know we belong. We know that God has made room for us, and we thereby make room for others.[5] Belonging to God is the basis of Christian identity, and therefore of baptism. Baptism is the act whereby we are incorporated, embraced, and welcomed. Baptism is a means of grace through which we participate in the identity of the triune God. Baptism bears witness to being born anew, the destruction of one life and the revelation of another, the drowning of the old person and the

---

3. For instance, see the work of Douglas John Hall, Stanley Hauerwas and William Willimon.

4. Taylor, *Secular Age*, 3.

5. Volf, *Exclusion*, 17, 29.

raising up of the new, to receive existence, to come into being. In short, baptism marks the beginning of our identity in Christ in God's world; baptism is the beginning of life.

If baptism is foundational for Christian identity, then it stands to reason that the way baptism is understood and practiced in the church reveals something about what is believed about Christian existence and identity. If baptism is a construal of Christian faith and life, and if it provides a narrative of the divine story into which we believe we are incorporated, then the baptismal theology and practice of a particular Christian tradition reveals the way in which it understands that story. In other words, differences between traditions on baptism are not simply differences about how a particular religious rite ought to be practiced. They represent distinctive ways in which Christian identity is construed and lived out. This understanding, it seems to me, is the most important starting point for any ecumenical discussion about baptism that intends to move towards convergence and consensus. In the first instance, it is not about baptism itself, but about Christian identity, about what it means to belong to God.

THE REFORMED TRADITION

The "Reformed" are those Christians who identify themselves with the Protestant tradition that traces its origins to the Reformation movement associated primarily with Ulrich Zwingli and John Calvin. Standing within the so-called "magisterial" Reformation, Zwingli and Calvin and their followers shared much in common with Lutherans and Anglicans, as well as a number of points of tension with Roman Catholicism and the Anabaptist movements of the so-called "radical" Reformation. With other Protestants, the "Reformed" emphasized the doctrines of salvation by grace alone, justification by faith alone, the reliance on Scripture alone, the centrality of Christ, and the glory of the sovereign God. By 1590 a theological distinction between Lutheran and Reformed teachings was clear, characterized by differences in a number of areas, including baptism. Accordingly, Queen Elizabeth I spoke of the "Calvinist" strand as "more reformed" than Lutheranism, and the name stuck. Historically, the Reformed tradition has often been identified theologically with a particular set of confessional statements (e.g., Scots Confession, Belgic Confession, Westminster Confession) and ecclesiologically with presbyterian polity. Having said that, there are many within Baptist and so-called "Free" churches as well as the Anglican tradition who would identify themselves as holding to a "Reformed" theology. Today, Reformed churches are found throughout the world, not only in the Netherlands, Scotland, and North America, but also, for example, in Korea, Ghana, and Cuba. This chapter, therefore, seeks to set out a baptismal theology and practice that acknowledges and draws upon the breadth and depth of the Reformed tradition, historically and globally.

Having said that, it is also important to note that I write from a particular ecclesial and social location. Born into a Dutch Calvinist immigrant family, I am now a Canadian Presbyterian, and my interpretation of a Reformed theology and practice of baptism reflects those realities. Canadian Presbyterians trace their origins, in the first instance, to the various strands of Scottish Presbyterians who settled Upper and Lower Canada in the nineteenth century. They were preceded, however, in Quebec, by the Huguenots who earlier settled New France, and succeeded by Presbyterian and Reformed Christians from places such as Ireland, The Netherlands, and Korea.

In an important article on Reformed spirituality, Howard Hageman notes that "it is difficult, if not impossible, to discuss piety in the Reformed tradition as a single concept."[6] The same may be said about baptism. It might be supposed that the Reformed doctrine and practice of baptism is identical to that of Calvin, but that is not exactly the case. Calvin was, to be sure, a dominant influence, but he was also a second generation Reformer and there was a Reformed theology and practice of baptism in existence before him. Furthermore, there were theological, liturgical, and pastoral developments subsequent to Calvin that continued to shape the understanding and experience of baptism in Presbyterian and Reformed churches. It is important, therefore, to sketch the historical, theological, and pastoral developments concerning baptism in the Reformed tradition by referring to the work of not only Calvin, but also Zwingli, Martin Bucer, Heinrich Bullinger, the Reformed orthodox theologians of the post-Reformation era, Jonathan Edwards, Friedrich Schleiermacher, the Mercersburg theologians, and Karl Barth, as well as the Reformed Confessions. The point is this: within the Reformed tradition itself there have been quite distinct ways of construing baptismal identity.

---

6. Hageman, "Reformed Spirituality," 55.

ZWINGLI AND BUCER

The story of baptism in the Reformed tradition begins with Zwingli who was born on New Year's Day, 1484, in the village of Wildhaus in the duchy of Toggenburg, a part of the Swiss confederacy. After studies at Bern, Vienna, and Basel (where he was educated in the *via antiqua*—the realist theology of the early scholastics such as Thomas Aquinas and Duns Scotus), Zwingli was ordained in 1506 and served a parish in Glarus. While he was at Glarus a friend introduced him to the humanist theology of Erasmus with its emphasis on the Church Fathers and the Bible, especially the critical study of the New Testament in Greek. In 1516 Zwingli became the people's priest at Einsiedeln and in 1519 he was called to the Great Church in Zurich. It was in Zurich where his interests as a biblical and humanist scholar converged with those of the Reformation. He began a series of sermons on the Gospel of Matthew, which are usually understood as the beginning of the Reformation in Zurich.[7] Soon Zwingli was challenging "a number of the late medieval worship practices such as penance and indulgences, fasting, veneration of saints, clerical celibacy, and pilgrimages."[8]

Zwingli's understanding of Christian baptism, therefore, was initially developed in response to the late medieval practices of the Roman Catholic Church. Like other first generation Reformers (especially Martin Luther), Zwingli was concerned about the appropriation of the sacraments, that is, the way in which the sacraments were efficacious for the faithful. Not surprisingly, therefore, Zwingli emphasized the importance of faith and the work of the Holy Spirit, but he rooted this in the concept of covenant. Initially, Zwingli emphasized a discontinuity between the old and new covenants in order to argue "from the lesser to the greater: the one temporal and of law, ordinances, and animal blood; the other eternal and of gospel, freedom, and the atonement of Christ."[9] There was continuity between the two covenants, however, because both represented God's pledge to humanity, ultimately confirmed and grounded in Jesus Christ. Christian baptism, therefore, represented the covenant promise in and through which the faithful might have access to God and experience the remission of sins. The efficacy of baptism for

---

7. Walton, "Zwingli," 414.
8. Riggs, *Baptism*, 22.
9. Ibid., 23.

Zwingli was, in the first instance, grounded in what God had done and was doing in and through the covenant promise fulfilled in Jesus Christ as attested by the Word of God, rather than in conceptions of sacramental grace mediated by the church through the priesthood.

During this early period of Zwingli's theology, he did make one change in his understanding of baptism that was decisive. In his *Proposal Concerning Images and the Mass*, Zwingli added, as John Riggs notes, "the idea that the sacrament was not only God's covenant toward humanity but also the believer's pledge and confession toward fellow believers."[10] Baptism was an initiatory rite or pledge by which one was publicly marked and bound to carry out the obligations of Christian faith and life. Baptism with water was a human act made in response to God's prior act and word. In baptism, one was not simply initiated into a new beginning but inducted into a new way of life. Baptism was a badge that identified the baptized as belonging to Christ. It was not surprising, then, that Zwingli increasingly came to doubt the propriety of baptism of infants.

Zwingli's flirtation with the rejection of the baptism of infants, however, came to a crashing halt with the well-known events of 1525 in Zurich. When Conrad Grebel baptized George Blaurock, an act of religious devotion became a symbol of political defiance that soon spread through Zurich and beyond. Zwingli saw this as an act that threatened the unity of the church and the integrity of the civic order. As the new teaching spread, the authorities in Zurich forbad "rebaptism" on penalty of death by drowning, a sad development in the history of Christendom. As the controversy around the issue of baptism, infant baptism, rebaptism, and believer's baptism ensued, Zwingli wrote a number of important treatises on the subject including his *Commentary on True and False Religion*, and his *Baptism, Rebaptism and the Baptism of Infants*.

In responding to the Anabaptists, Zwingli did not shrink from emphasizing the importance of baptism as a human act. Rather, he argued strongly that the sacraments were human covenants in which believers pledged their obedience to Christ. Baptism, he argued by analogy, was like being initiated into a monastic order in which one put on a monk's cowl and dedicated oneself to a lifelong process of learning a new way of life. Baptism was an external sign intended primarily as a guarantee to those who witnessed it that the one being baptized belonged to Christ, to

10. Ibid.

Christ's church, and was pledged to follow Christ's way. The connection to personal repentance and faith was therefore marginal, and the idea of baptism as a means of grace was not emphasized. Why?

In short, as John Riggs notes, "in responding to the Anabaptist movement, which Zwingli believed elevated the believer's subjective experience above the objective Word, Zwingli emphasized baptism as a confessional pledge."[11] The pledge of baptism, however, was not grounded in the subjective standpoint of a person's faith but was "an objective sign of membership in the Christian community that found fulfillment in God's blessings and promises."[12] Baptism was not the entire sum of faith for Zwingli: it was but the beginning of a life of discipleship according to the Word of God. The Anabaptists may have been right to insist on baptism as a human act, Zwingli contended, but they were wrong to equate it with the sum and substance of personal faith.

On this basis, Zwingli mounted a vigorous defense of the baptism of infants grounded in the biblical understanding of covenant. He now emphasized the continuity between God's covenant with Abraham and its fulfillment in Christ. In his *Commentary on Genesis,* his *Reply to Balthasar Hubmaier's Baptism Book,* and his polemical *Refutation of the Tricks of the Anabaptists,* he argued that this continuity comprised the whole promise of salvation. Just as the children of the old covenant were God's children, so too were Christian children included in the covenant promises of salvation. Specifically, and here Zwingli introduced a notion that became a staple in the Reformed argument for the baptism of infants, there was an analogy (or a parallel) between circumcision in the Old Testament and baptism in the New Testament. Since children were included in the rite of circumcision, so too should they be included in the rite of baptism, since both rites were grounded in the one covenant of grace. Children were to be included in the covenant of faith, including its outward signs, and raised according to the Word of God.

In sum, Zwingli's doctrine of baptism illustrates at least three important aspects of what became the Reformed understanding of baptism. First, it was forged as a response to late medieval Roman Catholic sacramental theology on the one side, and to the emerging theology and practice of the Anabaptists on the other. In his earlier theology, with Roman Catholic doctrine in mind, Zwingli emphasized the importance

---

11. Ibid., 24.
12. Ibid.

of the believer's pledge while later, when battling the Anabaptists, he emphasized the nature of baptism itself.

That being said, and this is the second point, Zwingli grounded his understanding of baptism in the biblical concept of the covenant throughout. To be sure, Zwingli may have emphasized baptism as an external and symbolic sign, but it was in the first instance a sign of God's unfailing covenant promises rather than believer's subjective experience of faith. While Zwingli may have shrunk from speaking clearly about baptism as a means of grace, he was nevertheless clear that baptism narrated the story of the Christian community into which believers were incorporated. Thus, he elevated the gospel above the believer's response to the gospel. Baptism was therefore grounded in God's grace rather than in the human response. And this in turn became the basis for his defense of the baptism of infants.

Third, Zwingli stressed the idea that baptism was but the beginning of lifelong faith and obedience. The one baptized was henceforth identified with the Christian community and committed to the disciplines of the Christian life under the Word of God. Thus was introduced the notion that baptism is not only identification with Christ's death and resurrection, incorporation into Christ's body, but also an initiation and induction into Christ's ongoing ministry through the Spirit.

While Zwingli labored in Zurich, his contemporary Martin Bucer was at work in Strasbourg. Born in 1491, Bucer was appointed pastor in Strasbourg in 1524 where he led the Reformation until he left for England to teach at Cambridge in 1549. Originally a Dominican, Bucer sided with Luther from 1518 and increasingly sought to provide a theology that would mediate between Zwingli and Luther. Like Zwingli and Luther, Bucer was initially concerned for the correct appropriation of the sacraments. Baptism, Bucer argued, did not produce salvation. Rather, it was efficacious only through the work of the Holy Spirit and human faith. Bucer never doubted that children should be baptized because the covenant preceded them (i.e., they already possessed the covenant), and because children were beloved by God and Christ.

By the 1530s, however, Bucer began to work on the grounds of baptism's efficacy on the validity of the sacrament itself rather than on its effect through the Spirit and human faith. In the Tetrapolitan Confession of 1530 (written chiefly by Bucer) the classical Augustinian position on the validity of the sacraments was introduced: the sacraments were "visible signs of invisible grace." This became an important element in later Reformed understandings of baptism. According to Bucer, baptism could mediate salvation because "it was the sign of God's saving covenant, made with Abraham, extending through his seed, and including within that covenant all the people of God from Moses through Christian infants."[13] Following Augustine, Bucer argued that the gospel was offered in both words and signs. As John Riggs notes, "When Bucer no longer needed to address the issue of proper appropriation and discuss what the sacrament did not do, he stood with the long tradition of sacramental validity and asserted that divine grace inhered to the external sign."[14]

Bucer believed that one's regeneration and renewal through the Holy Spirit were revealed through the words and water of baptism because baptism was a sign of God's good-will offered in the covenant of grace. In and with the sign of baptism God delivered and gave over his divine and hidden grace, and the redemption in Christ, as Bucer outlined in his first catechism. But Bucer was clear: it was Jesus Christ, the great High Priest and Savior, acting through his Holy Spirit, who acted and accomplished this. Christ used the outward ministry of the church in words and signs. While one thing happened inwardly through the power of Christ's Spirit, another thing happened outwardly in the ministry of the church.[15]

In summary, both Zwingli and Bucer, as first generation Reformers, were concerned about the appropriation of baptism and both set out their positions over against late medieval Roman Catholic and Anabaptist positions. Both distinguished "the institutional sign of God's grace from the subjective appropriation of the grace signified by the sign." Having done so, both then sought to ground the efficacy of baptism in the nature of baptism itself. At this point, however, each pursued a quite different strategy. Zwingli appealed to baptism as an external sign of the community created by the Word of God into which the believer was incorporated and to which the believer was committed. Bucer, on the other hand, re-appropriated the Augustinian theology of the sacraments and argued that baptism was truly a means of saving grace. That being said, both appealed to a conception of covenant to ground their respective understandings of baptism, and both argued in favour of the baptism

---

13. Ibid., 32.
14. Ibid.
15. Ibid., 32–33.

of infants. The tensions and trajectories introduced by both Zwingli and Bucer became characteristic features of the ongoing Reformed tradition.

BULLINGER AND CALVIN

Heinrich Bullinger (1504–1575) is best known as Zwingli's successor as head pastor and theologian of the church in Zurich, where he continued to develop and institute the reforms initiated by his predecessor. Recent Reformation scholarship, however, has emphasized the significance of Bullinger as a theologian in his own right, especially his conception of covenant theology. Following his education at the University of Cologne he taught for a time in Kappel before going to Zurich in 1523, where he worked closely with Zwingli. Bullinger was the sole author of the Second Helvetic Confession (1566), which was, according to Edward Dowey, "the most comprehensive and influential of early Reformed confessions."[16] He also wrote jointly with Calvin the Zurich Agreement (Consensus Tigurinus).

Bullinger's doctrine of baptism is closely tied to his understanding of sacrament, covenant, and predestination. In his 1559 *Catechesis*, Bullinger defined a sacrament as "a sacred symbol, or holy rite, or a sacred action, instituted by God through words, signs, and things, by which he retains in the memory of the church his greatest blessings, and he continually renews them. By these he also seals and represents what he executes for us and what he in turn requires from us."[17] As John Riggs notes, for Bullinger a "sacrament represented and sealed on us what God did on our behalf. At the same time it indicated for us what our duties were in response to the divine activity."[18] Bullinger's understanding of baptism was set within this covenantal framework. The true grounding for baptism is God's covenant with humankind in which God gives himself to us in Jesus Christ and in which we are bound by divine grace to God. There is a continuity of this covenant between the Old and the New Testaments; it finds expression beginning with Adam through to its fulfillment in Jesus Christ; its character is that of divine grace; and circumcision finds its fulfillment in baptism. Infants and children born

---

16. Dowey, "Heinrich Bullinger," 44.
17. Cited in Riggs, *Baptism*, 36.
18. Ibid., 36–37.

into this covenant are to be given the sign of baptism just as they had been given the sign of circumcision in the Old Testament.

In the Second Helvetic Confession, Bullinger affirmed that baptism was instituted and consecrated by God, that there is but one baptism in the church, and that to be baptized in the name of Christ "is to be enrolled, entered, and received into the covenant and family, and so into the inheritance of God's children." Bullinger emphasized God's sovereign grace and free mercy in his understanding of covenant and baptism. Baptism was a sign that God moved to embrace humanity in Jesus Christ but it was also a sign of our response to that embrace. To quote Riggs, "Baptism thus meant taking upon oneself, in personal responsibility, the covenant already embracing humankind, so that while from the human side baptism entered us into the covenant, from the divine side we were already included in that covenant."[19]

Similar notions of sacrament, covenant, and predestination can be seen in Calvin's doctrine of baptism. John Calvin was born on July 10, 1509 in Noyon, France. After studies in Paris in basic liberal arts (including Latin) and Christian humanism at the College de la Marche and the College de Montaigu, which led to his bachelor's and master's degrees, Calvin went, at the insistence of his father, to Orleans to study law. After receiving his license in civil law in 1532, Calvin returned to Paris to continue his humanist studies and in the same year published his critically acclaimed study of Seneca's essay *On Clemency*. By 1533 Calvin was clearly identified with the reforming movement in Paris, having been implicated in a controversial address delivered by his friend Nicholas Cop, the rector of the University of Paris. By 1534 Calvin had renounced his church benefice, and in 1536 he published, at the age of 27, the first edition of his magisterial *Institutes of the Christian Religion*. After periods in Basel and Paris and short ministries in Geneva (1536–1538 with Farel), and Strasbourg (1538–1541 with Bucer), Calvin was recalled to Geneva to be the head pastor and theologian, where he worked until his death in 1564.

Calvin understood himself as standing in the Reformation theology espoused by Martin Luther, and his early sacramental and baptismal arguments clearly reflected Luther's thought. Like Luther, Calvin affirmed that baptism was a sacrament and emphasized, initially, over against Rome, the importance of the proper appropriation of

---

19. Ibid., 39.

the sacraments, which occurred when faith was at work apprehending the divine promise that was represented in the sacramental sign. By the time Calvin wrote, however, Luther had already reworked his baptismal theology in response to the challenge of the Anabaptists. The sacramental validity of baptism, Luther argued, did not reside in human faith that appropriated the sacrament, but in the preceding promise of God upon which it was founded and of which it was a visible expression (or sign). This was the basic framework within which Calvin developed his baptismal theology and from which he never really departed.[20]

In the 1536 edition of the *Institutes*, Calvin defined a sacrament as "an external sign, by which the Lord represents and witnesses to us his good will towards us, in order to sustain the weakness of our faith." It is, he said, "a testimony of God's grace, declared to us by an external symbol" and it "is never without a preceding promise, but rather is joined to it as an appendix."[21] As a second-generation Reformer, Calvin assumed the importance of faith in the appropriation of the sacraments for which the earlier Reformers had fought so courageously. He now, like the later Luther, felt it was important to ground the sacraments, including baptism, in what God had done and was doing. The story of baptism was for Calvin a story about God before it was a story about us. It points to the promise of God of which we, by grace, through faith, are heirs. Our faith, our experience, and our story only make sense in light of the preceding promise.

It should be noted, however, that Calvin never underplayed the importance of faith expressed outwardly. Like Zwingli, Calvin was able to describe a sacrament as an outward sign identified with human action and he compared it to the solemn oath sworn by a soldier, a public profession of loyalty. In fact, in the 1536 *Institutes* he defined baptism initially in these terms: "Baptism was given us by God; first to serve our faith before him; and then to serve our confession before others."[22] But always underlying this was Calvin's emphasis that baptism was established as the sign of God's immutable promise, a promise that remained steadfast whether or not it was grasped by human faith. In short, Luther's "sign-promise" theology of baptism that treated a sacrament as "God's

---

20. Ibid., 39–42.
21. Cited in ibid., 42.
22. Ibid., 43.

personal visible promise of grace, appropriated only through faith" provided, it seemed to Calvin, the proper balance. Baptism was not, and could not be, grounded in the human response but rather in the preceding promise of God. As important as faith was, a sacrament was a divine action of grace instituted for the life of the church. It did not derive its meaning from human agency.

Having said that, Calvin's pastoral experience did affect his understanding of baptism. Initially, Calvin's concern, following Luther and Zwingli, had been to lay out a theology of baptism that forged a via media between Roman Catholic and Anabaptist understandings. That had been the presenting issue in the early years. But by 1539, after three years of church leadership in Geneva and Strasbourg, Calvin saw the need to develop the public pledge aspect of baptism. His earlier theology worked nicely when one thought of baptism in relation to the invisible church. But now he was faced with the reality of the visible church, in a local context, in two French-speaking cities. The issues of church discipline and worthy celebration of the Lord's Supper required a greater emphasis on the importance of faith and human response. Baptism was a visible means through which one was incorporated into the visible church, with all the privileges and responsibilities that pertain thereto. Faith, and its public profession, was therefore required. However, even here Calvin was careful to emphasize that only God knows the heart and only the elect truly respond. There is an invisible church within the visible church. But, and this is decisive, the invisible church is located within the visible church. There can be, for Calvin, no salvation outside of the visible church into which the elect (and the non-elect) are baptized.

This was the basic understanding of baptism that Calvin continued to develop and refine in subsequent editions of the *Institutes* and within the context of his ministry in Geneva for the rest of his life. Baptism was a sure bearer of God's promise. About that there could be no debate. At the same time, the response of faith was signally important, notwithstanding the weakness and frailty of the faith with which the elect appropriated the sacraments.

Another area that Calvin came increasingly to emphasize was the continuity of the covenant between the old and new dispensations, which was the basis for his affirmation of the baptism of infants. If in the Old Testament children were included in the covenant promise, and the covenant sign, then it stood to reason, Calvin concluded, that they should also be included in the sign of the covenant in the New Testament, namely baptism. Calvin incorporated most of the material of an earlier tract on the baptism of infants in later editions of the *Institutes*.

Before leaving Calvin, we must note that it is not difficult to see that there are at least two very thorny (some might argue intractable) problems in this theology of baptism. First, what is the significance of baptism in light of the doctrine of election? Isn't baptism only confirming something that is already a reality? And what does this mean for the effect of baptism on those who are not the elect (i.e., the reprobate)? For the elect, baptism seems to signify something that is already a reality; for the reprobate, it seems to signify nothing at all. Does baptism then become a hollow religious rite, its significance reduced to virtually nothing? Does the church have a valid sacrament at all?

Second, and related, if one assumes that children within the covenant of grace are part of the elect, what real effect, if any, would baptism have for them? Isn't baptism only affirming something that is already the case? Baptism does not offer a child of the covenant something that he/she does not already have. In short, is baptism really the means through which Christian identity is bestowed?

Calvin was sensitive to these criticisms, and he responded to them. In the first instance, a sacrament, he argued clearly, could be valid without being efficacious. In the second case, Calvin obfuscated by appealing to the metaphor of a seed: the seed of future repentance and faith in an elect child was concealed by the Holy Spirit to flower later. These issues, in various forms, and at different times, continued to plague the Reformed understanding of baptism.[23]

THE REFORMED CONFESSIONS AND REFORMED ORTHODOXY

While the theological work of individual pastors and theologians is important, the doctrine of baptism in Reformed churches has been most authoritatively set out in confessions of faith adopted by communities of faith. Creeds and confessions are intended to bear witness to (i.e., confess) the faith of the church in a particular time and place and to respond to particular challenges from other churches or the state. At the same time, they also serve as a summary of Christian teaching and provide

---

23. I am indebted to Riggs, *Baptism*, 69–70, for this material.

the basis for catechisms. In most Reformed and Presbyterian churches, ministers and elders are bound to these confessional standards. In this section I touch on only a few of the main emphases in what is a vast and varied set of Reformed creeds and confessions.

The Swiss Confessions of the Reformed tradition (First Helvetic, 1536; Genevan, 1536; Calvin's Genevan Catechism, 1545; Second Helvetic, 1561) reflect, for the most part, an irenic spirit and an attempt to reconcile the German and Swiss Reformations. A number of points of convergence emerge. First, there is a strong christological emphasis in the teaching on baptism. The sacrament of baptism is exercised in obedience to the command of Christ, it follows the example of Christ, and perhaps most important of all, it is the means through which Christ himself is offered to the elect. Baptism offers, to be sure, the benefits of Christ in the covenant of grace, but those benefits and that covenant are never to be divorced from Christ himself.

Second, baptism is a valid sacrament that offers regeneration in union with Christ by the Holy Spirit through an outward sign. The point here is that baptism is not a bare sign of an inner reality; rather, baptism is both a sign and a seal of the reality to which it bears witness. Or, to put it in words that dominate Reformed theology and practice: baptism is a means of grace. It is never simply an outward act, nor simply a social act in which a person is initiated into the Christian community. It is a spiritual act, a work of the Holy Spirit, who by grace binds the inner and the outer, and the individual and the community.

Third, the benefit of baptism is for the "elect," and infants are often assumed to be included in the elect. The First Helvetic Confession treats this practically and pastorally when it affirms that to repent and profess one's faith or to be raised in a Christian family and profess one's faith may normally be taken as a sign of God's election.[24]

Fourth, baptism testifies to the covenant of God's grace in which God's desire to adopt humankind as God's children is affirmed. The continuity of the covenant reminds us that baptism portrays the cleansing of sin through the shed blood of Jesus Christ, fulfilling the sacrificial system of the Old Testament. It also reminds us that children are included in the covenant, and the covenantal signs.

Finally, the administration of baptism is to be joined with the preaching and teaching of the Word of God. In a very real sense the

---

24. See ibid., 76.

sacraments are the visible words of God, enactments of the gospel. Those who present themselves or their children for baptism are to be catechized. The administration of baptism in a public service of worship is always to be accompanied by the reading of Holy Scripture and the proclamation of the gospel. The words of the baptismal liturgy, including the prayers, are to be biblical words.

The Continental Confessions of the Reformed tradition (French, 1559; Belgic, 1561; Heidelberg Catechism, 1563) emphasize many of the same points. The sacrament of baptism is understood as a "pledge" and a "seal" added to the Word of God as an outward sign of God's work and through which God works. The ideas of covenant and election are important, as is the existential question of faith and the benefits that accrue to the one who is baptized.

The British Reformed Confessions (Scots, 1560; Westminster, 1648) bear the marks, as do the Swiss and Continental Confessions, of particular social and political contexts. They often tend, however, to be more polemical. The Scots Confession, for example, written by John Knox and five others, was composed in four days so that the Scottish Parliament would have a theological basis to establish the Reformed faith as the Church of Scotland. The teaching on baptism in the Scots Confession is found scattered throughout the three chapters (21–23) on the sacraments. Most of the themes identified above are included, written in such a way as to distinguish Reformed Protestant teaching on baptism from Roman Catholicism.

The Westminster Confession of Faith has undoubtedly been the most influential theological document for Reformed churches in the English-speaking world. The Westminster Divines met over five years to compose a document that was intended to be the basis of the Reformation in England. The Westminster Assembly was convened by the Long Parliament in 1643 and consisted of 121 Puritan ministers, 30 members of Parliament, and 6 Scottish Presbyterian advisers. Charged with reforming the worship, discipline, and government of the Church of England, their work soon extended to include a confession of faith and catechism. The Parliament approved the Westminster Confession of Faith and the Larger and Shorter Westminster Catechisms in 1648. Ironically, the documents became the basis of the church, not in England, but in Scotland, and subsequently for many English speaking Presbyterian Churches in North America and around the world.

The Westminster Divines began by noting that baptism is a sacrament, ordained by Jesus Christ. As a sacrament, baptism is a "sign and seal of the covenant of grace" immediately instituted by God, to represent Christ and his benefits, and to confirm our interest in Christ (ch. 27.1). Sacraments make a visible distinction between those who belong to the church and the rest of the world, that is, they are marks of the visible church. Westminster emphasizes that the sacraments also signify our commitment to God in Christ, that is, they are pledges of discipleship. There is, they argue, a spiritual relation, or "sacramental union," between the sign and the thing signified. Sacraments are efficacious not because of any power inherent in them, and not because of the faith or power of the person administering the sacrament, but solely because of the Holy Spirit and the word of institution.

According to Westminster, of what is baptism a sign and seal? Well, as they state in chapter 28, baptism signifies and seals the covenant of grace, ingrafting into Christ, regeneration, remission of sins, and the renewal of life. But, and here Westminster tips its thoroughly predestinarian hand, the efficacy of baptism is not tied to the moment when baptism is administered. It depends on the will of God and the work of the Holy Spirit, which can never be predicted, manipulated, controlled, or domesticated. Notwithstanding that baptism is a sacrament, and that we may believe it really confers the promise of which it speaks, grace and salvation are not tied to baptism by any necessity. It would be wrong to conclude that "no person can be regenerated or saved without it" or "that all baptized are undoubtedly regenerated." The problems created by this formulation are not difficult to apprehend. On the one hand, as a sacrament, baptism seems necessary for salvation. It really confers the grace of which it speaks. On the other hand, God is sovereign, and no one should presume upon the will of God. Among the problems that such a formulation introduced to the Reformed tradition none was perhaps more pressing than the pastoral problem of the assurance of faith. Even the baptized might lack the assurance that they truly belonged to God. Rather then conferring and confirming one's identity in Christ, it was actually the case that for some, baptism injected a note of uncertainty.

Strangely, the Westminster Shorter Catechism is clearer and cleaner on this matter. Its definition of a sacrament is precise: "A sacrament is a holy ordinance instituted by Christ; wherein, by sensible signs, Christ, and the benefits of the new covenant, are represented, sealed, and applied to believers" (Q. 92). That follows a series of questions that have to do with the means through which Christ makes salvation effectual. Through the ordinary means of grace, especially the word, sacraments, and prayer, Christ by his Spirit works in the lives of the elect. The sacraments become effectual means of salvation by the blessing of Christ and the working of the Holy Spirit in the lives of those who by faith receive them. And when it asks, "To whom is baptism to be administered?" (Q. 94) it again lifts up the importance of faith: "Baptism is not to be administered to any that are out of the visible church, till they profess their faith in Christ, and obedience to him." Where the Westminster Confession and the Larger Catechism focus on God's sovereign will, the Shorter Catechism, while not negating this, emphasizes the right appropriation of baptism by faith.

Following the period of the first- and second-generation Reformers, and the Reformed confessions of the sixteenth and seventeenth centuries, the Reformed tradition moved into a period often described as "Protestant Scholasticism" or "Reformed Orthodoxy." The theological tradition needed to be consolidated and handed on to new generations. Both Lutheran and Reformed theologians turned to the scholastic theological method of the late medieval period to reformulate and refine the substance of Reformation teaching. It is true that this era may not have been a particularly creative period in Reformed theology, but contrary to the impression left by a good deal of twentieth-century scholarship, this was indeed a deep and rich period for the Reformed tradition. The theological achievement of people like Theodore Beza, Amandus Polanus, Johannes Wollebius, Johann Heinrich Heidegger, Francis Turretin, and Johannes Cocceius, among others, is to be admired.

A summary of Reformed orthodox theology of this era was written by Heinrich Heppe in the nineteenth century, called *Reformed Dogmatics*. This is a highly organized, lengthy, technical treatment of Reformed theology and has been influential on numerous people, including Karl Barth, who commended it to his students. Among the things emphasized in the chapter on baptism is the primacy of the Word. The water of baptism is an outward element to which the Word of God is added. The "Word" refers to the Trinitarian formula (the name into which one is baptized) and Christ's institution of baptism (the authority on which one is baptized), both supported with reference to Matt 28:19. The entire gospel, Heppe notes, is to be found in this text. The exterior act of baptism "was the means by which God sealed on the hearts of the elect the divine promise that they were participants in the covenant of grace."[25] Baptism administered with water and in the name of the triune God is always inherently valid. Its efficacy, however, rests solely upon the electing grace of God. The Reformed orthodox theologians tended to loosen the connection between the sign and the efficacy of baptism and therefore did not emphasize baptism as a means of grace. In the context of election and double predestination, the emphasis fell on baptism as a seal of the salvation already present rather than as a means of regeneration. Baptism was necessary, they argued, not for salvation, but due to its divine institution. All who belonged to the covenant were to be baptized, including the children of believers. As one summary of the Reformed orthodox position on baptism puts it:

> Baptism was the divinely instituted activity which sealed the participation of the elected person in the covenant of grace. This covenant was also described as the death and resurrection of the person in Christ, as well as the forgiveness of all sins of the person's life, and including their regeneration ... As such, baptism did not impart salvation but rather sealed it as a means of strengthening the person ... Salvation itself came from the promise of God to impart grace in Jesus Christ ... Such salvation as baptism sealed had efficacy only insofar as the person received the sacrament (and thus the divine promise) in faith ... The validity of the sacrament, however, was dependent not on faithful reception but on its proper administration with water and the triune baptismal formula instituted by Christ as the word of grace. ... All people were entitled to receive this sacrament who belonged to God's covenant of grace—both confessing adults and children of believers.[26]

It has to be said that a good deal of this summary is consistent with the position of Calvin and the other Reformers with two exceptions. First, during this period covenant theology emerged as the organizing principle of Reformed theology, partly to mitigate the harshness of the doctrine of double predestination. The language of covenant seemed less deterministic and more relational. Thus, Calvinist theology, or Reformed theology, was often referred to as Covenant theology. Secondly, there was less emphasis on the language of sacrament and thus on what the

---

25. Ibid., 88.
26. H. Heppe, *Reformed Dogmatics*, 611–26; see Riggs, *Baptism*, 89.

sacrament actually mediated or conferred. Many have noted that in this sense the Reformed orthodox theologians stood closer to Zwingli than to Calvin on the issue of baptism.

EDWARDS, SCHLEIERMACHER, MERCERSBURG, PRINCETON, AND BARTH

Jonathan Edwards (1703–1758) was a remarkable and prominent eighteenth-century New England pastor, revivalist, philosopher, educator, and theologian. After serving as minister of the church in Northampton, Massachusetts for twenty-one years (1729–1750) Edwards left to minister to North American aboriginals for six years (1751–1757). In 1758 he was called to be president of the College of New Jersey, but he died in Princeton after just three months.

In the latter years of his pastorate in Northampton, Edwards faced a good deal of opposition from church members over a variety of issues, including his theology and practice of the sacraments. Specifically, Edwards excluded from the Lord's Supper those who had not experienced conversion. Having experienced a full-scale revival in his congregation in the 1730s, Edwards was convinced of the need for what he considered to be true religion marked by religious affections. Baptism was important, but the revivals had underscored for Edwards the importance of genuine personal faith and repentance as the basis for Christian identity and life. The emphasis on personal decision and conversion stood in tension with a view of baptism that emphasized the sovereign work of God in salvation. It created a particular problem for those who saw the baptism of infants as the basis for growing up in the church "without a radical break before which they were not Christian and after which they are."[27] At the same time, Edwards emphasized the majesty, splendor, and glory of God, the utter and absolute dependence of sinful humanity on God for salvation, and the beauty of the life of holiness.[28]

In short, the theology and practice of Edwards underscores a number of tensions at the very heart of the Reformed understanding of baptism: the relation of divine agency to human agency (divine will and human will); the relation between what God has done (in Christ) and

---

27. Leith, "Sacraments," 226.
28. Noll, *History*, 97.

what God is doing (by the Holy Spirit); the relation between inner faith and outward church practice.

Edwards had been shaped by a rigorous Calvinist orthodoxy, revivalism, as well as the British empiricism and the continental rationalism in which he had been educated. Similar forces—orthodoxy, pietism, romanticism, and Enlightenment rationalism, provided the background for the most influential Reformed theologian and church leader of the nineteenth century in Europe: Friedrich Schleiermacher (b. 1768). Schleiermacher, however, moved in a different theological direction than did Edwards.

After serving as a tutor, pastor, and hospital chaplain, Schleiermacher taught theology, first at the University of Halle (1804–1806), and then at the University of Berlin (from 1810) where he remained until his death in 1834. His two most well-known writings are *On Religion: Speeches to Its Cultured Despisers* (1799) and *The Christian Faith*. In addition to teaching theology, Schleiermacher was active as a preacher and church leader throughout his life.

Schleiermacher's father was a Reformed minister whose life had been renewed through contact with the Moravians. Friedrich Schleiermacher was raised in a context, therefore, where the experience of faith was valued. His problem, however, was that he found it difficult to accept many of the traditional Christian doctrines. As a result, and in response to the Enlightenment, he began to reformulate Christian faith and practice around his basic insight and starting point: everyone has a "feeling of absolute dependence." This was not a particular emotion but a fundamental and primordial awareness of being dependent, a sense of being immediately related to the divine. This is the original experience of all human beings and accounts for the reality of all religions. From this basic insight Schleiermacher reformulated all Christian doctrine. Jesus became the man with a perfect God-consciousness. Redemption became our participation in that God-consciousness with him. The church became the body which received and continued that God-consciousness of Christ in the world.

Schleiermacher's conception of baptism fit into this basic theological framework. Baptism was the means through which one entered the church. It was "the act of the will by which the church receives the individual into its fellowship" as well as "the channel of divine justifying activity, through which the individual is received into the living fellowship of Christ."[29] Baptism is to be preceded by the preaching of the Word, and it presupposes the faith of the person being baptized. But even though faith is presupposed as the basis of salvation, Schleiermacher argued that the influence of Christ and the enjoyment of his blessedness "become real only within the fellowship of believers,"[30] of which baptism is the mark of initiation.

Furthermore, for Schleiermacher, regeneration consisted of justification and conversion together, and this occurred at baptism. This was true theologically, he argued, but the experience of the church was such that it was not always coincidental. There are imperfect baptisms. Some regenerate persons are not yet baptized, and some unregenerate persons are. This experiential inconsistency created the opportunity, indeed the justification, as Schleieramacher saw it, for the baptism of infants. On the basis of this inconsistency he then put forward a positive reason to baptize infants: the future of the children of believers was entrusted to the church whose duty it was "to bring them . . . into direct relation to the Word of God, and to maintain them therein until faith awakens."[31] Having made the case, however, he was open to the possibility that the baptism of infants could be abolished and felt that there was sufficient theological warrant within the Reformed tradition to do so. The baptism of infants could only be said to fulfill Christ's institution when it was accompanied by confirmation and profession of faith.

Two other developments in nineteenth century Reformed theology are worthy of note in relation to baptism, both occurring in North America. First, the so-called Princeton theology of A. A. Hodge, Charles Hodge, and B. B. Warfield represented a high point for Reformed Orthodoxy in American theology. The theology and practice of baptism taught by the "Old Princeton" theologians emphasized covenant, election and predestination, the primacy of grace and the profession of faith, and the church as believers together with their children. Secondly, the so-called Mercersburg theology of John Nevin and Philip Schaff was a serious effort to recover aspects of Calvin's theology and piety which Nevin and Schaff believed had been eclipsed by Reformed Orthodoxy. They focused particularly on Calvin's ideas of the church, ministry, liturgy, and the sacraments. They argued for a rather "high" doctrine of the

---

29. Schleiermacher, *Christian Faith*, 619.
30. Ibid., 630. See Riggs, *Baptism*, 92.
31. Schleiermacher, *Christian Faith*, 633–38.

church catholic, which they believed could be found in Calvin's theology, and pressed for the necessity and efficacy of the sacraments, including baptism. In a tradition that had emphasized the primacy of the Word, they argued for the importance of baptism and eucharist. In a tradition that had emphasized the importance of profession of faith, they argued for an emphasis on the mediation of sacramental grace. In a tradition that had often affirmed the sacraments as being good for the faithful, they argued for the necessity of the sacraments for salvation. The sacraments were essential and the believer was absolutely dependent upon them for Christian identity and life.

Finally, we turn briefly to the most influential Reformed theologian of the twentieth century, Karl Barth. Given Barth's emphasis on the primacy of the Word, the objectivity of God's grace in Jesus Christ, and the universal scope of the work of reconciliation, one might assume that Barth was a strong advocate for the baptism of infants. Such was not the case. In 1943 he published a book called *The Teaching of the Church regarding Baptism* in which he argued that the baptism of infants was exegetically unsupported, historically unjustified, and theologically unsound. Later, in volume 4:4 of the *Church Dogmatics,* he argued that baptism was the foundation of the Christian life but that it was not a sacrament. The only sacrament is Jesus Christ. He is the only means of grace. Furthermore, Barth distinguishes between baptism with water and baptism of the Holy Spirit. Our baptism with water, he argues, is to be construed as a free human act analogous to, in correlation to, and in response to the free act of God in baptism by the Spirit. Human agency finds its full freedom and authentic existence in relation to God. The case was pressed further by Barth's son Markus, a New Testament scholar, and later by Jurgen Moltmann.

BIBLICAL, CHRIST-CENTERED, TRINITARIAN FAITH

Having sketched the historical development of baptism in the Reformed tradition from Zwingli to Barth, we turn now to a summary of important theological themes, noting points of convergence and divergence with other Christian traditions, emphasizing the unique and decisive aspects of baptism in the Reformed tradition, and identifying the implications for the life and ministry of the churches today.

To begin, the Reformed churches share with other Christian churches the basic affirmation that baptism was taught and practiced in the New Testament as the rite of initiation into the faith and fellowship of the people of God. In the early church, those who confessed Jesus of Nazareth as God's crucified Messiah were baptized. Biblical scholars remind us that early Christian baptism emerged from earlier Jewish practice and therefore stood in continuity with earlier understandings, such as: baptism is the cleansing of the believer from sin (e.g., the baptism of John for repentance); baptism is incorporation into the community of faith (e.g., the baptism of the Essenes); and baptism is new birth (e.g., the baptism of proselytes to Judaism). Furthermore, the early church, especially the Jewish believers, understood its faith and practice in continuity with the tradition of the Hebrew Bible, which was still their sacred text.

At the same time, new and decisive understandings emerged: cleansing from sin, new birth, and incorporation into the community of faith were bound up with the life, teaching, death, resurrection, and ascension of Jesus of Nazareth and with the outpouring of the Holy Spirit on the day of Pentecost. The early church practiced baptism following the example of Jesus (who was baptized by John), in obedience to the command of Jesus (who gave the Great Commission), and in the power of Jesus (who promised the Holy Spirit).

These aspects of the New Testament understanding have been especially important for the Reformed tradition. Early in the Reformation, Zwingli understood the baptism of Jesus as a pattern for Christian baptism and although this was "a radical departure from scholastic theology, which understood John's baptism as being quite different from the apostles' baptism,"[32] his approach was followed by many others in the Reformed tradition. Christian baptism, in this understanding, stands as an ongoing witness that Jesus was baptized for us and that we are baptized in him. Reformed liturgies of baptism often begin with a reference to the baptism of Jesus, emphasizing his obedience to God the Father. In his baptism Jesus' ministry is inaugurated and his identity is affirmed as the beloved Son. The Spirit descends and he is empowered for his ministry. In baptism we are identified with the Christ who was baptized for us and this becomes, for the believer, an identity-affirming and ministry-inaugurating event. Martin Bucer made this point by affirming "that baptism stands at the beginning of the Christian life, just as it stands at the beginning of the Gospel, a prophetic sign of what will

---

32. Old, "Baptism," 21.

be, namely a turning away from the ways of this world and an entering into the life of the Spirit, a sign and seal of our conversion."[33]

In the Reformed tradition, the baptism of Jesus is often linked to Jesus' identification of his baptism with his crucifixion. Jesus himself said: "I have come to bring fire on the earth, and how I wish it were already kindled! But I have a baptism to undergo, and how distressed I am until it is completed." The Gospels make it clear that the baptism of Jesus by John was but a foreshadowing of the baptism that was to come. It was a prophetic display of the suffering into which Jesus was to enter. Jesus was affirmed as the beloved Son of God, but he was the Son who would give himself as a ransom for many. Jesus had a ministry given to him by the Father in the power of the Spirit, but it was a ministry that led to a cross. The death of Jesus was his baptism for us. And our baptism is a participation in his baptism, his death and resurrection. As Paul lays it out in Romans 6, those who have been baptized into Christ Jesus are baptized into his death. We are buried with him in baptism into death, "so that, just as Christ was raised from the dead by the glory of God the Father, we too might walk in newness of life" (Rom 6:1–11). Baptism is the beginning of our own mortification (death to sin and the old self) and regeneration (resurrection to new life and ongoing sanctification). Central to a Reformed understanding of baptism, therefore, is the Pauline understanding of union with Christ. Baptism is practiced not only in obedience *to* Christ, and in imitation *of* Christ, but in fellowship and union *with* Christ. For the Reformed tradition, this is decisive: it is the basis of Christian identity and discipleship.

If baptism was christologically enacted, it was also christologically instituted. Prior to the ascension, Jesus commanded his disciples to go into all the world to make disciples, to teach them everything that Jesus had taught them, and to baptize them in the name of the Father and of the Son and of the Holy Spirit. As we noted earlier, the Reformed Orthodox theologians emphasized the so-called "dominical mandate" of Christian baptism. The necessity of baptism did not emerge, for them, from a connection between the sign of water baptism and its efficacy (i.e., one had to be baptized to be saved), but rather from baptism's divine institution. The church baptized in obedience to the word of the Lord Jesus. That was warrant enough. Furthermore, the validity of Christian baptism resided in the triune identity of God.

---

33. Ibid.

As the Dutch theologian Herman Bavinck notes, baptism in the name of the triune God "does not prescribe what the apostles are to say but what they have to do. The name here indicates that the baptized person is placed in a relationship with the Father, Son, and the Holy Spirit."[34] The Trinitarian formula for baptism has been, until very recently, a non-negotiable element of Christian baptism for precisely this reason. Despite the difficulties that some might have with the exclusive character of the traditional Trinitarian language, it is difficult to see how Christian identity today can be grounded in anything other than the name of the triune God. The Reformed tradition can recognize any baptism done with water in the name of the Triune God.

But there was more. In the life of the early church baptism was practiced in the aftermath of Pentecost and it was connected to the work of the Holy Spirit. Baptism was pneumatologically empowered. In Acts 2 Peter preached the gospel to people from all nations gathered in Jerusalem. Note what is said in verses 38 and 39: Peter called the people to repentance and to be baptized in the name of Jesus Christ so that their sins would be forgiven, and that they would receive the gift of the Holy Spirit. Here again we see the pattern for Christian baptism: repentance, baptism, forgiveness of sins, and the gift of the Spirit. But Peter presses further: "For the promise is for you, for your children, and for all who are far away, everyone whom the Lord our God calls to him." The Reformed tradition has taken this to mean that the promise enacted in baptism is not for Jews only, but also for Gentiles, and for their children. Throughout the rest of the book of Acts there are numerous references to Gentiles being baptized, including some with their households (a group of Samaritans, Acts 8:4–11; an Ethiopian, Acts 8:26–40; a Roman centurion and his household, Acts 10; Lydia, a Greek businesswoman, Acts 16:14–15; and the Philippian jailer and his household, Acts 16:29–34). Many Reformed theologians have noted that if there is any biblical warrant for the baptism of infants and children in the practice of the early church, it would be found here: the promise enacted in baptism is not only for Peter's Gentile listeners, but also for their children, just as it had been for the Jews and their children. And, to make the point stronger, it depends, in the first instance, not upon their response, but upon the call of God (i.e., God's electing grace).

---

34. Bavinck, *Dogmatics*, 4:496.

In sum, the Reformed tradition has understood baptism as a visible expression of the sum and substance of the gospel as set out in a rigorously biblical Christ-centered Trinitarian faith. Baptism is biblically warranted and the Bible's teaching on baptism contributed to the development of a full Trinitarian theology in the life of the early church. The recent renewal of Trinitarian theology among Reformed thinkers has given a new and dynamic expression to this aspect of baptism. Among the many theologians who might be quoted here, I note again the writings of James B. Torrance:

> At the center of the New Testament stands not our religious experience, not our faith or repentance or decision, however important these are, but a unique relationship between Jesus and the Father. Christ is presented to us as the Son living a life of communion with the Father, presenting himself in our humanity through the eternal Spirit to the Father on behalf of humankind. By his Spirit he draws men and women to participate both in his life of worship and communion with the Father and in his mission from the Father to the world ... This unique relationship is described as one of mutual love, mutual self-giving, mutual testifying, mutual glorifying.[35]

Baptism in the name of the Triune God unites us to Christ by the power of the Holy Spirit. In baptism we are incorporated into participation in the divine life and mystery. Reformed theologians, having been influenced by Eastern Orthodox thinkers such as John Zizioulas, can speak of becoming fully human through baptism, becoming fully alive in the image of God, and coming to authentic human existence in relation to God. In the words of Baxter Kruger:

> It all boils down to three things. First, there is the Trinity and the great dance of life and glory and joy shared by the Father, Son and Spirit; second, there is the incarnation as the act of the Father, Son and Spirit reaching down, extending the circle, their great dance of life, to us; third, there is our humanity, which is the theatre in which the great dance is played out through the Spirit.[36]

Baptism is the beginning of our participation in the great dance. And, as Newbigin, Berkhof, Moltmann, and Guder have noted, it is the

---

35. Torrance, *Worship*, 30–31.
36. Kruger, *Dance*, 18.

beginning of Christian vocation and mission: just as the Father sent the Son, and just as the Father and the Son send the Spirit, so the Father and the Son send the church in the power of the Spirit. In baptism we are incorporated into the Trinitarian mission of God (*missio Dei*).

COVENANT THEOLOGY AND COMMUNITY

The understanding and practice of baptism in Reformed churches is incomprehensible apart from covenant theology, a perspective set out by Bullinger and Calvin in the sixteenth century and further developed and refined by seventeenth-century Reformed theologians. In an effort to mitigate the harshness of the doctrine of double predestination, as noted earlier, covenant theology provided a more relational emphasis by focusing on the ways in which the relationship between God and humankind has been framed by a "covenant." In its most basic sense, a covenant is a formal agreement, a contract, or a treaty that establishes a relationship between two parties in which mutual obligations and responsibilities are enacted. Such covenants, Reformed biblical exegetes argued, are found throughout the Old Testament, beginning variously with Adam, or Noah, or Abraham. Israel functioned as a covenant community in relationship with Yahweh who had agreed to be their God. Israel had agreed to be God's people. God binds himself to his people by these covenants (e.g., Gen 17:1–19, Exod 19–24). The people of God, similarly, are bound to God. Reformed theology often spoke of a covenant of grace (*foedus gratiae*), "a relationship into which God entered to provide, by grace, the promise of salvation to sinful humanity. It extends throughout the Old Testament by means of various covenants to its final fulfillment in Jesus Christ."[37] Some streams of Reformed theology ("federal theology") spoke about God's initial covenant of works (*foedus operum*) with humanity (Adam) before the fall into sin. In the state of original righteousness, it was argued, "a perfect relationship with God could be enjoyed if humans maintained a perfect obedience to God's law."[38] In the main, however, the Reformed tradition emphasized grace as the character of God's relationship to humankind, and therefore spoke about the one covenant of grace, from Adam forward, administered under two dispensations—the Old and New Testaments. There was continuity, therefore, between

---

37. McKim, *Westminster Dictionary*, 64.
38. Ibid.

the covenant with Israel and the covenant in Christ. Both Israel and the church are described as covenant communities. In short, the people of God are a covenant people.

Within this basic framework, then, Reformed theologians argued, Christian baptism should be understood in continuity with the history and experience of Israel. The Reformers emphasized that the New Testament understanding of Christ's saving work and the Christian life were shaped by Old Testament conceptions, especially the Old Testament sacrificial system. The Reformers were fond of quoting Paul's description of crossing through the Red Sea as a type of baptism (1 Cor 10:1–2) noting that baptism sets the Christian on a pilgrimage from the land of sin towards the promised land. They pointed out that 1 Pet 3:20–21 presents the flood as a type of baptism in which God's justice is satisfied, Noah and his family are saved (along with a host of other creatures), and a new beginning takes place. Most importantly, they saw that the covenant between God and humankind had certain outward signs. God's covenant with Israel was marked by circumcision as the rite of initiation and Passover as the ongoing celebration of God's deliverance of his people from slavery and oppression. Reformed theology has always insisted that circumcision be understood as a type of baptism, a shadow of things to come, grounding this insight in Paul's words in Col 2:17 and Rom 4:11. It concluded that baptism was a covenantal sign in which one is joined to Christ in his death and resurrection, incorporated into the church as the visible people of God, and committed to the Christian life.

For Calvin and most other Reformed theologians, this understanding of covenant theology provided the only real biblical basis for the baptism of infants. It is true that one can find other arguments in the Reformed tradition in support of the baptism of infants—the principle of vicarious faith (parents may exercise faith on behalf of their children, e.g., Mark 2 where Jesus healed a sick man because of the faith of his friends); the idea that while children may not have fully formed faith they may have a disposition (*habitus*) of faith; the silence of the New Testament on the baptism of infants because it was not an issue (the absence of any clearly undisputed case of the baptism of an infant or child might mean that it was indeed practiced and uncontroversial rather than not practiced at all); and the appeal to household baptism, as noted earlier (e.g., Acts 16:15, 33 and 18:8). It is not surprising that those outside the Reformed tradition have found these arguments weak, since even many within the tradition have found them less than fully persuasive.

But Reformed and Presbyterian churches have insisted, and for the most part continue to insist, that the children of believers are part of the covenant. In the Old Testament the children of Israel were included in the covenant agreement between God and his people and they participated fully in the covenant community. Children were not excluded from circumcision or the Passover. The New Testament church stands in continuity with this covenant. This covenant is fulfilled in Jesus Christ and expanded to include Jews and Greeks, slaves and free, male and female (Gal 3:28). How strange it would be, then, to conclude that children should be excluded from participation in the signs of the covenant to which they are party. The Reformed tradition has affirmed that the children of believing parents are included in the family of God and that this inclusion is marked by baptism. In fact, the visible church, as the covenant community, is defined as "all those throughout the world that profess the true religion, *together with their children*" (WCF 25.1).

SACRAMENTAL SIGN AND SEAL

In the sixteenth century, Reformed Protestant Christians, along with Lutherans, continued to use the term sacrament to describe the rite of baptism while Anabaptists and others in free church traditions preferred the term ordinance. The Magisterial Reformers, therefore, took over a concept that had been important in Roman Catholic theology and practice and tried to "reform" its meaning and use. The Latin word for "sacrament" (Latin *sacramentum*) was used in the Vulgate to translate the Greek word for mystery (Greek *mysterion*) in texts such as Eph 1:9; 3:2–3; 5:32; Col 1:26–27; and 1 Tim 3:16. In Latin the term could refer to the money that was deposited by a party in a lawsuit as a guarantee that was, if forfeited, often devoted to some sacred or religious purpose. It could also refer to the oath of loyalty taken by a soldier. In the background, then, are the concepts of mystery, oath, and guarantee. In the course of the church's tradition the word sacrament came to be understood as a religious sign with a hidden or mysterious meaning, a religious rite in which the mystery of salvation was somehow signified and mediated. Augustine's definition of a sacrament as "a visible sign of an invisible grace" was quoted approvingly by Calvin.

By the late medieval period the Roman Catholic Church had developed an entire theological system—soteriology and ecclesiology—on the basis of the sacraments. Among the characteristic features of this system were the following: the sacraments were necessary for salvation; the sacraments contained the grace of God and conferred the grace they contained; the sacraments were efficacious for salvation, that is, they were the efficient cause of grace by a virtue inherent in them when the act was performed (*ex opere operato*); baptism was one of seven sacraments, which also included eucharist, confirmation, ordination, marriage, penance, and last rites; baptism, confirmation, and ordination imprint an indelible mark on the soul; and the sacraments must be administered by priests. This understanding, which had developed through the medieval period, was set out clearly by the Council of Trent in response to the Reformation.

Luther and Calvin and the other Magisterial Reformers reformulated the concept of sacrament in ways that they believed were more consistent with the teaching of the Bible. First, they argued that a sacrament was an ordinance or rite instituted in direct obedience to the command of the Lord Jesus Christ. Thus, the only two sacramental acts expressly commanded by Jesus were baptism and the Lord's Supper. Second, they argued that the sacraments rightly administered constituted a mark of the true visible church. Third, the sacraments were to be administered in public worship. Fourth, the sacraments were always to be accompanied by the Word of God. Indeed, the Scripture principle of the Reformation demanded that the sacraments be subordinate to the preaching of the gospel and the teaching of the Bible.

Fifth, they understood the sacraments as an outward sign of an inward work of grace. In this sense a sacrament was a means of grace, a divinely appointed way by which the grace of God is mediated and received. God uses sacraments to unite us to Christ through the ministry of the Holy Spirit. Sacraments are signs of what has been accomplished *for us* in Christ, on our behalf (justification), as well as seals of that work in our lives, through the Holy Spirit's work *in us* (regeneration and sanctification). The sign participates in the reality to which it points, it participates in the truth which it bespeaks. Sixth, for the Reformed tradition, as noted above, sacraments are signs of the covenant.

Seventh, and finally, the Reformed tradition has never taught that the sacraments were efficacious in themselves. Any grace mediated by the sacraments is not conferred by any power in them. The efficacy of the sacraments does not depend on the piety, doctrine, faith, or intention of the person administering the sacrament or the recipient. Whatever efficacy may be attributed to the sacraments resides in the power of God's Word and Spirit. Faith is important, but faith is understood as the divinely created human response enabling the believer to receive and apprehend the grace of God in Jesus Christ. Faith is, as Calvin noted, like empty hands with which Christ is embraced. It is Christ who saves; faith binds us to Christ; but even this is an act of God. Or to quote Karl Barth, "the Gospel demands participation, comprehension, co-operation; for it is a communication which presumes faith in the living God" but it "creates that which it presumes."[39]

Baptism in the Reformed tradition has been practiced with some variation within this basic sacramental framework. According to the Reformers, the late medieval and Counter-Reformation Roman Catholic Church emphasized that baptism worked the forgiveness of sins so that the sign of the water in the act of baptism was by necessity bound to the forgiveness of sins. Luther and Calvin rejected this, and questioned the tradition following Augustine that argued that in baptism original sin was forgiven. Building on the response and reformulation of the Reformers, the Reformed tradition emphasized the following aspects of baptism as a sacrament.

First, baptism is a sign of the removal of the guilt of sin but it does not eradicate sin from the life of the believer (i.e., it does not do away with the sinful nature). That is the lifelong process of sanctification, which culminates in glorification. Second, baptism is a sign and seal of our union with Christ in his death, resurrection, and ascension (union with Christ is one of the central themes of Calvin's *Institutes*), or, as the Westminster Confession puts it, "of our ingrafting into Christ" (WCF, 28.1). It is also a sign and seal of the covenant of grace, of regeneration, of the remission of sins, and of a commitment to walk in the newness of life. Third, baptism is the sacrament of Christian initiation. It is a visible expression of the gospel given as a means of entering the Christian life. As such, it is to be administered but once to any person. Fourth, baptism is a sign and seal of the covenant of grace. It is the sacrament of initiation into the Christian community and extends, as noted above, to believers and their children. Finally, baptism is to be administered with

---

39. Barth, *Romans*, 28.

water, accompanied by the Word of God, in the name of the triune God, with prayer, and with profession of faith. The mode of baptism is not essential: dipping, pouring, or full immersion is permitted.

BAPTISM AND THE FUTURE

With the disestablishment of the Christian churches in the West comes a new opportunity to think together about the theology and practice of baptism. Christian baptism, as I have argued throughout this chapter, is a construal of Christian identity. Baptism defines who we are in relation to the Triune God, the people of God, and God's world. In our time, therefore, baptism is best understood in relational rather than ontological categories. The Reformed tradition has learned to think and speak of baptism in terms of participation and communion. In the Reformed tradition, baptism is an expression of the belief that God is before we are, and that we become who we are and do what we do because of who God is and what God has done. The identity and vocation of the Christian is located in Jesus Christ, and through union with Christ the believer becomes authentically human. Here Karl Barth's insight is helpful: baptism is a free human act analogous to, in correlation to, and in response to the free act of God in Jesus Christ. Baptism reveals the reality of grace in human existence. God does for us and in us what we can never do for and in ourselves. And yet, it is precisely because God has acted and acts in this way that human beings find their full freedom. The act of baptism, rightly understood, is the act in which human agency is fully exercised. In baptism we find our human freedom and our authentic existence in relation to God. For the Reformed tradition, this construal of Christian identity is rooted in a rigorous Christology and Trinitarian theology, the doctrines of election and covenant, and a conception of baptism as a sacramental means of grace.

The post-Christendom and postmodern context in which we now live creates a new occasion to think about the common identity all Christians share as followers of God's crucified Messiah, in whose one name we have all been baptized. Going forward, Reformed Christians have particular gifts and insights to offer to this ecumenical conversation, as well as things from which to repent. Since baptism in the Reformed tradition was shaped so dramatically during the Reformation in response to Roman Catholic theology on the one hand, and the Anabaptist movement on the other, Reformed churches have a particular responsibility to attend to these conversations as an ecumenical project. To start with, for example, Reformed Christians must surely seek forgiveness from those in the Anabaptist tradition whose forbears they persecuted because of their understanding and practice of baptism. At the same time, Reformed Christians must express their gratitude to sisters and brothers in the Eastern Orthodox tradition from whom we have recently learned much about the meaning of baptism.

Among the specific issues that require ongoing attention we might name, as examples, the following:

1. Baptismal regeneration: What is it that we actually believe happens in and through baptism?

2. The baptism of infants: This surely remains an ongoing issue of critical self-examination for the Reformed tradition, especially in the wake of Barth, Moltmann, et al.

3. Rebaptism: Can we ever expect to reach a consensus in which all Christian churches will recognize each other's baptisms as the baptism of the holy catholic church despite different theologies and practices?

4. The language of baptism: What latitude, if any, is there in the Trinitarian formula?

5. Water baptism and baptism in the Spirit: What can Reformed Christians learn from Pentecostal and Charismatic Christians concerning the meaning of baptism?

6. The global church: What can and must we learn—theologically, pastorally, and liturgically, from churches in the global south, especially among the poor and the marginalized, that are baptizing many more new Christians than churches in the West and in the older traditions?

That being said, the ongoing practice of baptism is a sign of hope in the Christian movement. It reminds us that God's Spirit is always at work, from generation to generation, bringing men and women and young people and children to saving faith. Baptism reminds us that God is always doing new things in the lives of those outside the church. And baptism reminds those within the church that Christian hope, in life and in death, in the words of the Heidelberg Catechism, is rooted in the reality that we belong, body and soul, not to ourselves, but to our faithful Savior Jesus Christ. Or, as John Calvin put it in the *Institutes*:

> We are not our own: let not our reason nor our will, therefore sway our plans and deeds. We are not our own: let us therefore not set it as our goal to seek what is expedient for us ... We are not our own: in so far as we can, let us therefore forget ourselves in all that is ours ... We are God's: let us therefore live for God and die for God. We are God's: let God's wisdom and will therefore rule all our actions. We are God's: let all the parts of our life accordingly strive toward God as our only lawful goal.[40]

We belong to God: when all is said and done, that is what baptism means in the Reformed tradition.

FURTHER READING

Calvin, John. *Institutes of the Christian Religion*, 4.15–16.

The Heidelberg Catechism, Questions 69 to 74.

The Westminster Confession of Faith, Chapters 27 and 28.

---

40. Calvin, *Institutes*, 3.7.1.

5

Baptism in the Anglican Communion

Alan L. Hayes

The Anglican Communion today is a family of forty-four autonomous national and regional churches, all of which have descended, directly or indirectly, from the Church of England. Until the 1960s almost all the churches in the Anglican communion used similar baptismal liturgies, since they all used service books that were adapted from the first Anglican prayer books of 1549 and 1552. Similar texts, however, did not lead Anglicans to common understandings; on the contrary, they disagreed about many things. Was baptism necessary to salvation? What happened to an unbaptized person? Did baptism actually effect or only signify God's grace? Was baptism complete or did it require later additions to be fully valid? Similar texts, then, did not decide the questions, but did help Anglicans have common conversations, and, for the most part, Anglicans practiced similar patterns of what is now often called Christian initiation (which includes baptism). Since the 1960s, however, most Anglican provinces have revised their liturgies more or less independently, and they no longer share common texts and patterns. Moreover, even within any one of these national and regional churches, there can be considerable variety in theology and pastoral approach. As a result, for the centuries up to 1960 it is possible to identify some common history, some texts generally acknowledged to be influential, some recurring patterns, and some intransigent controversies, all of which combined to create something like an Anglican way of baptism. For the period since 1960, however, the picture is much more scattered.

MEDIEVAL APPROACHES

Although non-Anglicans often think of King Henry VIII as the founder of the Church of England, Anglicans themselves trace their tradition back at least as far as 601, when the first archbishop of Canterbury was appointed, and indeed before that to the Christians in Britain when it was part of the Roman Empire. The success of the early Christian missions in Britain was measured in baptisms. Patrick, the apostle to the Irish in the fifth century, reports thousands of baptisms in his *Confession*, and Gregory, the pope who appointed the first archbishop of Canterbury, reported 10,000 baptisms among the English (but he may have been exaggerating).

Although the New Testament records a number of inconsistent patterns of baptism, the most influential on early Christian liturgy was that of the Ethiopian eunuch of Acts 8. This was a person who was curious about salvation, took instruction from the apostle Philip, requested baptism, and, after being baptized, experienced the power of the Holy Spirit and went away rejoicing. A typical early Christian pattern, then, was instruction followed by baptism with prayer for the gifts of the Spirit. In addition, from an early date, the laying on of hands became connected with baptism, partly from the influence of Heb 6:1–2.

As territories became Christianized, it did not seem right to leave children uninitiated into the church, especially since 1 Cor 7:14 suggested that the children of holy parents were also holy. So the pattern developed that everyone in Christendom, outside the small ghettoes of Jews, was expected to have their babies baptized. Often celebrations of baptism, especially for the more socially important people, became an important part of English community life. The decisive theological rationale for infant baptism, argued by the influential North African bishop St. Augustine in the years around 400, was that all persons inherited the sin of Adam, which was called "original sin." A primary piece of evidence for this conclusion was that all persons were mortal, and death was the wages of sin: "by one man [Adam] sin entered into this world and by sin death: and so death passed upon all persons, in whom all have sinned" (Rom 5:12). The value of infant baptism was therefore that it washed away the infant's original sin, and strengthened him or her against actual sin, even though (for various reasons) actual sin could not be avoided entirely. Occasionally some daring souls might question whether baptizing a child was actually of any real use; these dissidents often come to the historian's attention because they were hauled before an ecclesiastical court to answer for heresy. People in England called Lollards (the origin of the term is uncertain), who were particularly active in the late fourteenth and early fifteenth centuries, were reported to deny the sacramental power of baptism, and sometimes to be in possession of books expressing this view.

Among the theologians at Oxford and Cambridge (as on the continent) there was no agreement on the nature and meaning of baptism. One of them, John Duns Scotus, a scholar who was Irish, Scottish, or English, and who lived around 1300, argued that baptism worked because God had made a covenant with the church to bestow grace on each occasion that someone was baptized. The effect of baptism was remission of sin, spiritual birth, adoption as children of God, and church membership.[1] In this he was partly disagreeing with a slightly earlier Italian theologian, Thomas Aquinas, who thought that the very liturgical action of baptism was an "instrumental cause" of salvation, and God did not need to intervene specially at every occasion of baptism. This view was called *ex opere operato*, meaning that the effectiveness of the sacrament depended simply on "the doing of what was done." When baptism was administered with the proper intention, the proper matter (i.e., water), and the proper form (i.e., the words of administration), it was effective—not necessarily with an adult, indeed, since an adult might resist sacramental grace, but certainly with an infant, who was impressionable and who had committed no actual sin. Half a century later, however, John Wyclif, a teacher at Oxford University, contended that baptism in itself effected nothing at all; it was at most a sign, and then only for those elected by God to salvation. For the non-elect, it signified nothing at all. Debates of this kind extended beyond the Middle Ages, and indeed continue among some of the Christian intelligentsia to this day.

In addition to baptism, an extra piece of Christian initiation among the Christians of Western Europe was confirmation. By a probable account, it arose as a result of the popularity of infant baptism. In this theory, a typical pattern in the early church was that the bishop instructed an adult candidate, baptized him or her in water on Easter or Pentecost, laid hands on his or her head with prayer, anointed him or her with chrism, and administered Holy Communion. This pattern was disrupted as infant baptism became popular, and as Christians began to

---

1. Spinks, *Early and Medieval Rituals*, 145–48.

worry that an unbaptized infant would not be saved: increasingly babies were baptized soon after birth by a midwife or by whatever minister was available. A baby was too young to be instructed, and could not easily eat bread or drink wine for Communion, and who knew when a bishop might be on hand to lay on hands. Therefore, the laying on of hands by the bishop and communion were separated from baptism. The laying on of hands became a separate service, which the Latin West called confirmation, and by the twelfth century it was receiving its own theology distinct from baptism.

THE FIRST ANGLICAN PRAYER BOOKS

Although Anglicanism has a diverse and interesting medieval history, its character was most profoundly re-shaped by the English Reformation, which gathered momentum in the 1530s. Its most conspicuous political expression was schism from the Church of Rome; the king and Parliament came to believe that they had rightful jurisdiction over the Church of England, and that for centuries the Pope had illegally usurped it. Part of their rationale for denying papal authority was that the Pope seemed to them to be acting un-scripturally in many matters, and increasingly England became aligned with the Protestant movement, whose first watchword was "Scripture alone." There was nothing revolutionary about the English Reformation—the same clergy continued to minister to the same people in the same buildings within local administrative and financial structures that remained much the same. Yet English translations of the Bible were made publicly available; arrangements for administration and pastoral care were improved; resources for preaching and religious teaching, often reflecting a Protestant viewpoint, were written and published under government auspices; monasteries were closed, with some of their endowments going into education; and devotional observances that were considered superstitious, such as masses for the dead and the veneration of saints' relics, were abolished. Most importantly for our purposes, during a short period when a very Protestant group controlled the government, a book of worship services in English was published, called the *Book of Common Prayer* (BCP) or Prayer Book. Legislation was passed requiring all public worship in England to follow the Prayer Book. The first edition of the BCP in 1549 maintained a number of medieval forms but its texts reflected some Protestant adaptations; a revised edition of 1552 was more Protestant still. The BCP service of baptism would define the limits of the Anglican theology of Christian initiation for the next several centuries.

The principal author of the BCP was almost certainly the archbishop of Canterbury, Thomas Cranmer, a Protestant-minded divine who was well-read in classical theology and historical liturgies, and who also kept up with current religious controversies. His general approach to the revision of worship is summarized in a little essay called "Of Ceremonies," which was published as part of the BCP. It assumed that revision should begin with the texts currently in use. But elements that "obscured the glory of God," as understood from Scripture, would be "cut away," and godly practices that had been abused would be corrected. In addition, although the essay asserted that the purpose of revision was not to "satisfy . . . parties" but to "please God," it seems extremely likely that government and church leaders wanted their services of worship to accommodate a fairly wide diversity of religious opinion in England. A few strategic ambiguities in liturgical language might spare England some of the division, and indeed bloodshed, that marred religious reform on the Continent. Cranmer also borrowed ideas and texts from other lands, especially Protestant lands, if they seemed useful.

In revising the service of baptism, then, Cranmer sought to accommodate the acceptable range of religious opinion in England, to preserve as much of the late medieval liturgical structure and text as possible, and to adapt Protestant ideas and texts. The acceptable range of religious opinion at the time did not include Anabaptists, who rejected the practice of infant baptism. On the contrary, the few Anabaptists that could be found in England were savagely persecuted. There is evidence that Roman Catholics and what might be called the mainstream Protestants (the ones representing territorial churches), who disagreed on a great many other things, felt obliged to maintain a common front on baptism against the Anabaptists. There were theological principles at stake, of course; but in addition there was an important political principle. The leaders of the day generally understood that the integrity and security of their states and societies depended on an entirely Christian citizenry (with a few barely tolerated Jewish minorities), and they were deeply threatened by the Anabaptist view that people might decide at the age of discretion whether or not to become Christian, and that those who professed Christianity might then gather their own churches without state sanction.

In general, Roman Catholics and mainstream Protestants agreed that baptism was instituted as a sacrament (an outward and visible sign of an inward and invisible grace) by the authority of the Lord Jesus Christ; that it signified that a person's sin was remitted, and that he or she was born again, adopted as a child of God, and admitted into the church; that it primarily expressed the promises of God rather than anyone's individual faith; and that the infant children of believing parents should be baptized. There was, however, disagreement as to what it meant for the sacrament to be a "sign." Some signs (like five-dollar bills) actually are what they represent; but other signs (such as a McDonald's stylized M) point beyond themselves to something else. Did baptism simply point to God's promise, or was it in itself the actualization of God's promise, effecting a spiritual change in the person being baptized? Luther, especially in his later years, seems to have understood baptism as actually conferring grace, and it is hard to find any substantial disagreement between his *Larger Catechism* of 1529 and the statements promulgated by the Council of Trent of the Roman Catholic Church in 1547. This "high" view of baptism is implied in the provision for "emergency" baptism that was made by most mainline Protestants as well as Roman Catholics: that is, if an infant was in danger of death, he or she should be baptized immediately so as not to be eternally separated from the vision of God. The most prominent dissent from the mainstream consensus came from John Calvin, who re-wrote his section on baptism for the 1539 edition of his greatest work, *The Institutes of the Christian Religion*. Like John Wyclif, he thought that God's sovereign authority to decide whom to invite into eternal life—that is, the doctrine of election—relativized all the sacraments. If a minister in a certain congregation decided to administer a rite of baptism for someone, God was not thereby forced to decree that person's salvation. Baptism was not necessary for the elect, and could not save the non-elect. So-called emergency baptism was pointless. Nevertheless, he strongly endorsed public services of baptism. This sacrament, he emphasized, was founded in God's word; the church was required to honor it; it signified God's promises even if it did not in itself bring them to effect; and it had many spiritual benefits, notably the nourishing of faith. Although mainstream Protestants were divided on this point, they were generally agreed that, emergency baptism aside, services of baptism should be public, so that the witness to faith could be openly shared, in contrast to the frequent Roman Catholic practice of baptisms in households or in private chapels.

In the first English baptismal service in the BCP of 1549, we can see Cranmer's intention of comprehending both theological possibilities with texts and structures that maintain tradition where no Protestant theological principles would be compromised, but making changes where necessary.[2] For the essential structure, he used the Latin liturgy that was then current in most of England, called the Sarum rite, and he also adapted and translated many of its texts. The structure comprised introductory material, questions for the baptismal candidate, baptism in water, and an anointing with oil, with words of administration. He also maintained the assumption that the person being baptized would be an infant, and that godparents would answer the baptismal questions on the infant's behalf; and he kept a ritual blessing of the water in the baptismal font, although he demoted it from the service itself to an occasional rite, presented in a rubric (i.e., an administrative instruction) appended at the end. On the other hand, in a more Protestant direction, he eliminated a number of minor medieval rites and ceremonies, which Protestants often derided as "dark and dumb," and added material intended to make the intention and character of the service theologically perspicuous. Here one of his principal inspirations was a kind of manual of Protestant reform published in 1543 by the archbishop of Cologne, Hermann von Wied, who had grown sympathetic to the religious views of the German reformer Martin Luther. This manual, usually called the *Consultation* (its official title was exhaustingly long), was really compiled by the Lutheran leader Philip Melanchthon and the Strasbourg-based reformer Martin Bucer. Its recommendations for the service of baptism reflected Martin Luther's baptismal liturgy of 1526.

The service of baptism in BCP 1549 begins with a rubric that it should preferably take place in public on Easter or Pentecost. This takes aim against private baptisms, giving preference to Bucer's vision of the church as a Christian society where people would be built up in the faith by public ministry and shared witness. (A separate service in the BCP does provide for private baptisms, mainly for occasions when an infant was likely to die soon.) The service opens at the church door with an exhortation or teaching. Cranmer, like many other Protestants, wanted to be sure that worshippers clearly understood the meaning and intent of every service, ceremony, and sign, since otherwise liturgy had a way of degenerating into a set of meaningless canned rituals, or even super-

---

2. For changes, see Procter and Frere, *New History*, 570–72.

stition or idolatry. There follows a prayer making reference to the Old Testament story of Israel's rescue from Pharaoh through the water of the Red Sea (which was typological of baptism). Then there appears a relic of the early Christian practice of admitting a person into the catechumenate as a candidate for baptism: the child is named and signed with the cross. This rite is followed by a prayer, an exorcism ("I command thee, unclean spirit, ... that thou come out"), a Gospel reading from Mark 10 ("suffer little children to come unto me", as a Scriptural warrant for infant baptism), a short homily (adapted from the *Consultation*), the Lord's Prayer, the Apostles' Creed, and a prayer that the Holy Spirit might be given to the child. Then the baptismal party moves inside the church to the font, and the priest instructs the godparents in their duty. The child is asked the questions of the baptismal covenant: the godparents answer on his or her behalf. The first three questions invite renunciations of (1) the devil and all his works, (2) the vain pomp and glory of the world, and (3) the carnal desires of the flesh. The second set of three questions invites professions of faith; they correspond to the three paragraphs of the Apostles' Creed (belief in the Father; belief in the Son; and belief in the Holy Spirit). Each paragraph is followed by "I believe." The interrogatories conclude with "Wilt thou be baptized?" After the answer "I will," the priest, holding the child in his hands, dips the child in the water of the font three times in the medieval way (right side, left side, face forward), "so it be discreetly and warily done," or, if the child is weak, pours water on him or her, and says the words, "I baptize thee in the name of the Father, and of the Son, and of the Holy Ghost." The godparents take the child, and the priest clothes him or her with a white baptismal garment, called the chrisom, saying, "Take this white vesture for a token of the innocency which ... is given unto thee." Then the priest anoints the infant with oil on the head, signifying the unction of the Holy Spirit, and the "inheritance of eternal life." The service concludes with a further instruction to the godparents that they look after the child's spiritual welfare.

As the baptized infant grows into a child, Christian initiation according to the Prayer Book continues with instruction in the faith. Then when he or she comes to "the years of discretion," which might be anywhere from seven to fourteen years of age, the child makes a personal commitment to Christ in the rite of confirmation, and receives the laying on of hands from the bishop, with prayer for the strengthening gifts of the Holy Spirit. The service following baptism in BCP 1549, therefore, is confirmation, which begins (after several administrative rubrics) with a catechism or instruction for children. This service is not called a "sacrament," as it was in the continuing Roman Catholic Church, where it was typically numbered as one of the seven sacraments. The service of confirmation begins with a brief doxological dialogue between priest and congregation, followed by a traditional prayer for the sevenfold gift of the Spirit. The bishop makes a sign of the cross on the candidate's forehead with a prayer for strengthening, and then lays his hand on him or her. The service ends with a prayer and a blessing in the name of the Trinity.

Cranmer's intention for the service has been disputed, but it looks very much like a prominent provision for the instruction of children in the faith, followed by a rather brief version of the medieval rite of confirmation. The two are connected by a rubric providing that before the confirmation the bishop or his delegate can examine the candidate's knowledge of the Lord's Prayer, the Apostles' Creed, and the Ten Commandments; another rubric implies (questionably) that this examination amounts to a profession of faith. Did Cranmer regard the service as part of a process of Christian initiation? An argument that he did not is a rubric affirming that baptism is sufficient for salvation (in the absence of actual sin). An argument that he did is another rubric requiring confirmation as a condition of taking Holy Communion. In any event, BCP 1549 established the standard pattern of Christian initiation among Anglicans for the next four centuries: baptism as an infant, followed by catechetical instruction in the early years, followed by a personal commitment and receiving the laying on of hands in the service of confirmation, followed by first communion. Baptism and confirmation were connected, but had distinct rationales. In baptism, as a covenanted mercy, God forgave people their sins, granted them second birth, and adopted them as children; this grace was necessary to salvation. In confirmation, God gave people an additional strengthening of the Holy Spirit, and they then entered into full communion with the rest of the church.

In the more Protestant BCP 1552, Cranmer made numerous changes in the services of Christian initiation; only a few particularly important ones require mention. The whole service is said at the font. The exorcism, the anointing, the chrisom, and the appended rite for the blessing of the water in the font are deleted, mainly as unnecessary medievalisms that distract from the essence of the rite. The relic of the catechumenate is also deleted, and the child is first named immediately before baptism. Baptism itself has become a simple dipping in water. The sign of the cross is moved from the beginning of the service to a point after the baptism; it is no longer a sign of the catechumenate, therefore, but of something else—but what? One theory has it that Cranmer was taking one of the signs of western confirmation (and the principal sign of its counterpart in eastern Christianity) and moving it into baptism, to indicate that baptism completed Christian initiation. A similar purpose may have lain behind the new statement by the priest following baptism beginning, "Seeing now, dearly beloved brethren, that these children be regenerate." (This statement would later cause considerable controversy.)

BCP 1552 also made significant changes in the confirmation service. The bishop no longer made the sign of the cross on each child (perhaps because this sign had been moved to a new location in the service of baptism), but only laid hands on his or her head. Instead of the simple statement of BCP 1549, the bishop now said, "Defend, O Lord, this child with thy heavenly grace, that he may continue thine for ever, and daily increase in thy Holy Spirit more and more, until he come unto thy everlasting kingdom. Amen." The wording thus suggested a service of strengthening for lifelong sanctification.

THE ELIZABETHAN SETTLEMENT

The Protestant period when the BCP was promulgated was followed by a relatively short-lived Catholic reaction under Queen Mary, and in 1558 Queen Elizabeth acceded to the throne. She immediately moved to effect a "settlement of religion." Fortunately for her, few bishops of a Catholic persuasion were in office when she became queen, a circumstance that made it easier for her to resist pressure from a traditionalist direction. On the other hand, many advanced Protestants, usually called Puritans, were agitating for further reforms in the Church of England. The queen and her church leaders, managing Parliament skillfully, generally agreed to hold the line at a moderate and broad Protestantism. In 1559, her Parliament re-established BCP 1552 with several revisions (none of substance in the services of baptism or confirmation). Her general policy was to accommodate as many consciences as possible, whether of Catholic or Protestant disposition, as long as they respected the uniformity of worship defined by BCP 1559, and acknowledged the royal supremacy in the Church. The defining characteristic of Anglicanism for the next several centuries would be a liturgy, rather than a confessional statement of faith, an influential theologian, or an ecclesiastical discipline. Anglicanism has been called a "reformed Catholicism," with such catholic elements as bishops and some traditional symbols and ceremonial, and such reformed emphases as a vernacular Scriptures, vernacular worship, and moderately Protestant formularies.

In 1571, an Elizabethan Parliament adopted a formulary that perhaps has been, second to the Prayer Books, the most authoritative and influential document of Anglican history. The Thirty-Nine Articles of Religion of the Church of England had originally been drafted as forty-two articles by Archbishop Cranmer; they had more recently been shortened and revised in a rather less Protestant direction. They were not a confessional statement and carried no specific authority for the laity, but until the 1960s clergy in most parts of the Anglican Communion were required to subscribe to them before they could be ordained. Most of the articles stated the Church's position on certain theological matters that were in dispute either with Roman Catholics or with Anabaptists (or sometimes both), but they were typically expressed in language that was intended rather to exclude unacceptable opinion than to make narrowly precise affirmations. Baptism was discussed in Article XXVII:

> Baptism is not only a sign of profession, and mark of difference, whereby Christian men are discerned from others that be not christened, but it is also a sign of Regeneration or New-Birth, whereby, as by an instrument, they that receive Baptism rightly are grafted into the Church; the promises of the forgiveness of sin, and of our adoption to be the sons of God by the Holy Ghost, are visibly signed and sealed, Faith is confirmed, and Grace increased by virtue of prayer unto God. The Baptism of young Children is in any wise to be retained in the Church, as most agreeable with the institution of Christ.

This pithy but substantial statement was consistent with the Prayer Book service of baptism that required persons (almost always through godparents) to make a profession of faith before baptism, and its list of the benefits signified by baptism was familiar: forgiveness of sins, spiritual birth, adoption by God, and entrance into the Church. The article did not, however, specify whether the "sign" of baptism was effective in itself, or pointed to a grace that might be independently conferred by God.

The phrase "as by an instrument" perhaps suggested the former, while the phrase "by virtue of prayer unto God" perhaps suggested the latter, but neither was clear and specific. Calvin in his *Institutes*[3] had agreed that baptism was an "instrument," but an instrument of God's assurance, not an instrument of God's conferral of sacramental grace. The word "sealed," too, had Calvinist associations: the *Institutes* had compared the sacraments to the seal on a legal document, which attests the legitimacy of the document but does not make it effective.[4] Thus those both of a Catholic and of a Calvinist disposition could accept the article, but the last sentence clearly excluded Anabaptists.

Two works by Elizabethan theologians have usually been regarded as classic expressions of Anglicanism. *The Apology of the Church of England* (1562) by John Jewel, bishop of Salisbury, was intended chiefly as a defense of Anglicanism against Roman Catholic criticisms. It had extremely little to say about baptism, however, other than to affirm the similar mind of the two communions: "We say that Baptism is a Sacrament of the remission of sins, and of that washing, which we have in the blood of Christ; and that no person which will profess Christ's Name ought to be restrained or kept back therefrom; no, not the very babes of Christians; forsomuch as they be born in sin, and do pertain unto the people of God."

The other representative theological work of Elizabeth's reign was *On the Laws of Ecclesiastical Polity* (1594–1597) by a learned Anglican divine and parish priest named Richard Hooker. This work defended Prayer Book Anglicanism chiefly against the Puritan Anglicans. Later generations of Anglicans would regard Hooker as an important spokesperson for their tradition, although the Puritans, too, were members of the Church of England, and have been considered by some Anglicans as part of an evangelical Anglican tradition extending from Wyclif through Cranmer to the modern period. The Puritans, as Hooker understood them, had developed Calvin's thought so far as to reduce the sacraments to useful instructional symbols, and therefore unnecessary. Hooker, by contrast, contended that the sacraments were "ordained" by God "as means conditional which God requireth in them unto whom he imparteth grace."[5] In the case of baptism, he contends that a verse in John 3

---

3. Calvin, *Institutes*, 4.15.1.
4. Ibid., 4.15.22.
5. Hooker, *Polity*, 5.57.3.

can and should be taken literally: "Unless a man be born again of water and of the Spirit, he cannot enter into the kingdom of heaven." Baptism in water, linked to the gift of the Spirit, assures entry into salvation. On the other hand, he himself mitigates this principle when it comes to unbaptized infants: the presumed desire of the parents and of the Church for a child's baptism is accepted by God as equivalent to the material baptismal water. The necessity on the individual of receiving baptism is therefore not absolute, he concludes; but the necessity on the Church to administer baptism is more "strait and narrow."[6]

For the service of confirmation, which Puritan Anglicans, following Calvin, rejected entirely, Hooker's claims are muted. Like the earlier generation of English reformers, he saw no biblical warrant in the service. He had little reason to leap to its defense, since in practice confirmation services happened infrequently; indeed, Hooker complained of the "deep neglect of this Christian duty."[7] (There were very few English bishops, serving a sizable, widely distributed population, and many of them spent more time in London than in their dioceses.) In the end Hooker had little more to say for confirmation than that "there is a certain congruity and fitness to honour prelacy" by reserving to bishops the right to lay on hands.

THE SEVENTEENTH AND EIGHTEENTH CENTURIES

Beginning modestly in Elizabeth's reign, England for the next three centuries pursued a policy of global exploration, colonization, and territorial expansion that would create the British Empire and the worldwide Anglican Communion. As a result, the challenge of evangelizing and baptizing non-Christians arose for the first time since about the eleventh century. In 1607, under King James I, Virginia was founded, partly to serve as a base for converting the Indians. Would Anglicans administer indiscriminate baptism according to the required theological criteria of intention, matter, and form in order to save souls? In fact, they were unwilling to baptize adults without instructing them in the Christian faith and persuading them of the gospel of Christ. Infants might be susceptible of being baptized on a proxy or proleptic faith, but not adults. Unfortunately this policy excluded African and aboriginal slaves from

---

6. Ibid., 5.60.
7. Ibid., 5.66.8.

the purview of the missionaries, since slave-owners did not want their property instructed. In fact, some feared that baptism might confer legal freedom. On the other hand, most free Native Americans were available for evangelization, if the colonists were not at war with them. A few missionaries to the Indians did make serious efforts. In Virginia, Alexander Whitaker worked with the Powhatan nation; about 1612 he instructed the princess Pocahontas in the Christian faith, "who after she had made some good progress therein, renounced publicly her country idolatry, openly confessed her Christian faith, was, as she desired, baptized."[8] In New York, an Anglican missionary named Henry Barclay began learning the Mohawk language in 1734, set about teaching Christianity to the Mohawks, and by 1742 had reportedly baptized almost all their nation.

Back in England, disagreements continued about the services of Christian initiation and other parts of the BCP. Almost immediately after his accession in 1603, King James I tried to address these disagreements by calling together some religious leaders of diverse views to meet with him in his palace at Hampton Court. The Puritan group reportedly protested several parts of the Prayer Book service of baptism: making the sign of the cross (which seemed to them to be superstitious, and highly identified with the much disliked Roman Catholic Church), asking questions of infants (a silly fiction, since they could not answer for themselves), and retaining the service of confirmation (which seemed to lack biblical justification). They also opposed baptism by midwives, since, following Calvin, they did not think that any baptism could be an "emergency baptism." In the end, the king and his advisers made a few modest accommodations of Puritan opinion: they placed certain restrictions on private baptism, including the requirement of a minister (not a midwife) to administer it. They also created a canon, or church law, to explain the sign of the cross as a mere "significative," and not a pretended "sign effective." The sign of the cross, it said, was "no part of the substance of that Sacrament," but an ancient and lawful ceremonial recalling the cross of Christ.[9]

These minor adjustments did little to assuage the Puritans, who enjoyed little standing under James I and his intransigent son Charles I. A reversal was in store when Charles I, who like his father had inherited the crown of Scotland as well as that of England, tried to impose the

8. Whitaker's letter is reprinted in Hamor, *True Discourse*, 55.
9. Canons of 1604, Canon 30.

Prayer Book (in a revised form) on the Church of Scotland. At the first Prayer Book service at St. Giles's Cathedral in Edinburgh, on Sunday, July 23, 1637, the story goes that an outraged street seller named Jenny Geddes threw a stool at the minister, setting off angry demonstrations and leading eventually to war between Scotland and England, followed by a civil war in England. As a result, an anti-Anglican faction took control of the English government, and eventually executed the king. The BCP was outlawed from 1645 to 1660. During this period also, many English Christians were challenging infant baptism. This unstable period came to a close in 1660 when King Charles II was invited to return to England to take the throne. The Church of England once again became the established religion of the country. The Prayer Book was revised again, and was promulgated by an Act of Uniformity in 1662.

In BCP 1662, the service of baptism was changed to take into account the fact that for many years many had been baptized irregularly, or not baptized at all. Affirming the tradition of the church, and St. Paul's prescription (Eph 4:5) that no one should be baptized more than once, the BCP 1662 required the minister to satisfy himself at the beginning of the service that the person to be baptized had not been previously baptized. It added a third baptismal service, in addition to the public and private services for the baptism of infants, for "such as are of riper years": this would serve both those in England who during the recent disruptions had not been baptized as infants, and aboriginals and others in the overseas English colonies who might be converted as adults. The rubric making confirmation a prerequisite to communion was changed to read, "And there shall none be admitted to the holy Communion, until such time as he be confirmed, or be ready and desirous to be confirmed." This change served England's overseas colonists, who had no bishops, and therefore could not be confirmed. Several additional textual changes were made. The number of godparents was specified as three. The font was to be filled afresh at every baptism. A phrase for the sanctifying of the water in the baptismal font was added to a prayer. The catechism was separated from confirmation in a separate section. In the confirmation service, those being confirmed were required explicitly to affirm their baptismal vows.

An influential Anglican theological movement began in the 1640s and gathered momentum in the remainder of the century. It is named by some historians Caroline Anglican "moralism,"[10] and it provoked controversy by its reinterpretation of Anglican baptismal teaching. Against the Reformation teaching of justification by the free grace of God, the moralists affirmed that the salvation signified by baptism depended on a person's scrupulous attention to the obligations of morality and personal piety. They argued that in baptism Christians entered into a legal conditional covenant with God by which they promised sincere obedience and God promised salvation; those who fell short violated the covenant, and lost their salvation. A bishop named Jeremy Taylor was a leading exponent of this school of thought. By the end of the century, this view that baptism was an entry into a conditional covenant of works had influenced two church parties: the high church and the whiggish latitudinarians. The former predicated salvation on an obedient attachment to Anglican polity and tradition; the latter, though more ecumenically minded and less fussy, predicated salvation on living "soberly, righteously, and godly,"[11] reflecting their reaction against the Calvinist emphasis on revelation and doctrine.

In the eighteenth century, an evangelical revival, or rather a series of revivals, that swept Great Britain can be seen partly as a reaction against Anglican moralism. Evangelicals taught that through a personal commitment of faith a Christian could experience acquittal of sin and the enlivening fruits of the Holy Spirit. This was an attractive message that left Anglican moralism looking grim, dull, and repressive. But it was not an easy thing for Anglican evangelicals to find a place for baptism. Their allegiance to their church order prevented them from either abandoning infant baptism or adding a second baptism for converts. Their quandary is illustrated by the best known of the Anglican revivalists, John Wesley (1703–1791). He was firmly committed to the practice of infant baptism, and in a treatise of 1756 he renewed the rationale for it that was familiar to generations of Anglicans. But in 1755, when he was trying to discourage his preachers from beginning an unauthorized sacramental ministry, he told them that not one soul would perish for lack of the sacraments if they refrained (which, he said, was not true of preaching). One of Wesley's most astute modern students concludes that he never quite reconciled his ideas of a second birth in baptism and

---

10. Cf. Allison, *Rise of Moralism*.
11. Titus 2:12.

another second birth in an adult commitment of faith.[12] A long-term impact of evangelical revivalism on the Anglican doctrine of baptism was that, from then on, terms like "regeneration" and "second birth" and "being born again" were associated by a great many people primarily with adult conversion, which left the theology of infant baptism confused. A more precise agreed definition of "regeneration" was required, but failed to materialize.

FROM 1810 TO 1959

A prolonged and sometimes bitter controversy erupted among Anglicans about baptism in the nineteenth century, particularly about two issues: Did the sacrament of baptism effect regeneration in every person, including infants? And was baptism only the beginning of Christian initiation, requiring a later service of confirmation to be completed?

The first issue was launched in 1812 in a prestigious annual theological lectureship at the University of Oxford, called the Bampton Lectures. The lecturer that year was Richard Mant, an Oxford-trained parish priest who despised evangelicals and Methodists. Prefacing his lecture with John 3:5, and quoting the Prayer Book and such Anglican moralists of the seventeenth and eighteenth centuries as Jeremy Taylor, Mant argued that water baptism was ("humanly speaking") the necessary and sufficient instrumentality of the blessing of spiritual regeneration. Evangelicals responded with insistences on the necessity of personal faith; high-church writers counter-replied. A few years later the cause of baptismal regeneration was taken up by the Anglo-Catholic movement, which is usually dated as originating in Oxford in 1833. One of the most influential of the Anglo-Catholics, Edward Pusey, sought to address Wesley's quandary by affirming that an adult conversion was necessary only when one was estranged from God after baptism; but estrangement, if it happened, did not invalidate the baptism. "In Holy Baptism," Pusey wrote, "we were all 'made children of God,' and we never need have left our Father's house."[13] The most heated and enduring controversy about baptismal regeneration arose in 1847 between George Gorham, a slightly antiquarian Cambridge-trained evangelical Anglican priest, and Henry Philpotts, the cantankerous and conservative high-church bishop

---

12. Baker, *John Wesley*, 156.
13. Chadwick, *Oxford Movement*, 107.

of Exeter. Gorham, who had been nominated to be the minister of a parish in Philpotts's diocese, denied that regenerating grace was always connected to the baptism of an infant, though it might be activated if, for instance, the infant grew up and became a faithful Christian. After examining Gorham for thirty-eight hours over five days on the doctrine of baptismal regeneration, Philpotts found him doctrinally unsound and refused to allow him to minister in the parish. Gorham sued. A church court took two years to mull over the history of the doctrine of baptismal regeneration, and found in favor of the bishop. Gorham then appealed to the highest court in the British Empire, which in 1850 decided that he had not, after all, taught clearly against the formularies of the Church of England. The case was one of the most embittering episodes in an increasingly polarized Victorian church.

Not quite so divisive, but very controversial, was the question of confirmation. This service, as we have seen, had been held infrequently before the nineteenth century. When it was held, the bishop typically made a perfunctory pass of his hands over a very large crowd, and the event did not seem particularly personal and reverent. In the nineteenth century, however, many bishops were determined to give more attention to their pastoral duties; the construction of railways made episcopal travel easier; and the Anglo-Catholic revival was focusing attention on sacramental theology and episcopal ministry. Some of a catholic disposition began to contend that confirmation was a sacrament, just as Roman Catholics said it was; that it was necessary to the Christian life, and that baptism was incomplete without it. Some short devotional tracts were published, and some referred back to a treatise on the subject by the busy Jeremy Taylor. Then in 1891 a 23-year-old Cambridge graduate named A. J. Mason published a lengthy argument for confirmation as the sacramental completion of baptism, adorned with numerous quotations from ancient authors.[14] In baptism, he contended, sin was forgiven and new life begun; but only in confirmation did the "objective, personal indwelling of the Holy Spirit" begin, with the many spiritual blessings attendant thereon. Among many writers who followed Mason, one of the most influential was an Anglican Benedictine monk named Gregory Dix, who began writing about it in 1936. Dix took the eccentric view that confirmation was the Christian counterpart to Jewish circumci-

---

14. Mason, *Relation*.

sion and originally preceded baptism.[15] Wags called the argument for confirmation as the sacramental completion of baptism "the Mason-Dix Line." The most influential voice on the other side was G. W. H. Lampe, a professor of divinity at Cambridge.[16] Apart from any arguments from Scripture or ancient theologians, Lampe pointed out that "the doctrine that no person unconfirmed by a bishop can be possessed of the Holy Spirit, unless it be by some uncovenanted act of mercy, is flatly contrary to all experience." But he did have his own arguments from Scripture and early authorities, which agreed that not just forgiveness of sins, but the seal of the Spirit as well, occurred, actually or in anticipation, in water baptism, and not only later in an accessory rite. The baptized infant did indeed receive the indwelling of the Spirit, even if he or she could not become aware of it until an older age. That awareness might come gradually, or in a moment of conversion.

The debate has not been resolved, and there are those in the Anglican Communion who lean more in the direction of the Mason-Dix Line, and others who lean more in the direction of Lampe. The Anglican Communion does not have machinery, and would not want to develop machinery, to render authoritative doctrinal interpretations for all its members.

SINCE 1960

Several forces converged in the 1960s to overthrow the picture of Anglican baptism that we have been observing so far. First, an aggressive new school of thought called the Liturgical Movement created a new liturgical agenda. Second, Anglicanism was profoundly influenced by the Second Vatican Council in the Roman Catholic Church. Third, many British colonies achieved independence in the 1960s, and their Anglican churches began questioning the models they had been taught by their missionaries. Fourth, Anglicans entered into ecumenical conversations that broadened their horizons.

The Liturgical Movement originated in the Benedictine order of the Roman Catholic Church, and received some encouragement from Pope Pius X in 1903. Consistent with its Benedictine roots, it always exalted liturgical and especially sacramental worship as the central re-

---

15. His developed argument ten years later is in Dix, *Theology of Confirmation*.
16. Lampe, *Seal of the Spirit*.

ality of Christian life. Originally marked by an in-group spirit and an intellectualizing irrelevance (which it never entirely lost), it expanded ecumenically and pastorally, and by the 1920s it was percolating away in the Anglican world. It took early Christian worship as the model to follow, which helped free it from denominational narrowness and appealed to those of a catholic temperament. It advocated worship with solid Scriptural teaching, clear purpose, pared ceremonial, and lay participation, which appealed to those of a Protestant temperament. It sought relevance to modern culture, which appealed to liberals. It was explicitly antagonistic to sixteenth-century liturgy, whether Cranmer's Prayer Books or the missal of the Roman Catholic Council of Trent. By the 1960s it was ruling over processes of liturgical revision in the Roman Catholic, Anglican, and Lutheran worlds. It lavished a considerable amount of its attention on baptism. As Christendom was expiring and infant baptism could no longer be taken for granted as a social norm, baptism stood out, it thought, as the defining expression of Christian identity, as well as the point of admission to the world of Christian worship. Indeed, all worship functioned partly as a reminder and reaffirmation of the covenant established and the grace signified in a Christian's baptism. While it fully endorsed infant baptism, it gave fresh thought to the baptism of adult converts, whose number was increasing both in the old Christendom and in the global mission field. For this purpose, it advocated a reinvigorated catechumenate for the instruction and formation of converts, leading to a dramatic and memorable service of baptism. Instead of taking infant baptism as the norm and adapting it *ad hoc* for those rare occasions when an adult convert happened along, as Anglicans had been doing for centuries, the Liturgical Movement derived its theology of baptism from the norm of adult baptism.

In the Roman Catholic Church, which had more members than all other Christian groups put together, the Second Vatican Council (1962–1965) was an epoch-making event, and it captivated the Anglican world. Its watchword was *aggiornamento,* "updating"—bringing expressions of doctrine, forms of worship, and pastoral practice fully into the modern world. When it came to baptism, it was clearly influenced by the Liturgical Movement. It directed a revision of rites of baptism to remove medieval and possibly superstitious accretions, and to focus on the central biblical meaning of the rite. In its decree on ecumenism it embraced all Christians as brothers and sisters (though in imperfect communion) on account of their baptism. In the wake of the Council, the pope in 1971 issued an "apostolic constitution" on confirmation that connected it much more intimately with baptism. He decreed that the essential act in the rite was not the laying on of hands but the chrismation (signing with holy oil), a decision that overturned centuries of western assumptions. He affirmed that in confirmation the candidate receives the Holy Spirit.

Before 1960 all the world's Anglican churches (except for a few that were evangelized from the United States) had been planted in the context of the political and commercial power of the British Empire, and were imbued with British values and cultural symbols. In the nineteenth century, Canada, Australia, New Zealand, and South Africa had become independent, and their Anglican churches had become technically autonomous, although until after the Second World War they remained so steeped in anglophilia that they still functioned as satellites of the Church of England. In Africa, Anglican churches were shunned by many locals, and sometimes violently attacked, as instruments of imperialism. With decolonization in the 1960s, however, African Anglicanism increasingly indigenized, that is, came under African control and identified with African realities. Its credibility increased dramatically, and in many parts of Africa the result was an exponential increase in membership and activity. Today the Anglican church in Nigeria has the largest active Anglican membership of any country, about 18 million. The Anglican Church in Kenya comes second. Increasingly these and other churches revised their liturgies with attention to "inculturation," the expression of gospel truth in a local, non-European intellectual and social context. "For four hundred years," Archbishop Henry Luke Orombi of Uganda has written, "Anglicanism represented both the theological convictions of the English Reformation and the culture of the Christian Church in Britain." East Africans, he said, deserved an Anglicanism of their own, one that in particular would reflect their own history and values, and not least the evangelistic zeal of the East African Revival of 1935.[17] Therefore, since the Second World War, as the British Commonwealth countries of both the global north and the global south have developed clearer national identities independent of England, their Anglican churches have decentralized and diversified in their baptismal theology, pastoral practice, and liturgy. The Episcopal Church in the United States, of course, has had an independent ethos for a great deal longer.

17. Orombi, "What is Anglicanism?"

Anglican churches had joined in ecumenical work in the nineteenth century and helped found the World Council of Churches in 1948, but in the 1960s the Anglican communion established or joined a number of ecumenical dialogues that expanded its theological horizons. Among the most important fruits was the statement "Baptism, Eucharist and Ministry," released by the World Council's Faith and Order Commission in 1982. Identified as the "most widely distributed and studied ecumenical document," it represented the common mind of representatives from a very broad Christian spectrum. Its general approach was not to analyze divisive terms and ideas, like regeneration, but to find consensus in the rich and varied language used in the Bible for baptism, and especially in Paul's affirmation that through baptism Christians participate in the life, death, and resurrection of Jesus. At many points it left strategic ambiguities, notably with the word "sign." While not excluding infant baptism, it affirmed that personal commitment was necessary for responsible membership in the body of Christ. Although most Christian communities have expressed reservations about pieces of the document, it has been very successful in increasing ecumenical understanding, and in its general approach it has reinforced the Anglican tendency to comprehend and value different approaches to baptism.

All these developments together have moved Anglicans to review their practices and understandings of Christian initiation. They all played a part in a report on Christian initiation presented in 1968 to the decennial "Lambeth Conference" of Anglican bishops worldwide. The report called for a review of received patterns, and commended consideration of several new alternatives, including the communion of children and a change in the timing of confirmation (either earlier or later). The bishops then passed the following resolution: "The Conference recommends that each province or regional Church be asked to explore the theology of baptism and confirmation in relation to the need to commission the laity for their task in the world, and to experiment in this regard."[18]

ANGLICAN DIVERSITY TODAY

The pre-1960 Anglican pattern of infant baptism, childhood Christian education, and confirmation in early adolescence followed by first communion, is now a minority practice, although it is by no means obso-

---

18. Resolution 25.

lete: it remains the norm in the West Indies and the Church of Ireland, for example. In Kenya and some other parts of Africa, this traditional pattern has been adjusted by inserting, between baptism in infancy and confirmation in adolescence, a rite for admission to communion for children aged about nine or ten. In addition, in Kenya's inculturated prayer book *Our Modern Services* (2002), confirmation was transformed into a service of confirmation and commissioning, so that the emphasis was changed from inward strengthening to outward service and mission. North America generally went in a quite different direction, partly because of its theological doubts about the purpose of confirmation, but also because, pastorally, confirmation seemed to produce results opposite of those desired: young people were confirmed, and then left the church. (According to an Anglican joke, the best way to chase bats out of the belfry was to confirm them.) By 1971, the Episcopal Church in the United States was proposing that those baptized, whether in infancy or adulthood, had completed Christian initiation. This represented a significant change, and it became the norm in the American BCP of 1979. One indication of its new understanding was the transfer of the traditional confirmation prayer for the sevenfold gift of the Spirit into the service of baptism. The Anglican Church of Canada accepted the American re-thinking in its *Book of Alternative Services,* although since this was an "alternative" book, parishes were generally free to continue in the older pattern. Many local variants aside, Anglican children in the U.S.A. and Canada commonly take communion, but confirmation services are infrequent and serve small numbers. This practice is also increasing in some other parts of the Anglican world, including the Church of England.

In many parts of the Anglican world today, including the Church of England, "increasing numbers of people are not being baptized as infants."[19] Some leaders and parents encourage the deferral of baptism until a person can make his or her decision. In some parts of the Anglican world a renewed catechumenate has been developed both for those of Christian upbringing who are ready to prepare for baptism, and for converts from a non-Christian background. The catechumenate is usu-

---

19. In April 2009, in response to a 56-year-old atheist's petition, the diocese of Southwark agreed that the record of his infant baptism would be cross-referenced to his protest that he had not agreed to it. See http://news.bbc.co.uk/2/hi/uk_news/7941817.stm (accessed February 20, 2010).

ally modeled after the restored catechumenate of the Roman Catholic Church. The *Book of Occasional Services* of the Episcopal Church in the United States, the book *Making Disciples* in the diocese of Toronto, and the Catechumenate Network in the United Kingdom, reflect this development.

The services of Christian initiation themselves can vary quite considerably from national church to national church, and indeed, because of options written into many national liturgies, the services can vary from parish to parish. All services of baptism include water and the words of administration, but baptism can be done by sprinkling, effusion, or immersion. Because the Liturgical Movement enjoyed dramatic symbolism, some of its exponents have promoted immersion. Some Anglican liturgies provide that the presider may apply chrism to the baptismal candidate with the sign of the cross, lay on hands, or hand a lit candle to the candidate; others do not. Some Anglican churches continue to have godparents for a baptized infant; some have godparents for adults too; but in some places the parents may be the godparents, while in still others the entire congregation may be invited to be godparents. Different liturgies will highlight different theological emphases. In addition to the differences on the large questions already discussed, a more modest example is that while many Anglican services speak of being baptized "in Christ," in Anglican baptism in Southern Africa persons are baptized "into Christ." This word is used, it is explained, because baptism should be seen as leading people in a new direction rather than giving them a completed destination. In Africa, Anglican liturgies are often characterized by Scripture, testimony, zeal, and elements of African culture, such as joyful African song and dance. In Kenya, *Our Modern Services*, published in 2002, moved strikingly ahead in this respect. In February 2008 the Anglican Church in Nigeria announced a revision to replace a "cold and lifeless" service with a more engaging one.

In Africa a particular issue after 1960 was whether polygamous converts could be baptized. The tradition had been against it, but the unhappy results were, first, that some men put away all but one of their wives, which left the discarded women as social outcasts, and, second, that Muslim missionaries had a distinct advantage over Christians. In 1988, the Lambeth Conference, which has no juridical authority but does have some moral influence, recommended a new policy in the matter. While upholding "monogamy as God's plan," it gave support to the baptism of a polygamist with his believing wives and children on the condition that he promise not to add more wives, and that his local Anglican community approve.

In this as in other matters, Anglican diversity reflects partly historical development, partly ethos, and partly theological principle. Currently the forces towards diversity and even disagreement appear stronger than the forces towards harmony and consensus, and although all Anglicans can officially agree that baptism is an obligation and promise of the gospel, it seems unlikely that in the foreseeable future they will agree on when, how, where, or precisely why it should be done, or what its implications are for a person's life in Christ or membership in the church.

FURTHER READING

The First and Second Prayer Books of King Edward VI, London: Everyman, 1976.

Hooker, Richard. *Of the Laws of Ecclesiastical Polity.* London: Everyman, 1922 (especially book V, chapters 49–66).

Irons, William J. *The Judgments on Baptismal Regeneration.* London: Joseph Masters, 1850.

6

Baptism among Baptists

Anthony R. Cross

THE WORLDWIDE COMMUNION OF Baptists comprises various unions, conventions, and bodies of churches that exhibit many common emphases yet considerable diversity. Bill Leonard writes,

> Baptist identity is configured in a variety of ways by groups, subgroups, and individuals who claim the Baptist name. This identity extends across a theological spectrum from Arminian to Calvinist, from conservative to liberal, from open to closed communionist, and from denominationalist to independent.[1]

On the subject of baptism, Anthony R. Cross's conclusion of the baptismal theology and practice of twentieth-century British Baptists equally applies to all Baptists over their four-hundred-year history and their geographical dispersion:

> [T]here is no single Baptist theology or practice of baptism, only theologies and practices, and this diversity accords with Baptist ecclesiology which continues to tend towards independency, each local church and individual minister exercising their liberty in the administration and interpretation of Christ's laws.[2]

---

1. Leonard, *Baptist Ways*, xiii. He helpfully summarizes Baptist distinctives and the differences of interpretation and expression these receive among various Baptists (see also 1–10 and 14–15).

2. Cross, *Baptism and the Baptists*, 455. See also Leonard, *Baptist Ways*, 1–3. It is equally important to recognize that even the present attempt to summarize the theologies and practices of Baptists runs the risks of over-generalization and simplification.

If other Christian traditions are to understand Baptists it is important for them to understand this variety of doctrine and practice, not just on the subject of baptism, but on any subject. There is no hierarchy that can legislate or impose in matters of doctrine or practice, for, as the "Declaration of Principle" of the Baptist Union of Great Britain expresses matters in its first principle, "our Lord and Saviour Jesus Christ, God manifest in the flesh, is the sole and absolute authority in all matters pertaining to faith and practice, as revealed in the Holy Scriptures, and that each Church has liberty, under the guidance of the Holy Spirit, to interpret and administer His Laws."[3]

Baptists, together and individually, seek the mind of Christ for what they believe and do, recognizing the central place of the Bible in this,[4] and trusting in the guidance of the Spirit who has been given to the church community and individual believers.[5] While they have always valued the counsel of others (whether other local churches, regional associations, national unions/conventions, the international community of Baptists, or the wider, catholic church and the historic Christian faith) they have not been tied to their decisions. While Baptists have often adopted confessions of faith, these "statements of belief are not equal with Scripture or binding on individual conscience"[6] and over time have been replaced

---

3. Baptist Union of Great Britain website, online: http://www.baptist.org.uk/baptist_life/what_is_a_baptist/dec_of_principle.html.

4. Cf. the Preamble to the 1963 Southern Baptist "Baptist Faith and Message," in George and George, *Baptist Confessions,* 138, which states, "4. That the sole authority for faith and practice among Baptists is the Scriptures of the Old and New Testaments."

5. Leonard, *Baptist Ways,* 14: "the compelling ideal that informs Baptist identity theologically and pragmatically seems to be the belief that the people can be trusted to interpret Scripture aright, *in the context of community* and under the guidance of the Holy Spirit" (italics added emphasizing that, while individualism in the worst sense is a bane to all Christian traditions in the contemporary church, the Baptist ideal recognizes the corporate dimension of seeking the mind of Christ).

6. Leonard, *Baptist Ways,* 8. Cf. Lumpkin, *Baptist Confessions,* 16–17, who observes that "The Baptist Movement has traditionally been non-creedal in the sense that it has not erected authoritative confessions of faith as official bases of organization and tests of orthodoxy. An authority which could impose a confession upon individuals, churches, or larger bodies, has been lacking, and the desire to achieve uniformity has never been strong enough to secure adoption of a fixed creed even if the authority for imposing it had existed. Still, Baptists have recognized the valuable uses to which confessions of faith might be put. Their earliest confessions were called forth for apologetic and propaganda purposes in response to criticism from other church groups."

by others.[7] Confessions of faith are historical expressions of the faith of a particular group of Baptists at a particular time and in a particular place, but they are no replacement for Scripture. This also applies to creeds, and while Baptists have been more wary of creeds than they have been of confessions, they have nevertheless often recognized the usefulness of the historic creeds.[8] Baptists, then, are biblicists in the sense that "their devotion to the Bible [is] the result of their belief that all spiritual truth is to be found in its pages," though when it comes "to determining the implications of inspiration ... there [are] notable divergences."[9] Recognizing this will help other Christian traditions understand why New Testament baptism is determinative for Baptists.

HISTORICAL ORIGINS[10]

The first Baptist congregation originated in Amsterdam in 1609 among a group of English Separatists from the East Midlands led by John Smyth and Thomas Helwys, who had fled from the religious persecution of Dissenters the previous year. Their reading of Scripture, as well as the widespread Separatist unease with the baptism they had received from what they saw as an apostate Church of England, led them to the conviction that New Testament baptism was that of believers.[11] So Smyth first

---

7. See the collections of these in Lumpkin, *Baptist Confessions*, and George and George, *Baptist Confessions*.

8. For instance, the General Baptists' *The Orthodox Creed* (1678/79), article XXXVIII, in Lumpkin, *Baptist Confessions*, 326, which says that the three creeds, "viz. Nicene creed, Athanasius's creed and the Apostles creed ... ought throughly to be received and believed."

9. Bebbington, *Evangelicalism in Modern Britain*, 12–13. While Bebbington is here discussing the characteristics of Evangelicals, this is equally true of Baptists. On these divergences on the nature of the inspiration and interpretation of Scripture, see Leonard, *Baptist Ways*, 1, 4–6. It is important to note that this is not to suggest that Baptists are bibliolaters; they do not worship the Bible, but the Lord of the Bible.

10. See McBeth, *The Baptist Heritage*, 21–63; and for a succinct overview, Leonard, *Baptist Ways*, 10–13.

11. See Cross, "Adoption of Believer's Baptism." It must also be noted that the Baptist adoption of believer's baptism is wholly consistent with the biblical, and also the reformers', emphasis on the necessity of faith for salvation—hence it is the baptism *of believers* that is practiced, not of infants who are unable to believe for themselves. Baptists clearly, then, reject any notion of vicarious faith, even for the children of one or more Christian parents, as these children must come to personal faith in Christ if they are to be received into the kingdom of God. Baptists agree, therefore, with the view expressed so clearly by Schnabel, *Early Christian Mission*, 1:358, that "there is a new

baptized himself out of a basin (hence he is known as the Se-Baptist) and then the others. Smyth did not seek baptism by the local Mennonites (Dutch Collegiants/Waterlanders) for several reasons: he did not see them as a true church;[12] he had doctrinal reasons;[13] and he had a difference of opinion on succession in ordination.[14] Smyth baptized himself and the others by affusion (i.e., pouring), which appears to have been the mode adopted by other English Separatists in exile.[15]

In his 1609 treatise, *The Character of the Beast*, Smyth argued that infants were not to be baptized as there is no scriptural warrant for the practice and because infants are incapable of confession with their mouth. Further, those converted are to be admitted to the church by baptism, for the true church is comprised of believers only. In holding this position, Smyth and Helwys, and all Baptists subsequently, adopted a doctrine of the church that rejected the idea of Christendom, along with its concomitant that the state controls the church. Smyth went on to reject the doctrine of original sin and guilt and so set the tone for the predominant Baptist view that infants are born in a state of innocence,[16]

'missionary situation' in every family in which a baby is born. The 'missionary situation' will never end until the second coming of Christ." Cf. Barth, *Church Dogmatics*, 4:4, 184: "The Christian life cannot be inherited as blood, gifts, characteristics and inclinations are inherited. No Christian environment, however genuine or sincere, can transfer this life to those who are in this environment. For these, too, the Christian life will and can begin only on the basis of their own liberation by God, their own decision." Baptists reject the paedobaptist argument from the household baptisms recorded in the book of Acts (Acts 10:24–48; 11:14; 16:15; 16:30–33; 18:8; cf. 1 Cor 1:16), because in each of these accounts the gospel is proclaimed (of which baptism was an integral part and the response of faith is either explicit or implicit, cf. Acts 10:33; 11:14). See Beasley-Murray, *Baptism in the New Testament*, 312–20; and Stein, "Baptism in Luke–Acts," 61–63.

12. John Smyth, *The Character of the Beast, or The False Constitution of the Church* (1609), 1, for which see Cross, "Adoption of Believer's Baptism," 5–6 n. 20.

13. White, *English Baptists*, 19. It is possible that he viewed their docetic Hoffmannite Christology as an obstacle to fuller fellowship, though later, in 1610, he and those of the congregation who remained with him in Holland sought to join the Mennonites. They eventually did so in 1615, three years after his death.

14. Wright, *Early English Baptists*, 34–35.

15. White, *English Baptists*, 19; Cross, "Adoption of Believer's Baptism," 7–14.

16. Cross, "Adoption of Believer's Baptism," 19. Though this is a weakness in the Baptist theology of initiation, there has been an increasing number of Baptist studies on the theology of the child in recent decades. For example, see Miller, "Baptist Theology"; *Believing and Being Baptized*; and West, "The Child and the Church," 75–110.

thereby doing away with one of the key arguments for infant baptism, since a child who dies in infancy is accepted by God.

Smyth's theology was deeply covenantal, covenant understood as the mutual consent of both parties. Covenant theology in its Roman and Reformed forms, especially coupled with the understanding of Christendom entered into by baptism, required the baptism of babies, which was understood as the seal of the covenant. However, according to Smyth, two covenants were made with Abraham: one with his physical children in which the covenant seal was circumcision,[17] the other with his spiritual children of which the baptism of the Holy Spirit is the seal.[18] From the first, therefore, Baptist understanding of the baptismal covenant was firmly based on New Testament teaching. While many Baptists have not so sharply distinguished Spirit- and water-baptism in the way that Quakers and, later, many Pentecostals and Charismatics have,[19] they have nevertheless tended to emphasize the spiritual dimension of conversion, often to the detriment of its physical expression. This was less so

17. Cross, "Adoption of Believer's Baptism," 22–23. While Baptists accept the continuity between the old and new covenants, they do not equate circumcision with baptism in a way that is comparable to type and anti-type. Rather they see the new covenant as new in the sense that entry into the covenant community is not sealed by familial or racial membership, but by personal faith in Christ. This is supported by the observation that in the New Testament the gifts attributed to faith are all also attributed to baptism and that, therefore, New Testament baptism is faith-baptism (see n. 48 below). Jewett, *Infant Baptism*, 235–36, criticizes the paedobaptist argument from the covenant on the grounds that "it stresses the covenant idea as the unifying concept of redemptive history to the point of suppressing the *movement* of redemptive history, a movement from the age of anticipation and promise to the age of realization and fulfillment." While he applauds paedobaptist affirmations "of the centrality and perpetuity of the covenant concept as a fundamental category of biblical revelation" he nevertheless cautions that it must not overshadow the truth that "the old covenant made with the Jewish people has now become the new covenant in Jesus Christ." Jewett argues against the equation of baptism and circumcision (see 85–104, 229–30, 238–40). Schreiner, "Baptism in the Epistles," 78, says: "The typological antecedent to baptism . . . is not physical circumcision but spiritual circumcision." See the whole of his discussion of Col 2:11–12 on pages 75–79. Also on the covenant/circumcision argument, see Wellum, "Baptism."

18. Cross, "Adoption of Believer's Baptism," 18–19, 21. Many Baptists either reject or are reluctant to accept the New Testament language of "seal" (e.g., 2 Cor 1:21–22; Eph 1:13; 4:30) as a reference to baptism because of its connection with the rite of confirmation, though those with a more sacramental theology do not have such a difficulty. For instance, see Beasley-Murray, *Baptism in the New Testament*, 171–77; Schreiner, "Baptism in the Epistles," 86–87.

19. Many British Baptists, for example, have been influenced by this second blessing theology of baptism in the Spirit. Cf. Cross, *Baptism and the Baptists*, 348–57.

early on, but over time believer's baptism became just as separated from conversion as infant baptism, only coming after rather than before it.

While Smyth and part of the congregation remained in Amsterdam, a group of the first Baptists, under the leadership of Helwys, left the safety of exile and returned to England in 1612 to found the first Baptist church in Spitalfields, London. These General Baptists held to a general view of the atonement, that Christ died for all.

A second Baptist stream, like their Arminian predecessors, developed out of a Separatist, Independent/Congregational church in London in the 1630s. The first Calvinistic Baptists appeared when a group of ten left this church under the leadership of Samuel Eaton who, like Smyth, was baptized as a believer by affusion. A further six were dismissed from the mother church in 1638 and joined the Particular Baptist church, being convinced that "Baptism was not for Infants, but professed Believers," and by 1640 they had become convinced that baptism "ought to be by diping ye Body into ye Water, resembling Burial & riseing again," citing Col 2:12 and Rom 6:4 in support. One of their number who spoke Dutch, Richard Blunt, was then sent to the Netherlands where he either received baptism at the hands of the Collegiant Mennonites or a letter of commendation, which he brought back to England in January 1641. He then baptized those "persuaded Baptism should be by dipping ye Body."[20] This is regarded by many historians as marking the introduction of immersion into Baptist practice.[21]

In adopting believer's baptism, the first Baptists were charged with the ancient crime of re-baptism,[22] something they repudiated at the time and ever since. Thus, for example, the first Particular Baptist confession of 1644 declared on its title page and its opening words, "The Confession of Faith, of those Churches Which Are Commonly (Though Falsely) Called Anabaptists."[23] As such, Baptists are antipaedobaptists, a position

---

20. "The Kiffin Manuscript," reproduced in McBeth, *Sourcebook*, 26–27. (Ibid., 27, notes that at first this church was an open membership fellowship.) Historians are divided on whether Blunt was baptized by the Mennonites or his colleague Mr. Blacklock on his return to London. On this, see Leonard, *Baptist Ways*, 29–30.

21. Though Wright, *Early English Baptists*, 66–68, 75–110, argues for a slightly earlier date.

22. Under various emperors, re-baptism was proscribed under a series of Roman mandates (e.g., from AD 377 to 428), which ranged from condemnation to the death penalty. See Coleman-Norton, *Roman State*, documents 163, 230, 335, and 395.

23. *London Confession* (1644), in Lumpkin, *Baptist Confessions*, 153. Cf. the similar

they have adopted because they do not see the practice of the baptism of infants as anywhere in or consistent with the teaching of Scripture (both Old and New Testaments).

However, for the first Baptists baptism was not used as a means of exclusion, for they identified themselves with historic Christianity,[24] frequently sought fellowship and worshipped with Paedobaptists,[25] and set themselves within the catholic/universal church. On this latter point, for instance, the *Second London Confession* declares "Of the Church": "The Catholick or universal Church, which ... may be called invisible, consists of the whole number of the Elect, that have been, are, or shall be gathered into one, under Christ the head thereof; and is the spouse, the body, the fulness of him that filleth all in all."[26] Rather, baptism was a means of preserving a pure church comprised of genuine Christians (and as such shows continuity with their Puritan-Separatist origins) and this was why baptism should be applied only to believers old enough to profess their own faith in Christ. It was not until later that baptism began to act as a way of keeping the non-baptized outside of the church. This increasing insularity and setting themselves against other groups is hardly surprising among the three streams of early Baptists (the third being the Seventh Day Baptists)[27] who were severely persecuted throughout much of the seventeenth century, a persecution that still continues to this day in

---

opening statement of the General Baptists' *The Standard Confession* entitled *A Brief Confession or Declaration of Faith* ... (1660), in Lumpkin, *Baptist Confessions*, 224.

24. In their positive views of the major creeds of the church. See n. 8 above. This is the argument of Riker, *Catholic Reformed Theologian*, in his study of probably the most important seventeenth-century Baptist thinker, Benjamin Keach. For a contemporary discussion of this stream of the Baptist tradition, see Harmon, *Towards Baptist Catholicity*.

25. For example, see the mixed congregations (Baptists and Independents/Congregationalists) of the Bunyan tradition in and around Bedford, Broadmead in Bristol, New Road in Oxford, and, in time, union churches. See Cross, *Baptism and the Baptists*, 91–96; and Haymes et al., *On Being the Church*, 85 and 98, esp. nn. 112 and 156, and the literature cited there. Such united churches reappeared during the twentieth century in various parts of the world: in Britain through Baptist participation in what are now known as Local Ecumenical Partnerships. See Cross, *Baptism and the Baptists*, 289–315 and *passim*. Baptist–Paedobaptist congregations are also to be found in South Africa and the Church of North India, on which see Roy, *Baptism, Reconciliation and Unity*, 118–22, and for wider discussion the whole of Roy's book.

26. *Second London Confession* (1677), chap. XXVI, par. 1 (see also pars. 2–4), in Lumpkin, *Baptist Confessions*, 285. On this, see Renihan, *Edification and Beauty*, 38–42.

27. Sanford, *A Choosing People*.

some parts of the world.²⁸ This persecution, perpetrated by the state and the state church, inevitably focused a great deal on the Baptists' rejection of infant baptism and, both implicitly and explicitly within this, their rejection of the state-church ecclesiology and the idea of Christendom itself. It also goes a long way to explain why the issues of the subjects and mode of baptism came to figure so prominently in Baptist writings, often to the detriment of the theology of baptism proper, for those were the issues on which Baptists were being challenged.

BIBLICAL-THEOLOGICAL FOUNDATIONS AND PASTORAL IMPLICATIONS

For all Baptists, faith and practice must come from an understanding of God revealed in Jesus Christ, the living Word, as witnessed to in Scripture,²⁹ and this is nowhere more true than baptism, because in New Testament times there were *no* unbaptized believers³⁰ and the Christian church was, therefore, the baptized community. Recognition of this is the only explanation why the various New Testament writers could appeal to baptism as the basis for the exhortation, admonition, and instruction of the Christian communities (cf. Rom 6:1–11; Eph 5:25–27; 1 Tim 6:12; Heb 6:1–5; 1 Pet 3:8–22).³¹

The predecessor of Christian baptism was John's baptism of repentance and confession (Matt 3:1–2, 6, 11; Mark 1:4–5; Luke 3:3; John

---

28. In the early 1970s Romanian Baptists had to apply to the inspector of cults for permission to perform a baptism, even though constitutionally every Romanian citizen was free to believe or not believe, or change or renounce their religion. Pastors who declined to follow this oral regulation faced dismissal by the inspector. See "The Situation of Baptists in Romania, 1973," in McBeth, *Sourcebook*, 602–3. For other instances in six eastern European countries, see Jones and Randall, *Counter-Cultural Communities*.

29. The "Statement of Identity" of the European Baptist Federation, which comprises over 800,000 Baptists in fifty-one unions, says: "[Together those Assembled] . . . 4. Declare that the divinely inspired Old and New Testament Scriptures have supreme authority as the written Word of God and are fully trustworthy for *faith and conduct*" (italics added). See http://www.ebf.org/about-ebf/statement (accessed 27 September 2008).

30. Cf. 1 Cor 12:13, note "all."

31. While the Faith and Order paper *Baptism, Eucharist and Ministry*, IV.A.11 (p. 4), concedes that "baptism upon personal profession of faith is the most clearly attested pattern in the New Testament," for Baptists it is the only baptism in the New Testament. This being so, it should be recognized that paedobaptism is, therefore, a departure from the norm, not the norm itself from which believer's baptism is a departure. This should have implications for the whole issue of re-baptism (see below).

1:26–28; Acts 19:4.). It anticipated Pentecost when the Spirit would be given by Christ to his people in fulfillment of the Baptist's prophecy (Matt 3:11; Mark 1:4–5, 7–8; Luke 3:16), and Jesus' baptism at his hands was one of identification with humanity and a revelation to John and others that the Son of God had come (Matt 3:13–17; Mark 1:9–11; Luke 3:21–22; John 1:31–33).

Christian baptism originates in the post-resurrection command of the exalted Christ (hence "ordinance," i.e., that which is ordained by Christ) to "Go and make disciples of all nations, baptizing . . . and teaching them" (Matt 28:19–20; cf. Mark 16:16), and in the apostolic church it was an integral and essential part of the preaching of the gospel/the *kerygma* (cf. on 1 Cor 1:17 below). All those who repented and accepted Christ were baptized immediately (see Acts 8:12; 8:36–38; 10:44–48; 16:14–15, 31–33; 18:8) and were assured that in this expression of their faith they would receive the forgiveness of their sins and the gift of the life-giving Spirit (Acts 2:38, 41; cf. 1 Cor 12:13). New Testament baptism was conversion-baptism/conversion-initiation into the triune God. New converts were then discipled in the faith both in what they should believe (doctrine) and how they should live as followers of Christ (ethics, cf. Rom 6:3–4, "live a new life").[32] Baptism is, therefore, inseparably linked with discipleship, and whether baptism is administered before any teaching can take place it most certainly should be followed by a life of learning more of God's word and living it out in daily life, following Jesus Christ.[33]

Because baptism is an ordinance of Christ, and the God-ordained response to the preaching of the gospel, it is not an optional extra and it should not be encouraged to be so. Often people say "I'm not ready to be baptized," or "I am waiting for Jesus to tell me to be baptized," or "It's

---

32. On this position, see Beasley-Murray, *Baptism in the New Testament*; Stein, "Baptism in Luke–Acts"; Cross, "Evangelical Sacrament." However, this position is by no means accepted by all Baptists. The only issue of disagreement in the statement of faith adopted by both West and East German, Austrian, and Swiss Baptists in the early 1980s came from the East Germans over the more sacramental view of baptism held by the others when it emphasized "the togetherness or the oneness of faith, baptism and church membership and even receiving the Holy Spirit." See "Wolfgang Mueller, Interview about German Baptists, 1983," in McBeth, *Sourcebook*, 598.

33. Recent years have witnessed a revival of Baptist interest in discipleship, what other traditions often call the catechumenate. See, Colwell, *Promise and Presence*, 132: "Baptism . . . should mark the beginning of a life-long 'catechumenate' rather than the conclusion of a preliminary and 'qualifying' catechumenate."

not my kind of thing." This is largely due to Baptists having a low view (impoverished theology) of baptism and not including it in the proclamation of the gospel. Baptists have tended to spiritualize becoming a Christian so that Spirit- and water-baptism have become separated in a way that is untrue to the New Testament (see Acts 2:38; 1 Cor 12:13; Eph 4:5; John 3:5; cf. John 1:32–33)—this separation did not begin to happen until the fourth century.[34] Baptists would do better to avoid the danger of over-spiritualizing and internalizing conversion and Christian faith. As a matter of fact, there have always been Baptists who have avoided the spirit-matter dualism that was characteristic of the Hellenistic world in general and Gnosticism in particular (and was restated by Zwingli),[35] and, instead, restore a healthy view of God as Creator, and matter as the means in and through which he works for the salvation of his bodily creation, humanity.[36] He has done this through the incarnation of his Son, our Savior. With this understanding of the goodness of God's creation and the way he uses ordinary, material means as vehicles of his gracious working, we can see that baptism becomes the meeting place of the initiating divine-human encounter (the grace of God meeting the faith of the repentant believer),[37] and, linked to this, that Christ can take physical bread and wine and spiritually nourish his people.

Contemporary Baptists tend to prefer the term "ordinance" for both baptism and the Lord's Supper, and many deny the use of sacramental language in connection with the rite. However, there have always been

---

34. See Cross, "Spirit- and Water-Baptism."

35. On this spirit-matter dualism, see Pinnock, "The Physical Side of Being Spiritual." Cf. Freeman, "To Feed Upon by Faith," 204, who identifies "a *latent Gnosticism* [in Baptist theology] that sharply distinguished between spiritual and material and is thus skeptical of identifying the divine presence with anything in the physical (or biological) world often accompanied by an *incipient Marcionism* that separates the spheres of creation and redemption" (italics original); and on this dualism and Zwingli, see Rainbow, "Confessor Baptism," 196–200.

36. See Fiddes, "Baptism and Creation."

37. This is not to suggest that God is limited to working through the sacraments, or any other means he chooses. Colwell, *Promise and Presence*, 124 (see the whole of his discussion, 120, 124–25), writes, "the sacraments are not God's prison. He has promised to act by his Spirit through these ordained means but he is not entrapped by such means, he remains free to act elsewhere and through other means (though he has not promised to do so)." This is what Thompson calls "the freedom of God" (see Thompson, *The Freedom of God*).

Baptist sacramentalists,[38] and, in recent years, this revival of baptismal sacramentalism has been led by British Baptist scholars.[39]

The word that gives us baptism/baptize comes from the Greek word βαπτίζω meaning "to dip, to plunge," and this is why baptism is by total immersion, expressing the dying and rising of the Lord Jesus. This is in full accord not just with the meaning of the Greek but also with the practice of the New Testament: both Philip and the Ethiopian eunuch "went *down* into the water" (Acts 8:38), while Jesus "went *up* out of the water" (Matt 3:16). The physical going down into the water, being immersed into it and the being raised up from it provides baptism with its powerful symbolism. Paul uses the symbolism of a watery grave to show us that "all of us who were baptized into Christ Jesus were baptized into his death" and were "buried with him through baptism into death in order that, just as Christ was raised from the dead ... we too may live a new life" (Rom 6:3–4), and this is arguably the strongest argument for total immersion. It also ties in with baptism in the New Testament being the occasion where the forgiveness of sins is first experienced (Acts 2:38) and we are washed clean (cf. Acts 22:16; 1 Cor 6:11; Eph 5:26) by the working of the Spirit (Titus 3:5).

For the majority of Baptists, baptism is an outward symbol of what has already taken place inwardly. For instance, in the 1920s, Bulgarian Baptists stated that they

> do not believe in "baptismal redemption" or in "baptismal rebirth" as others wrongly do. We believe that salvation is a purely spiritual connection with God in Christ Jesus and that baptism is an outside physically-religious ordinance, which represents the death of Christ and resurrection, and a Symbol of death of the believer toward sin and resurrection into new spiritual life. (Rom 6:3–5; Col 2:12; Gal 3:26, 27).[40]

It is important to emphasize that this is the predominant view of baptism amongst Baptists, but it is equally important to note that this position is maintained over against the theology and practice of

---

38. See the definitive study by Fowler, *More than a Symbol*.

39. See Fowler, *More than a Symbol*, 98–126, 341–48 and *passim*; Fiddes, ed., *Reflections on the Water*; and Colwell, *Promise and Presence*.

40. Kendall, "Evangelical Foundations," 9, cited and translated by Teodor B. Oprenov, "The Theology of Baptists in Bulgaria as Reflected in *Evangelist* (1920–1939)," in Jones and Randall, *Counter-Cultural Communities*, 193.

infant baptism, and in particular the view that infant baptism is *essential* for salvation. As has already been noted, there has always been a sacramental tradition in Baptist thought. For example, when, in 1959, a group of young British Baptist ministers and scholars published *Christian Baptism*,[41] the biblical and theological chapters propounded a sacramental interpretation of New Testament baptism. In his defense of this position against attacks from other Baptists, George Beasley-Murray had repeatedly to assert that "This teaching relates to *baptism in the apostolic Church*, not to baptism in the average modern Baptist church."[42] The key to the sacramental understanding of baptism is that it is *faith*-baptism[43]—that baptism is the expression of the believer to the prevenient, gracious act of God in Christ through his Spirit. In both interpretations of baptism, non-sacramental and sacramental, faith is key, and Baptists of both schools of thought oppose the view that baptism's efficacy operates *ex opere operato*, that is, in mechanical isolation from the faith of the believer[44]—hence their rejection of vicarious faith, whether of parents, godparents, or the church. Salvation for Baptists is personal, as people must come to faith in Christ for themselves.[45] The corporate dimension of this is not unimportant, for the church indeed mediates the gospel through its life, preaching, and witness, and the believer enters the church through faith, and—when faith is a part of the conversion process—through faith-baptism, but Baptists repudiate any suggestion that the church controls the means of grace—for this is God's prerogative.[46]

However baptism is more than a symbol; it is an *effective* symbol. (It is not necessary that the understanding of baptism as an ordinance excludes it from also being a sacrament; in fact, "ordinance" and "sacra-

---

41. Gilmore, ed., *Christian Baptism*. On this, see Fowler, *More than a Symbol*, 113–33, and his "Baptist Sacramentalism," 196–97, 200–201, 227–43 and *passim*.

42. Beasley-Murray, "Baptism Controversy," 130. Beasley-Murray does continue, "Where baptism is sundered from conversion on the one hand, and from entry into the Church on the other, this language cannot be applied to it; such baptism is a reduced baptism." See below on the movement among Baptist scholars to reform baptism.

43. So White, *Biblical Doctrine of Initiation*, 226.

44. For a nuanced interpretation, see Fiddes, "*Ex opere operato*."

45. As such, Baptists are in total agreement with Tertullian's dictum that "people are made, not born, Christians" (*Apology*, 18).

46. However, for sacramental understandings of the church, see George, "Sacramentality," 27–35; and Colwell, *Promise and Presence*, 65–87.

ment" are complementary.) It is in this sense a sacrament, understood as a divinely appointed *means of grace*.[47] New Testament baptism is faith-baptism, and this is clearly shown in the fact that the full range of the gifts of salvation that are attributed to faith in the New Testament are also attributed to baptism.[48] However, this is *not* to succumb to the idea that baptism acts automatically. Faith is always essential, otherwise the actions are meaningless. Any suggestion of the mechanical operation of baptism is excluded in key New Testament passages. For example, in 1 Pet 3:21 we read that "baptism now saves you" but it is "not the removal of dirt," as happens in an ordinary bath, rather it is "the pledge/prayer of a good conscience towards God." In fact, "It saves . . . *by* the resurrection of Jesus Christ." Elsewhere, Paul tells us that we are "saved . . . through the washing of rebirth and renewal/regeneration by the Holy Spirit" who is poured out through Jesus Christ so that "having been justified by his grace, we might become heirs having the hope of eternal life" (Titus 3:5–7; regeneration is Paul's expression for what John records as rebirth/birth from above, cf. John 3:3, 5).

In the present day, baptism normally takes place in the baptistery in a church building, but it has often taken place in a river, lake, or the sea, wherever there is running water. Sometimes, however, this simply is not possible, and in areas where there is drought, for example, valid baptisms have been performed where there is no water at all, or, if only a little water is available, or the candidate is prevented from being immersed due to some disability, or has a fear of water, baptism can be performed by affusion/pouring (this was, as we have seen, the mode the first Baptists used before a deeper understanding of the New Testament led them to the practice of immersion). Further, baptism is into the name of the triune God (Matt 28:19) and Baptists often use this as a baptismal formula spoken at the moment of immersion. It means this, but it also means

---

47. Cross and Thompson, "Introduction," 3: "most Baptists have been happy to accept the definition of sacraments as 'means of grace.'"

48. See Cross, "Evangelical Sacrament," 206–8: forgiveness, cf. Rom 4:5–7 with Acts 2:38; justification, cf. Rom 3:28 with 1 Cor 6:11; union with Christ, cf. Eph 3:17 with Gal 3:27; being crucified with Christ, cf. Gal 2:20 with Rom 6:2–11; death and resurrection, cf. Rom 8:12–13 with Col 2:12; sonship, cf. John 1:12 with Gal 3:26–27; the Holy Spirit, cf. Gal 3:2–5, 14 with Acts 2:38 and 1 Cor 12:13; entry into the church, cf. Gal 3:6–7 with Gal 3:27; regeneration and life, cf. John 3:14–16, 20:31 with John 3:5 and Titus 3:5; the kingdom and eternal life, cf. Mark 10:15 and John 3:14–16 with 1 Cor 6:9–11; and salvation, Rom 1:16 and John 3:16 with 1 Pet 3:21.

more than this. It is a Semitic phrase that means that in baptism a person is brought into an existence that is fundamentally determined and ruled by God—Father, Son and Spirit.[49] Use of the Trinitarian formula is not at odds with the testimony of Acts that the earliest baptisms were into the name of "Jesus Christ" (e.g., Acts 10:48; Rom 6:3; Gal 3:27) or "the Lord Jesus" (e.g., Acts 8:16; 19:5), because the Persons of the Trinity cannot be divided, and to be baptized into Christ is to be baptized into the triune God. There are some who baptize "into the name of (the Lord) Jesus Christ" and this is quite legitimate. The norm for Baptists appears to be a single act of immersion using the Trinitarian formula of Matt 28:19, but it can equally be a threefold immersion with each person of the Trinity named at the corresponding immersion (this practice has ancient precedent).

Baptism is an occasion where baptized believers profess/confess their faith in Christ (e.g., Rom 10:9–10; 1 Tim 6:12), and this is why baptized believers either respond to questions and/or give their testimony of how they came to faith in Christ. First Timothy 6:12 shows us that this normally happened "in the presence of many witnesses," so baptismal services are generally not private affairs, but usually take place in the context of the church's worship and often this will include many non-Christians, thereby providing an evangelistic opportunity for the preaching of the gospel in word and drama.

This raises the question of the age for baptism. From what we have seen of New Testament baptism, it is not age that determines whether people should be baptized, but whether they have come to faith in Christ. This is evidenced in the phrase "believer's baptism," or credo-baptism. Many Baptists insist that baptism should not be administered until teenage years, sometimes early (13 or 14), sometimes later (17 or 18). But this upper age range changes baptism altogether from believer's baptism to adult baptism.[50] Many people become Christians before their teenage years—sometimes earlier. If this is the case then, as far as the

---

49. Beasley-Murray, *Baptism in the New Testament*, 90–92.

50. When Baptists insist on the candidate's reaching a certain "adult" age, whatever that age may be (usually somewhere in the teenage years), rather than when they have become a Christian, they do, in fact, alter believer's baptism to adult baptism—though they often refute this charge. However, the charge is faced by Colwell, *Promise and Presence*, 129. This issue exposes the weakness of Baptist theological consideration of children, a subject that is receiving increasing attention. For example, see *Believing and Being Baptized*, and n. 16 above.

New Testament is concerned, they are eligible for baptism. To separate baptism from conversion is to depart from New Testament baptism. However, the younger the child the more complicated matters become pastorally, requiring knowledge of the young person, discernment as to whether their request comes from a true commitment to Christ or from peer pressure, the desire for attention, or some other reason. If the young person comes from a Christian family then the pastoral decision is more straightforward than if the young person comes from a family where either one or neither of the parents are believers. In all cases, the pastor and the church need to consult with the parents and the candidates themselves before the decision to baptize is taken. There might also be legal reasons why care needs to be taken, such as if the child is in foster or some other kind of care. There are other reasons often given as to why baptism should be postponed. If it is, "They are too young to be baptized," then the answer is, "If they are old enough to believe in Christ they are old enough to be baptized." If it is, "It will mean more to them when they are older," this is, again, to divorce baptism from conversion and it thereby becomes something other than New Testament conversion-baptism. Sometimes young people are deterred from baptism on the grounds that they might backslide, but this is true of anyone at any age in life.[51] The fear of post-baptismal sin should not be a reason for the deferment of baptism for either a young or older person, for baptism belongs to the beginning of the Christian life. Since Baptists ground their theology and practice in the New Testament they seek to be faithful to it even when Baptist tradition says something different, and trust the Lord that he will honor those who seek to honor him.

That baptism normally takes place within the church's worship also shows that baptism has a corporate dimension—it is not just an individual's act. According to Paul, "we [are] all baptized by one Spirit into one body" (1 Cor 12:13) and enter God's family ("children of God through faith in Christ Jesus," Gal 3:26; cf. Eph 2:19, "members of God's household"). Baptism is the initiating rite through which a person enters the church. Here Baptists have frequently understood baptism in covenantal terms.[52] One is in covenant relationship with the triune God, and in and through this relationship they are in covenantal relationship with all other members of the body of Christ. This is a great privilege, but

51. See Haymes, "Baptism," 121–26.
52. Fiddes, "Walking Together."

with it comes responsibility to be fully committed to the work of Christ in the local church. This is why Baptists have frequently practiced closed membership—although there have always been Baptists who have not excluded others who understand baptism differently to themselves (i.e., those who support infant baptism). John Bunyan is perhaps the best known example of this "mixed congregation" practice. In New Testament times, however, when all believers were conversion-baptized, it was true that baptism was initiatory into the body of Christ, the church. But as soon as baptism is separated from conversion (by Paedobaptists who put it before conversion, and by most Baptists who put it after conversion) it becomes less easy for us to claim the fullness of the New Testament theology of baptism for our baptismal practice, because it is different from that of the earliest church.

Baptists in the seventeenth century were the first to claim universal liberty of conscience and religious freedom in Britain, i.e., not just for themselves but for everyone—of other Christian traditions, other religions, and even atheists.[53] The practice of open membership, then, is a recognition that other believers interpret Scripture differently to ourselves (after all, we all "see in a mirror, dimly" 1 Cor 13:12), but this is not to suggest that they are thereby not true Christians or their churches not true churches, that is, members of the body of Christ (1 Cor 12:12–31; Rom 12:4–8; Eph 4:1–16). Open membership is a growing practice among Baptists[54] and, so long as candidates for baptism have been baptized/initiated into their traditions, advocates of open membership are willing to accept them into membership if they believe their baptism as infants is still valid. However, there are several Christian traditions that do not practice baptism (or the Lord's Supper)—such as The Salvation Army and the Society of Friends[55]—so Christian love and acceptance needs to be shown to those from these traditions who come to fellowship with Baptist churches.[56]

---

53. The argument for religious liberty, it must be stressed, is a theological, not a political, principle for Baptists. See Haymes, "Religious Liberty"; and Coffey, "From Helwys to Leland."

54. There are open membership Baptist churches, for example, in Australia, Canada, Estonia, Great Britain, New Zealand, Sweden, and the USA. Some Baptist churches that cannot go this far, perhaps due to restrictions in their trust deeds, have adopted associate membership for those from paedobaptist traditions.

55. See the article by Macy in this volume.

56. See the whole of the discussion of membership of the church and baptism in Haymes et al., *On Being the Church*, 80–87.

What open membership Baptists need to avoid is accepting into membership those from within the Baptist tradition who have not been baptized at all. Yet when candidates for membership from outside the Baptist tradition have come to the conviction that baptism is for believers, the vast majority of Baptists will baptize them as believers and will not see this as re-baptism (even though this is how infant-baptism communions regard it).[57] However, in ecumenical discussions, there are some Baptists who encourage such applicants for membership not to be "re-baptized" so as not to cause offense or suggest that Paedobaptist churches are not genuine churches and their patterns of initiation are not legitimate — this is simply recognizing the work of God in confessedly Christian people. There are also Baptists who are not willing to dismiss the validity of infant baptism completely,[58] and these are more likely to be willing to consider not "re-baptizing" those from Paedobaptist communions.[59] However, a 1996 British Baptist report offers a promising way forward that recognizes both Baptist convictions and the ecumenical context in which all churches now live:

> [T]here is a growing realization that we need to be more sensitive to the way other Christians feel about this, and to the hurt that can unwittingly be caused by Baptist practice. Such awareness belongs to living and working in relationship with others. We must seriously ask ourselves how we shall respond to the request from our partner churches that we desist from actions that look to them like re-baptism. At the same time, we ask them to understand that for us the issue of "re-baptism" depends upon the prior question of whether infant baptism can be recognized as a form of baptism.[60]

---

57. When *Baptism, Eucharist and Ministry*, IV.A.13 (p. 4), declared "Any practice which might be interpreted as 're-baptism' *must* be avoided" (italics added), it failed to acknowledge that this is not as simple a matter as many Paedobaptists apparently imagine. It is repeated in the Council for Christian Unity's *Pushing at the Boundaries*, 68: "Rebaptism is inconceivable, impossible, a contradiction in terms, a complete nonsense." As infant baptism is a theological conviction for Paedobaptists, so believer's baptism is a theological conviction for Baptists.

58. See the Swedish Baptist Bergsten, "Baptism," 125–31 and 162–71, esp. 166–71; and the change of position by Beasley-Murray, "Infant Baptism," 1–14; Colwell, *Promise and Presence*, 134. See also the more detailed study by Johnsson, *Baptist Reconsideration*.

59. Winter, "Ambiguous Genitives."

60. *Believing and Being Baptized*, 13.

Many Baptist churches have baptismal candidates wear white robes, the symbolism of which is linked to baptism as the cleansing/washing from sin, while others have them wear their ordinary, day-to-day clothes symbolizing that they are committing the whole of their everyday lives to Christ. Yet the change of clothing for baptism reminds us that the Christian's new life is to be lived according to God's ways. In baptism we "clothe ourselves with Christ" (Gal 3:27; Col 2:11–12), but, when linked to Christ's death and resurrection and our death to our old lives and resurrection to new life in Christ, it also reminds us that, as baptized believers, we have "put away [our] former way of life, [our] old self" and are to "clothe [ourselves] with the new self" (Eph 4:22, 24), because "in Christ" we are "a new creation," the old has gone and the new has come (2 Cor 5:17; cf. Col 3:5–11 with vv. 12–17). Baptism, then, has ethical implications: those in Christ are to live the baptized Christian life (cf. Rom 6:1–11). This is a life of discipleship, worship, and witness.

Building on this, the church as the baptized community is a witness to the gospel of Christ in that it shows that here, in contrast to the world, is an image of the way the world was intended to be and can be when Christ is Lord, for here there are no worldly divisions between race, social class, or sex, for all are "one in Christ" (Gal 3:26–28; cf. 1 Cor 12:12–13), the new international community of brothers and sisters, and here a new, counter-cultural way of life is lived (cf. Matt 5–7).

Ephesians 4:4–6 sets out seven essential "onenesses" for the people of God, and baptism's inclusion here shows how important it is, more important than is often recognized by many Baptists. The frequent Baptist fixation on the subjects of baptism (believers) and the mode of baptism (immersion) often means that they fail to do justice to the richness of New Testament baptism. Often Paul's statement in 1 Cor 1:17 is taken to justify this position and is interpreted to mean that preaching the gospel is more important. However, this fails to do justice to what Paul is saying (and what the rest of the New Testament says about baptism). In 1 Cor 1 and 3, Paul is opposing the disunity of the Corinthian church in which different key figures—and baptism by them—were being used as an excuse and justification for the divisions in the church. Yet as Paul shows later in 1 Cor 12:13 and Eph 4:5, a proper theology of baptism is integral to Christian life and witness. Its importance is nowhere more clearly seen than in the fact that Jesus commands it as one of the two aspects of making disciples (Matt 28:19) and in the New Testament church it was an essential part of the preaching of the gospel (e.g., Acts 2:38, 41).

WAYS FORWARD

One proposal that came out of the World Council of Churches' *Baptism, Eucharist and Ministry* document was the search for affirmation of a "common baptism,"[61] the recognition of infant baptism followed by confirmation and believer's baptism as equivalent alternatives. Clearly, if common baptism is the way forward then the issue of re-baptism becomes a major obstacle. Baptists, however, look instead for a common faith.[62] A recent alternative has been advocated by Paul Fiddes, which sets out to see baptism as one moment in a larger process of initiation.[63] These are fruitful avenues to pursue, and Baptists are involved at all levels of ecumenical discussion, not least at the grassroots. However, many Baptists, out of theological conscience, are unable to pursue such courses. With this in mind, three Baptists have suggested an alternative that "cannot be prescribed, and is dependent upon Christians' ability to accept one another (cf. Rom 15:7) in all our diversity and differences":

> What matters, surely, is that Christians seek the Lord's will and to be faithful to that? Baptists are rightly proud of their forefathers having pioneered universal religious tolerance and freedom of conscience, and so we need to live by it. In the same way that we strive before God to understand his word and his ways and to live accordingly, so we must allow and respect others as they seek to do likewise, even when they do not come to the same conclusion(s) we do. And they must show us the same respect.[64]

In recent years there has been a growing number of Baptist scholars who have followed George Beasley-Murray's call for the reform of baptismal theology and practice according to the word of God.[65] It is fitting, then, to conclude with Beasley-Murray that

---

61. *Baptism, Eucharist and Ministry*, II.D.6, 3 and Commentary (12), 5.

62. Haymes et al., *On Being the Church*, 86.

63. See his unattributed contribution to "One Baptism: A Baptist Contribution," in Council for Christian Unity, *Pushing at the Boundaries*, 31–57, which, from 41–57, explores the route of "Common Initiation."

64. Haymes et al., *On Being the Church*, 87.

65. See Beasley-Murray, *Baptism in the New Testament*, 387–95; George, "Reformed Doctrine," 251–52; Schreiner, "Baptism in the Epistles," 95 n. 67; Rainbow, "Confessor

All of us in all of the Churches need to consider afresh our ways before God, with the Bible open before us and a prayer for the guidance of the Holy Spirit and a preparedness to listen to what the Spirit is saying to all the Churches. With such a prayer answered—and it would be unbelief to assume that it will not be—and obedience pledged to guidance vouchsafed, the inadequate insights of frail individuals and of our very fallible traditions would surely give place to a fuller understanding of the divine will made known, and the glory of God in Christ be furthered through the Church by the Spirit.[66]

FURTHER READING

West, W. M. S. "Towards a Consensus on Baptism? Louisville 1979." *Baptist Quarterly* 28.5 (January, 1980) 225–32.

———. "Baptism: Report of the Faith and Order Consultation, Louisville 1979." *Baptist Quarterly* 28.5 (January, 1980) 232–39.

"Baptist Union of Scotland" and "Baptist Union of Sweden," in *Churches Respond to BEM: Official Responses to the "Baptism, Eucharist and Ministry" Text*, edited by Max Thurian, 3:230–45 and 4:200–213. 6 vols. Faith and Order Papers 129, 132, 135, 137, 143, and 144. Geneva: World Council of Churches, 1986–88.

"Towards Baptist Identity: A Statement Ratified by the Baptist Heritage Commission in Zagreb, Yugoslavia, July 1989," in *Faith, Life, and Witness: The Papers of the Study and Research Division of the Baptist World Alliance—1986-1990*, edited by William H. Brackney and Ruby J. Burke, 146–49. Birmingham, AL: Samford University Press, 1990.

Baptism," 205; Cross, "Evangelical Sacrament"; and Haymes et al., *On Being the Church*, 93–100.

66. Beasley-Murray, *Baptism in the New Testament*, 395. That this openness to learn more of God's ways is no innovation is seen in "The Conclusion" to the 1644 *London Confession*, in Lumpkin, *Baptist Confessions*, 149: "we confess that we know in part, and that we are ignorant of many things which we desire and seek to know: and if any shall doe us that friendly part to shew us from the word of God that we see not, we shall have cause to be thankfull to God and them."

7

Baptism and Quakers

Howard R. Macy

THE FRIENDS (OR QUAKER) movement emerged in the 1650s in England, in the middle of the Commonwealth period. This was a contentious and passionate time, full of new religious ideas, of vigorous debate over old practices (including baptism), and of government coercion to practice what the rulers in power considered true religion. In the previous century, King Henry VIII had established the Church of England and partisans still struggled over whether England would remain Anglican or return to Roman Catholicism. In addition, many folks now referred to as Puritans were eager to purify the Church. Some worked within the system; some gave up and left the Church to become Independents, Non-conformists, or Separatists. All in all, it was a tumultuous time out of which new life emerged.

A BASIC STATEMENT OF FRIENDS' APPROACH TO BAPTISM

At their best, Friends teach that they believe in and practice baptism as a spiritual reality, but that they do not use water or ritual to effect or symbolize that reality. Similarly, they regard communion with Christ (the Lord's Supper, Eucharist) as a vital and continuous spiritual reality that does not require ritual or physical elements. Friends intend to make a positive witness. They cherish living in the baptism of Jesus, known by the Holy Spirit and fire, and living steadily in intimate communion with Christ who is constantly present to his people. Indeed, rather than seeing their stance as diminishing the demands of discipleship, many understand not using the established forms as a way of entering more fully into the meaning of the New Covenant.

The three quotations included here illustrate this basic view. Robert Barclay, the earliest major Quaker theologian, offered these words in introducing his discussion of baptism:

> [The baptism of Christ] is a pure and spiritual thing (Gal 3:27), namely the baptism of the Spirit and of fire, by which we are "buried with him" (Rom 6:4; Col 2:12) so that being washed and purged of our sins, we may "walk in newness of life" (Rom 6:4).[1]

In her *A Short History of Quakerism* (1923), British Friend Elizabeth B. Emmott addressed common misunderstandings on this basic stance:

> It is not true, as we sometimes hear people say, that Friends do not believe in baptism and the Lord's Supper. We do believe both in spiritual baptism and spiritual communion.... Baptism to us means the Holy Spirit's power so known and yielded to in our hearts that we live in continual dependence upon His help and guidance. He brings us into such conscious fellowship with God and Christ that we can truly say, "The life which I now live in the flesh I live by the faith of the Son of God, who loved me and gave himself for me." "I live, yet not I, but Christ liveth in me" (Gal 2:20).[2]

A current excerpt from the Faith and Practice of Northwest Yearly Meeting of Friends widely represents many Friends today:

> We believe Christ's baptism to be the inward receiving of the promised Holy Spirit, whereby the believer is immersed in Jesus' power, purity, and wisdom. This baptism is the essential Christian baptism: an experience of cleansing from sin that supplants old covenant rituals.[3]

Friends themselves have often contributed to misunderstanding when they use verbal shortcuts to explain not using physical elements, and say wrongly that Friends do not baptize and do not have communion. Sometimes they also misrepresent the roots of Quaker practice by suggesting that it came about in response to abuses of baptism and communion in the churches they knew. That is not the case. Surely

---

1. Freiday, *Barclay's Apology*, 301.
2. London Yearly Meeting, *Christian Faith and Practice*, par. 213.
3. Northwest Yearly Meeting of Friends, *Faith and Practice*.

abuses and hypocrisy abounded in the tumult of the seventeenth-century English churches, as in many other times and places, but Friends did not witness that their understanding and practice was a reaction to abusive practices. Instead, they explained that it grew out of a transforming experience of the power and presence of Christ. It was rooted in spiritual encounter, not in disgust at abuse.

THE SPIRITUAL ROOT OF THIS WITNESS

The Friends witness about "sacraments" first finds expression in the experience and preaching of George Fox, who is regarded as the principal founder of the Friends movement. George Fox grew up in an ordinary but religiously attuned family. His father earned the nickname "Righteous Christer," and while George was still a lad, people around him thought he would be well suited for ministry. When he was nineteen years old, his keen sense of integrity pushed him into a search for authentic Christianity. He saw far too many folk who, in his judgment, "did not possess what they professed." Seeking guidance toward religious experience that penetrated all of life, he approached some of the leading ministers of his time, both Anglican and Separatist, only to be disappointed. In answer to his spiritual hunger they suggested he should sing in the choir or take up tobacco, go get his blood let or get married. Some used their private conversations with him for gossip with the milkmaids or even as sermon material.[4]

With his hopes repeatedly dashed, Fox despaired. He spent long days in solitude, fasting, and the reading of Scripture, but without finding the spiritual root he longed for. Then in the midst this solitariness, Fox claimed to have an encounter with Christ that energized him and, with other experiences of God's love and power, shaped the whole Friends movement as it arose. He wrote in his journal:

> And when all my hopes in them and in all men were gone, so that I had nothing outwardly to help me, nor could tell what to do, then, Oh then, I heard a voice which said, "There is one, even Christ Jesus, that can speak to thy condition," and when I heard it my heart did leap for joy. Then the Lord did let me see why there was none upon the earth that could speak to my condition, namely, that I might give him all the glory; . . . that Jesus Christ

---

4. Eugene Peterson rightly uses this series of ministers as telling examples of how not to offer spiritual direction (see Peterson, *Working the Angles*, 122–27).

might have the pre-eminence, who enlightens, and gives grace, and faith, and power. Thus, when God doth work who shall let [=prevent] it? And this I knew experimentally.[5]

In this experience Fox knew Christ directly, without aid of priest or sanctuary, prayer book or ritual. It went beyond and outside of the experiences he had known in the life of the church. It was direct and unmediated (in any ordinary sense). It brought guidance, transformation, and empowerment. Out of this experiential root Fox began to invite others, often preaching, "Christ has come to teach his people himself," and living boldly, knowing that "the power of the Lord is over all." As others warmed to his message and shared his experience of intimacy with Christ, this keen sense of Christ's presence shaped Friends' thinking and practice in many ways, including their approaches to worship and decision-making, their understanding of who might offer valid public ministry, their convictions about how God guides people directly and through Scripture, and, of course, their understanding and practice of baptism and communion. Friends' witness to "spiritual baptism" certainly has its early root in George Fox's powerful encounter with Christ.

THE BASIS IN SCRIPTURE

Although Friends have rooted their witness and practice about baptism in spiritual experience, they have neither dismissed nor neglected biblical teaching on the meaning of baptism. On the contrary, early Friends and many Friends since have known the Bible well and have relied on it to guide their Christian discipleship. Over the years Friends have come to display wide theological diversity, some attending to the Scriptures more than others, but the guiding discussions on the issue of baptism are deeply informed by reflection on biblical teaching.

One teaching that Friends often call attention to is the New Testament's frequent contrast between the baptism of John and the baptism of Jesus. Wherever the baptisms of John and Jesus are mentioned together (Matt 3:11; Mark 1:8; Luke 3:16; John 1:26–33; Acts 1:5; 11:16, perhaps also Acts 13:23–25; 18:25; 19:1–7) they are distinguished from one another in both character and importance. John the Baptist's preaching in Matt 3:11 offers a good example: "I baptize you with water for repentance, but one who is more powerful than I is coming after me;

---

5. Nickalls, *Journal of George Fox*, 11.

I am not worthy to carry his sandals. He will baptize you with the Holy Spirit and fire." Without diminishing the importance of his baptism for repentance, John himself presents baptism with "the Holy Spirit and fire" as greater than his own and as part of the new reality that will come with the greater one to come, the Messiah. Jesus draws the same contrast clearly when he teaches his disciples just before he is "taken into heaven." He tells them to wait in Jerusalem for "the promise of the Father." "This . . . is what you have heard from me; for John baptized with water, but you will be baptized with the Holy Spirit not many days from now" (Acts 1:4–5).

John's baptism takes place in the context of, and in contrast to, well-established traditions of water baptism and ritual washing in the Jewish tradition. In Joseph John Gurney's thorough article on baptism, he offers examples to show that baptism "actually formed a part of the customary Jewish ritual," to argue against those who, at least in his time, insisted that baptism was "of Christian origin." Some examples include washings, bathings, and immersions in order to move from uncleanness to purity in keeping with ceremonial requirements. Appealing to rabbinic texts, Gurney also notes the use of baptism as part of the process of conversion, eventually used with the conversion of proselytes who would enter into the Israelite covenant through "circumcision, baptism, and sacrifice." The proselyte was considered "a child new born" and, in Gurney's words, "immersion in water was evidently used as the expressive sign."[6] Given this precedent, he argues, it is "nearly indisputable" that Christian baptism "was borrowed" from Jewish practice.

Since Gurney's ministry in the first half of the 1800s, we have learned even more about Jewish ritual purification baths in connection with the Jerusalem Temple, at the community of Qumran, and even in homes. Among other things, we have learned that participants would descend into these cleansing pools by one set of stairs, ascend by another, and running ("living") water would refresh the purity of the pools.[7] Of course, this confirms and expands our understanding of Jewish baptismal practice; however, it also sharpens our understanding of John the Baptist's ministry.

Paul Anderson points out that John's baptism would have "jarred" the Jewish folks who heard and observed him, but not because it was

6. Gurney, *A Peculiar People*, 106–12.
7. Anderson, "Jesus and Transformation," 313.

creating a new ritual. For one thing, "John's immersion of people in the Jordan and elsewhere [served] as a declaration of the prolific availability of divine grace and the life of the Spirit. John's ministry should be viewed as a *contrast* to confining access to the grace of God to ritual means of purification, whether in Jerusalem, Qumran, or other cultic settings."[8] Also, John's baptizing in the muddy Jordan River called his hearers to genuine repentance, not ritual purity. His prophetic witness called people to a purity of life, not a purity in form. This recalls the prophets Amos, Isaiah, and Jeremiah, among others, who brought scalding judgments of elaborate but empty ceremonies that masked corrupt living. John's baptism, even in its form, made the same point.

The Jewish leaders' response to John the Baptist confirms this judgment. Clearly the Pharisees and others who would have most strictly engaged in acts of ritual purity were not eager to embrace John's ministry. When Jesus asked them whether the baptism of John had come from heaven or had human origin, they declined to answer, knowing in part that their negative judgment of John would offend the people (Mark 11:27–33). The Jewish leaders smarted under John's witness, but Jesus and his disciples honored and embraced it. They shared his call to holy living, to genuinely transformed lives. And they delighted in his pointing toward the coming kingdom of God, to the new era of life and power inaugurated by the coming of Jesus, God's Messiah.

The church, too, embraced John's baptism as a prophetic contrast to the forms of ritual washing in his culture, and they remembered and honored John's role as forerunner and predecessor. His pattern and witness set the stage, but they were not to set precedent. His baptism with water would be superceded by Jesus' baptism with the Holy Spirit and fire.

ONE LORD, ONE FAITH, ONE BAPTISM

In the light of the sharp contrasts the New Testament draws between the baptism of John and the baptism of Jesus, Friends have often called attention to Paul's appeal for Christian unity in Eph 4:4–6: "There is one body and one Spirit, just as you were called to the one hope of your calling, one Lord, one faith, one baptism, one God and Father of all, who is above all and through all and in all." Specifically, from this text Friends

---

8. Ibid.

argue that there is only one baptism and that is the baptism of Jesus, the baptism of Holy Spirit and fire.

George Fox often uses this language in his pastoral letters, very much in the spirit of Paul. For example, he writes, "And so, all strive to be of one mind, heart, soul, Spirit and Faith, living together in Unity, in the Love of God, all drinking into one Spirit, by which you are baptized into one body, having one Head."[9] Robert Barclay's summary characterizes how this text is often used:

> The "one baptism" in Eph 4:5 which acknowledges "one Lord," "one faith," and so forth, is the baptism of Christ. It is not a washing or dipping in water, but a baptism by the Spirit. The baptism of John was merely figurative of this, and as a figure it was intended to give way to the substance. Although baptism by the Spirit was to be continued, John's baptism was to cease.[10]

Certainly in this letter Paul intends mainly to gather people into unity, so some may wonder whether Friends' traditional appeal to this text is appropriate. Yet, given that Paul had to scold Christians at Corinth over their pride and quarrels about baptism (1 Cor 1:10–17), Friends teaching here may well help point the way to being joined together in the love of God.

THE APPEAL TO NEW COVENANT AND NEW PRACTICE

In still another important direction, Friends have explained their practice of baptism by noting that Christ introduced a New Covenant and new ways of approaching and worshiping God. Gurney notes that virtually all Christians agree that "when the New Covenant was established in the world, by the death of Christ, the ceremonies of the Jewish law were abolished"—except for two that most Christians still insist on, baptism with water and the physical practice of the Lord's Supper. He continues: "It is our belief that we have been led out of the practice of these rites by the Spirit of Truth; . . . and that, in fact, they are not in accordance with the entire spirituality of the Gospel dispensation."[11]

Often Friends point to Jesus' conversation with the woman at Samaria, who seems ready to defend ancient local tradition that the proper

---

9. Jones, *Power of the Lord*, 353, letter 341.
10. Freiday, *Barclay's Apology*, 305.
11. Gurney, *A Peculiar People*, 99–100.

worship of God should take place on Mount Gerizim, not in Jerusalem. Jesus replies that true worship is not tied to either place. Instead, "the hour is coming, and is now here," he says, "when the true worshipers will worship the Father in spirit and truth" (John 4:23). Quakers have understood this to mean that the new time that Jesus introduces frees worshipers not only from the traditional forms and places of Jewish worship, but also from set forms, places, or rites of any sort. In Robert Barclay's words: "no set form of worship under the purer administration of the new covenant is prescribed for his children by Jesus Christ, the author of the Christian religion. He merely tells them that the worship which is now to be performed is spiritual, and in the Spirit."[12]

To make this approach even clearer, often Friends appeal as well to the teaching of the Letter to the Hebrews, which so dramatically and thoroughly contrasts the Old and New Covenants. Throughout the epistle it speaks of old and new, of the shadow to be replaced by the true form, of better hope, better promises, a better covenant. The old covenant written on stone and full of ceremony is now replaced by a new covenant written on worshipers' minds and hearts. The old covenant with its symbols of sanctuary, sacrifice, symbols of "food and drink and various baptisms," was only to stand "until the time comes to set things right" (Heb 9:10). Then, God "abolishes the first in order to establish the second" (Heb 10:9). That time has now come in Jesus Christ. Friends understand the New Testament to teach that the person and work of Christ is fully sufficient, unaided by sign or ritual.

In *Why Friends Are Friends*, Jack Willcuts calls attention to Paul's teaching that tries to bolster Christians at risk of being misled by "empty deceit" and "human tradition." Paul encourages, "you have come to fullness in [Christ], who is the head of every ruler and authority. In him also you were circumcised with a spiritual circumcision, by putting off the body of the flesh in the circumcision of Christ; when you were buried with him in baptism, you were also raised with him through faith in the power of God, who raised him from the dead" (Col 2:10–12). A few verses later Paul is very direct: "Therefore do not let anyone condemn you in matters of food and drink or of observing festivals, new moons, or sabbaths. These are only a shadow of what is to come, but the substance belongs to Christ" (Col 2:16–17).[13]

12. Freiday, *Barclay's Apology*, 263.
13. Willcuts, *Friends*, 25–33.

Friends generally identify Christians' physical practice of baptism and communion with Jewish practice under the Old Covenant, as of *"precisely the same nature* as the ceremonies of the ancient Jews." So, Gurney continues, it is "plain (in the opinion of Friends) that such practices do not consist with that spiritual worship, which is described as so distinguishing a feature of the dispensation of the Gospel."[14] Certainly over the history of the church these forms have developed in a great variety of ways, but that should not obscure the fact that they have root in and grow out of Jewish practices of ritual washing and the observance of the Passover feast. Friends have often wondered that, given all the Jewish ceremonial practices that the church discontinued, these two have endured.

USES OF THE WORD BAPTISM

All interpreters of baptism face the challenge of the varied ways the New Testament reports or speaks of baptism. On the one hand, the reports of baptism show that the church's practice did not draw from a single or uniform pattern. On the other, the language about baptism sometimes refers clearly to water baptism yet at other points uses baptism with metaphorical or figurative meanings.

New Testament scholar James D. G. Dunn points out, as Quakers often have, "*the diversity of form and pattern* in conversion-initiation in Acts." He concludes that the first Christians did not intend "to establish a particular ritual procedure, far less to determine the action of God in accordance with a cultic action." Instead, they wanted to "underline the freedom of God to meet faith when and as he pleases."[15] In any event, it is clear that the early church did not have a single pattern and was not responding in a uniform way to normative instructions.

In a number of places, the New Testament uses the word "baptism" in ways that are metaphorical or figurative and that do not refer to water at all. For example, when Jesus asked James and John whether they could be baptized with the same baptism he was to be baptized with, he clearly meant a baptism of suffering, not of water (Mark 10:38; cf. Luke 12:50). In his highly figurative reference to the Exodus, Paul says that the Israelites "were baptized into Moses" (1 Cor 10:2). Paul uses figurative

---

14. Gurney, *A Peculiar People*, 105.
15. Dunn, "Sacraments," 157.

language also when he speaks of how Christ cleansed the church "with the washing of water by the word" (Eph 5:26). Gurney discusses at length why we should also regard as figurative Jesus' words to Nicodemus that people need to be "born of water and Spirit" (John 3:5).[16]

The figurative uses of the word "baptism" also provide a context for understanding other New Testament phrases about being "baptized into Christ," "baptized in(to) the name of Christ," "baptized into Jesus' death," and others. Certainly such phrases do not evoke the necessity of water baptism, though many of the early believers would have had that experience. So Robert Barclay, anticipating modern biblical interpreters' understanding of "name theology," asserts that baptism into the name of Jesus is being baptized into the virtue and power of Jesus.[17]

Barclay regards Paul's teaching that "As many of you as were baptized into Christ have clothed yourselves with Christ" (Gal 3:27) in a similar way. He says that this is "not merely a form of words to be added to water baptism" but points instead to being baptized "into the power and virtue" of Christ.[18] It is an immersion into the reality of Christ in which we are saturated with and take on the characteristics of the One into whom we are immersed. As Paul uses the other part of the metaphor here, "clothed," in his letter to the Colossians, that meaning is clear: clothed with "compassion, kindness, humility, meekness, patience . . . Above all . . . with love" (Col 3:12–14).

MATTHEW 28—THE GREAT COMMISSION

Friends generally understand the "Great Commission" in Matthew in this larger context of how the idea of baptism is used in the New Testament as a whole. "Go therefore and make disciples of all nations, baptizing them in the name of the Father, and of the Son and of the Holy Spirit, and teaching them to obey everything I have commanded you. And remember, I am with you always, to the end of the age" (Matt 28:19–20). More recent study of the textual and literary history of the New Testament text has brought some Friends to wonder (with interpreters from many traditions) about when these words, including a Trinitarian formula, became part of the Gospel of Matthew. Biblical scholars ask

---

16. Gurney, *A Peculiar People*, 119–22.
17. Freiday, *Barclay's Apology*, 316–17.
18. Ibid., 317.

similar questions about the "second ending" of Mark (Mark 16:9-20), which does not appear in the earliest Greek manuscripts. This contains a commissioning sentence followed by a teaching on baptism (and controversial teachings about picking up snakes and drinking deadly things). Though in this chapter these textual issues in New Testament interpretation need to be mentioned, by and large the Friends understanding of the Great Commission has not been shaped by technical points like this. It is relevant to note, however, that there are no examples in the New Testament of a Trinitarian formula like that in Matthew 28 being used with baptism.

All four Gospels report the risen Lord commissioning the disciples for service (Matt 28:19-20; Mark 16:15; Luke 24:45-53, cf. Acts 1:8; John 20:21-23). They emphasize the importance of taking the good news to the whole world, even "the whole creation," of drawing people to Christ, of teaching them in obedience to immerse themselves in the virtue and power of Christ and to lead transformed lives. Friends do not believe that the Matthew 28 text should be narrowly interpreted to point to a ceremony of water baptism. Indeed, given the other uses of "baptism" in the New Testament, they believe that it more properly refers to the Spirit-and-fire baptism of Jesus that replaces and supercedes the water baptism of John.

Some regard water baptism as an outward evidence of responding to God's grace, of entering the kingdom of God. But Friends believe that Jesus gave a simple and clear evidence of grace at work when he told his disciples, "By this everyone will know that you are my disciples, if you have love for one another" (John 13:35). The reports about the church in the Book of Acts show precisely that evidence. After the disciples received the baptism of the Holy Spirit at Pentecost, their love for one another, practically lived out, was winsome and widely noticed.

JESUS' TEACHING AND PRACTICE

Taken as a whole, Jesus' teaching and practice preserves the distinction between John's baptism and his own. Jesus seeking and receiving John's baptism offers a fascinating intersection of the two men and their ministries.

As Jesus came to be baptized, the writer of Matthew reports (alone here among the Gospels) that John objected and countered that Jesus should more rightly baptize him. John knew that Jesus did not need to submit to a baptism for repentance. Nonetheless, Jesus responded, "Let it be so now; for it is proper for us in this way to fulfill all righteousness" (Matt 3:15). This is a notoriously difficult passage to interpret. A review of commentaries and sermons reveals a wide variety of approaches with many creative but few compelling suggestions. Often, it seems, the suggestions are based on reading back to Matthew from the baptismal practices of the interpreter's own Christian tradition, obviously a risk for all who interpret. Perhaps Matthew, too, was puzzled by why Jesus submitted to John's baptism. Did God require it? Did it forgive Jesus' sin or make him righteous? Did it make a statement?

Without resolving such questions, what the text does not say seems quite clear. It does not say that the occasion of Jesus' baptism sets an example that requires all Christians to follow. It does not teach that the occasion of water baptism is what, in fact, brings Jesus' baptism with Spirit and fire then and now. It does not teach that the righteousness of believers will come about through water baptism.

In an outstanding article, Alan Kolp offers an interesting interpretation of Jesus being baptized, following the work of Edward Schillebeeckx on sacrament. Schillebeeckx defines sacrament as an effective sign of grace, a sign to "be found wherever the unknown God is revealed by and through visible means." Rather than being "things," sacraments are "encounters." So "it is the encounter with this divine realm, with the Lord of heaven and earth, which is sacramental . . . The sacramental occasion is that moment when one experiences the revealed God."[19]

In applying this understanding of sacrament to Jesus' baptism by John the Baptist, Kolp notes that the heart of the experience was "a theophany, that is, a revelation or manifestation of God to Jesus." In the images of the Spirit of God descending like a dove and of the voice from heaven declaring "This is my son," God's real presence came on Jesus, and the images, not the water, occasioned the sacramental encounter. "The dove and the voice, then, were visible signs by which Jesus knew and related to a spiritual encounter with the invisible God in heaven."[20] In this connection it is interesting to observe that the Gospel of John reports only the dove and the voice, not that Jesus was actually baptized in water by John (John 1:29–34).

---

19. Kolp, "Friends, Sacraments," 39–43.
20. Ibid., 47–48.

More traditionally, Friends have denied that Jesus' baptism by John set a precedent that all Christians should submit to water baptism. As we have noted, Jesus would not have had to do this, even as a good Jew. Quakers sometimes point out that even if he had, Jesus was a good Jewish lad who did all manner of things Jewish that do not continue to be part of Christian faith and practice. After all, he was circumcised and properly dedicated in the Temple. He observed Jewish holy days and festivals, though the Pharisees thought he was shaky on the Sabbath. Jesus probably also ate kosher though he was clearly not as good at hand-washing as his Pharisee critics. These are all matters that the church eventually decided not to require of new believers. Clearly, Jesus seeking John's baptism was a particular witness at its time, but it is not presented as and should not stand as a precedent required of Jesus' followers.

In reading the Gospels it seems clear that Jesus did not require water baptism of his followers. They simply left their boats and nets, tax collectors' booths, and homes to follow him. Surely some of his disciples had received John's baptism, but apparently Jesus did not baptize any of them. Friends often point out that even though the repentant thief executed with Jesus was not baptized, Jesus promised that he would that day enter Paradise (Luke 23:42–43). Some of Jesus' disciples baptized (John 3:22), but the writer or editor of the Gospel of John makes clear that Jesus himself baptized no one (John 4:2). As Paul Anderson notes, "Again, the purpose here is not to denigrate water baptism, but to show its historical origin as residing not with Jesus, but with his followers."[21]

Quakers usually observe as well that Jesus did not teach that his followers should use water baptism. This is consistent with the sharp contrast drawn between the baptism of John and the baptism of Jesus. Matthew 28:19–20, the "Great Commission," is the single text that many see as a command to use water baptism. (See fuller discussion above.) Even if this verse could be rightly interpreted to mean water baptism, it is striking that a practice regarded by most as crucial should be grounded in a single text.

In considering what Jesus commanded disciples to do, Friends have often made the point that Jesus more clearly told his disciples to wash each others' feet (John 13:14–15) than to baptize with water or to keep observing a ritual meal. Of course, some Christians understand Jesus to have commanded foot-washing and do incorporate it in their regular

---

21. Anderson, "Fourth Evangelist," 35.

practices. However, most do not, seeing Jesus as giving a stunning lesson about service rather than instituting a ritual act.

PRACTICES IN THE EARLY CHURCH

When the disciples began their life and work together after Jesus ascended into heaven, they were finding their way together, looking to the Spirit to guide as well as empower them. They did not have complete instructions, they had no manual, so they relied on Jesus' words to them that "when the Spirit of truth comes, he will guide you into all the truth" (John 16:13). The Book of Acts reports that they did very well. It also reports that they struggled to settle some controversial new issues: Should they require Gentile converts to be circumcised? Does everyone have to follow the old dietary laws? Is it okay to hang out with Gentiles? and more. At first many of them continued to observe Jewish practices they had known all their lives as they followed the Messiah for whom they had longed. But change was clearly afoot.

One of the issues the new Christian community was trying to figure out was the practice of baptism, reflected still in both the baptism of John and the baptism of Jesus. The reports in Acts show that there was a diversity of practice "in conversion-initiation in Acts—baptism prior to Spirit, Spirit prior to baptism, Spirit without baptism, baptism followed by laying on of hands."[22] In speaking of baptism, Friends often point to this lack of uniformity and suggest that the reason for such variety is that they had no specific instruction about whether and how baptism should be practiced. If it were important for Christians to use water baptism, surely Jesus would have taught and showed them.

Jack Willcuts reviews how often the word "baptism" in some form occurs in the New Testament letters. In fourteen letters of Paul (generously including Hebrews here), some form of the word occurs seventeen times, and one time in Peter's epistles. "If in the 21 epistles," he continues, "14 are entirely silent on the subject, we could assume that baptism is not of first importance in their teaching."[23] Significantly, the word "water" is not connected with the word baptism in any of these passages, and, as noted earlier, the uses are often clearly figurative.

Paul uses these words six times in 1 Cor 1:13–17 as he tries to get the Corinthians to stop quarreling in bouts of spiritual one-upmanship

---

22. Dunn, "Sacraments," 157.
23. Willcuts, *Friends*, 30.

about who was baptized by whom and who had the greatest spiritual gifts. At first Paul thanks God he has baptized only two persons—oh, and one household, as far as he can remember. This is a scant number for three years of service founding this new church. Then Paul speaks of his mission: "For Christ did not send me to baptize but to proclaim the gospel" (1 Cor 1:17). Though Paul does not reject the practice as such, Friends point out that Paul did not regard water baptism as a central or necessary part of proclaiming the good news. Such a response to controversy may also suggest why Paul wrote to the Ephesians about "one Lord, one faith, one baptism."

HISTORIC PRACTICE AND VARIATIONS AMONG FRIENDS

Though the Friends movement has grown to be widely international and theologically diverse over its 350 years, most Friends still do not practice a physical water baptism. However, Friends vary in their understandings or attitudes about this historic approach.

One group believes that by not using physical elements, Friends can most clearly witness to the power and steady presence of the baptism of Jesus. They want to point toward the reality of baptism with Spirit and fire. To put it more boldly, they believe that using physical elements actually hinders or blocks witnessing to and experiencing the baptism of Jesus. Occasionally someone will put this case forward with such passion and earnestness that Friends will have to take the edge off with a bit of joking about how he (or we) did not really intend to say that water baptism is wicked. At their best, Friends do not believe that. But many do believe that practicing water baptism may in fact obscure the importance of entering into the inward spiritual reality of Jesus' baptism.

Another segment of Friends are satisfied to say simply that water baptism is not necessary. It is not required of Christians, is not an expected visible sign of discipleship, and is not needed to bring people into Christian maturity. They generally try to explain clearly why they believe water baptism is not necessary, and they avoid the practice of physical sacraments. While not talking of physical sacraments as a hindrance, they do understand how speaking of non-necessity on the one hand while regularly practicing physical sacraments on the other sends an ambiguous message. Practically speaking, they understand that witnessing to non-necessity makes it necessary not to use physical elements.

This witness and practice, though important, rarely takes a disproportionately central place in the Friends message.

In varied times and places, some groups have re-examined and modified traditional Friends teaching about the sacraments. Among the first to do this were Friends who often use the phrase "freedom from, freedom to," that is, they are free from any requirement to use physical elements, but free to use them if they wish. They hold that Friends are correct in not requiring physical sacraments and generally agree that the New Testament does not institute such practices. However, they also hold that Friends congregations may use the physical sacraments on occasion without abandoning historic Friends teaching on this. This approach first emerged among some Friends in Ohio during the last decades of the 1800s, apparently under the influence of cooperation and strong relationships between Christian groups in the powerful revival movements of that century. Friends leader David Updegraff's friendship with revival leader Charles Finney is often noted as historically important in this change. The frequency and character of sacramental practice seems to vary widely among those in this tradition.

Since that time, discussion and controversy about traditional practice has emerged among Friends in a variety of places and for a variety of reasons. Sometimes leaders will disagree with Friends' historic approach to interpreting the Bible, though it is often the case that these leaders have not investigated Friends teaching very thoroughly. Sometimes Friends are trying to be sensitive to folk who have become part of their congregations but still feel attachment to sacramental practices they may have known with other groups. Sometimes in trying to draw new people into their congregations, Friends, seeking not to be seen as odd, try to minimize the ways in which they think Friends will appear different from other Christians. In these circumstances, traditional Quaker approaches to the physical sacraments may be set aside along with other Friends commitments about a whole Gospel, such as their witness to peace and social justice. Still other Friends wish not to seem harsh in an ecumenical environment and wish to be careful in speaking. Some even incorporate occasional practice of physical sacraments alongside traditional Quaker practice. Even with controversies and exceptions, however, the more traditional approaches still seem to prevail.

While the community of Friends acts in accordance with their understanding of sacrament, individuals often feel freedom to join in physical sacraments with others. For example, Friends ministers may discern that they should agree to an individual's request to be baptized. Or in settings where the invitation is extended, Friends might join with other Christians in the Lord's Supper, either occasionally or sometimes regularly. The community generally respects individual leadings in such matters, particularly if it does not undercut the common witness.

Currently the great majority of Friends are those who have emerged as a result of missionary outreach in the twentieth century. There are many Friends in Africa (especially Kenya) and Latin America, and well-settled and emerging groups throughout Asia. Ron Stansell, a Friends missiologist with wide experience, reports that around the world they tend to follow traditional Friends practice about the sacraments. The exception he notes is in India, where the mission work was initiated by Friends from Ohio who embraced "freedom from, freedom to."[24] In some settings, Friends teaching about spiritual baptism has helped bring people into new life. Jack Willcuts writes of serving in Bolivia in a religious environment shaped by an eclectic mix of traditional Christian sacramental practice and animistic belief. He says of new believers, "Upon finding the Lord Jesus and His infilling of the Holy Spirit, their spiritual needs were met in a wonderful and fresh revelation of truth and reality. This experience deepened my appreciation for spiritual communion."[25] In every setting, however, Friends throughout the world regard the real evidence of becoming a Christian as a transformed life.

CONCLUSION

Even with their diversity, all Friends would insist that the true mark of being a disciple of Jesus is a transformed life, not a public ceremony. They want individuals and the community together to be people who, in Fox's words, "possess what they profess." Friends often use the phrase "sacramental living" to speak of their conviction that Christ is among us at all times and that our lives should be creative signs of God's presence in the world.

Certainly people in any tradition might become complacent about or routinize their core convictions. Thus, Quakers might carelessly fall

---

24. From personal conversation with Ron Stansell, Professor of Religion, George Fox University, Newberg, Oregon.

25. Willcuts, *Friends*, 37.

into not using water baptism and yet neglect bringing people into Jesus' baptism with Spirit and fire. They might too easily speak of all of life as sacramental without living as visible symbols of God's presence and grace, without being so tangibly part of the Body of Christ broken for the world that in encountering them people sense somehow that they have encountered God. Yet Friends are eager to be faithful. They want to live deeply immersed in the life and power of Christ the Present Teacher, who is among us to guide and empower. They want to be Children of Light through whom God's glory shines in the world.

FURTHER READING

Freiday, Dean, ed. *Barclay's Apology: In Modern English*. Elberon, NJ: Hemlock, 1967.

Gurney, Joseph John. *A Peculiar People*. Richmond, IN: Friends United, 1979.

Willcuts, Jack L. *Why Friends Are Friends: Some Quaker Core Convictions*. Newberg, OR: Barclay, 1984.

8

Baptism in the Restoration Movement

Curt Niccum

IMAGINE A REPORTER RANDOMLY querying people on the street, "What is the most important decision you have ever made?" One would expect a wide variety of responses. "Getting married." "Joining the Navy." "Switching careers." "Having children." However, those answering, "Being baptized," probably belong to a church within the Stone-Campbell Movement (alternately known as the Restoration Movement). If further pressed, they could probably even recite the precise date and time of their immersion.

Many reading the above paragraph from within the Restoration tradition will immediately identify with this scenario. Others may find the choice of words rather strange and a little disconcerting. This particular view of baptism, along with a few other tenets, loosely binds together groups identifying themselves as Churches of Christ, Christian Churches, and Disciples of Christ. A sometimes fierce adherence to congregational autonomy and the resulting lack of a centralized body governing doctrine and polity have resulted in an amazingly broad spectrum of beliefs, making the task of summarizing the group's perspective on baptism quite daunting.

This chapter will attempt to outline the general shape of baptism as it has developed within Restoration churches (primarily from a Church of Christ background). The place to begin is first and foremost in Scripture. Indeed, an unwritten creed for the group is "Speak where the Bible speaks; be silent where the Bible is silent." Although not always recognized, this itself has roots within a particular historical setting.

Therefore, the presentation begins with the historical contexts behind the inception and development of the Movement. This will help inform the second section which addresses its biblical and theological bases for immersing adult believers. The last section investigates consequent pastoral application.

HISTORICAL DEVELOPMENTS

Although the seeds of the Stone-Campbell (or "Restoration") Movement were planted long before the late eighteenth century, the American experiment provided the fertile soil necessary for its sprouting and growth. In the face of ancient Christian divisions and a staggering number of new Christian groups emerging in the four decades immediately following the signing of the Declaration of Independence, some looked to the Scriptures, practices, and beliefs of the earliest Christians as the most suitable model for bringing about one church. In the beginning, leaders of the movement inherited baptismal practices from previous generations, but eventually baptism became an important topic in that effort.

Certain factors contributed to a thorough reexamination of all things related to this sacrament. First, the philosophies of the age significantly impacted American religious thought. For Alexander Campbell, the works of John Locke carried nearly the importance of the Bible. Whereas he rarely went anywhere without toting a copy of each in one of his coat pockets, the thoughts of the Scottish Common Sense philosophers he also carried about in his head. Furthermore, the recent successes of the American and French revolutions seemed to validate on a practical level the Enlightenment's theory that power rested upon man's rationality,[1] not in authorities set and determined by political or religious hierarchies. This encouraged a reasonable rejection of suspected foreign, especially "papist," intrusions on practical religion. Additionally, the Enlightenment's call to return "to the sources" shaped the developing belief that Scripture offered the only basis for pure, and hence unified, Christianity. The Bible also appeared to provide the answer to growing dissatisfactions with church traditions and creedal formulae.

---

1. I employ the word "man" here to emphasize the patriarchal nature of the ideas expressed during this time period. Although the concept of "all men" being created equal was rooted in American identity, political and religious discussion almost unanimously limited the phrase to white, educated males.

God's Word apart from human fallibility, so it was thought, would unite Christendom.

Second, personal experiences served as catalysts for reinvestigating baptismal theology and practice. Sometimes they were born of pastoral ministry. Barton W. Stone, for example, wrestled with the large number of penitent believers responding to the gospel message but who remained without any relief of assurance. His Presbyterian background emphasized human depravity. Salvation, the forgiveness of sins, and divine pardon came from God's call alone, apart from any sincere response by a disciple. Typically, visible signs such as falling, dancing, and "barking," would accompany the divine call so that some assurance might be granted those blessed by God, but frequently even these remarkable manifestations proved insufficient. So many, though sorely desirous of God's favor, continued in agony, keenly aware of both their sin and God's silence. Stone concluded that the preaching must be at fault and so turned to Scripture for answers. Among other passages, the story of Peter's preaching on the day of Pentecost (Acts 2) caught his attention.

Sometimes these personal experiences were born of theology. Alexander Campbell's first real interest in baptism came as he attempted to oppose the teaching of adult believer's immersion. Seeking additional help from denominational leaders, he was informed that pedobaptism could not be found in the Scriptures. This did not present an obstacle to many, for church tradition came with sufficient weight to instill within any ordained practice an authority all its own. Campbell, to the contrary, remained unsatisfied. Still, he did not further pursue the matter until another significant event in his life, the birth of his daughter in 1812. Now the issue of infant baptism mattered immensely. Scripture interpreted through the lens of Scottish Common Sense philosophy alongside, ironically, the spurning of European ideas, convinced him not to submit his daughter to the sacrament but to allow her eventually to choose for herself whether or not to place her faith in the risen Lord.[2]

In any event, people were responding to these stimuli with the assumption that the Bible alone provided the sufficient answer. That

---

2. It should be noted that ongoing conversations with Walter Scott, a significant leader in the Restoration Movement and able preacher in Ohio, also contributed to this decision. (Scott himself had been persuaded by a Haldanian pamphlet he had come across while studying baptism.) Others arrived at similar conclusions about the same time. If not chronologically the first, Scott certainly was the most influential in the earliest years. For more information on Scott's role, see Hicks, "Rational Religion."

several groups in different regions of the USA developed similar ideas simultaneously seemed only to confirm the rising confidence in the ability of rational man to determine universal truths and the inevitability of church unification around those truths. Thus a movement was born.

As of that time, nobody in this loosely associated movement had yet hammered out a definitive position on baptism. Ongoing interreligious discussion forced the issue. Formal arenas for discussion were arranged as proponents of adult immersion encountered opposition from pedobaptists, and then from Baptists with a strong Calvinist background. Campbell's debates in particular provided impetus for a detailed development and formulation of baptism peculiar to the Restoration Movement. Most notable were those held with John Walker (1820) and W. L. McCalla (1823). Eventually Campbell codified his thoughts in *The Christian System* (1835), further explicated in detail eight years later in a debate with N. L. Rice.[3]

From this a general consensus emerged. First, God offers salvation to all humanity yet it depends on individual human will to respond to the invitation. Second, faith in Jesus Christ and repentance from sins belong to the human element of the equation. Third, the effective work of salvation, the forgiveness of sin, and the imparting of the Holy Spirit come only from God and take place when one unites with the death, burial, and resurrection of Christ in baptism. Fourth, teaching and faith are prerequisites for those baptized, since the biblical narratives indicate adult response. Finally, the lexical meaning of "baptism" and descriptions of the earliest practices clearly point toward immersion. More than anything, the first three provide the distinctive character of baptism in the Restoration Movement.

These broad conclusions still allowed for considerably different application. For example, if one comes into contact with the grace of God, the blood of Christ, and the gift of the Holy Spirit through baptism, and the "one baptism" of the early church was immersion, then does it not follow that those receiving other forms of baptism stand outside of the "one Lord"? Campbell himself responded to such a question posed by a woman from Lunenburg, Virginia. He did not doubt one bit the need to restore ancient Christianity, but he refused to reduce it to exactitude in just a few commandments. What ultimately matters is "the image of

---

3. Walker and Campbell, *Infant Sprinkling*; Campbell, *Debate*, 1824 (with McCalla), cf. *Debate*, 1844 (with Rice); and Campbell, *System*.

Christ" and a devotion to God's truth "as far as known" by any one disciple.[4] Some found his answer unsatisfactory; perhaps he himself later did too.

Since that inaugural period, this movement for unity has, ironically, divided into three main branches: the Disciples of Christ, independent Christian Churches, and Churches of Christ. Although the Civil War cemented the disintegration of the Movement, each sect generally representing a particular geographical area (the North, border states, and the South respectively), the seeds for division, as noted in part above, already existed.

For a group so closely tied to the American experiment, this comes as no surprise. Indeed, many of the antebellum conversations about scriptural interpretation in Restoration churches mirrored the ongoing dispute between Federalists and Republicans concerning how best to read the Constitution. In other words, should one view the silence of the Bible/Constitution as permissive or prohibitive? In the political realm, did those items not specifically mentioned in the U.S. Constitution belong under the scope of the federal government (permissive) or that of the states (prohibitive)? Concerning baptism, does Scripture allow alternative methods (permissive) or only one mode (prohibitive)? The North, both politically and religiously, leaned toward the former, the South the latter. As a result, the Disciples of Christ and the Churches of Christ represent opposite ends of the spectrum, the Disciples of Christ preferring immersion but respecting other forms of baptism and the Churches of Christ largely recognizing only the immersion of an adult penitent believer as valid.

For the most part, publications about the mode and effects of baptism in Restoration Movement churches have rehearsed and rehashed the arguments of previous generations. Campbell's work in particular was so extensive that one could add little new, at least from the perspectives he addressed. As a result, churches began focusing on the consequences of their distinctive practices.

Among the Disciples, the tension between the ecumenical interest of the Movement and the sectarian nature of Restoration was eased by more strongly focusing on unity. To that end there developed a broadening of the scope of baptism. In opposition to what they perceived as an

---

4. For the larger issue see entries in the *Millenial Harbinger* 8 (1837) 411–14, 506–8, and 561–67.

exaggerated emphasis on its mode, they argued that Christian initiation encompassed much more than the ritual, therefore "baptism" in the New Testament bore greater meaning. In other words, what mattered was its "functional view," not its lexical definition.[5] Scripture does speak clearly of adult immersion, but one finds the power of the ritual in the work of God and not in conformity to the first century pattern itself. Although adult believer's immersion supersedes all others in terms of meaning and an implicit and explicit confession of unity with Christ and his church, alternate practices can share in the basic character of biblical baptism as part of one's initiation into the kingdom.[6] This made it possible for the Disciples to provide open membership and engage in ecumenical dialogue. The latter subsequently has also led to a more sacramental interpretation of baptism.[7]

Not all of the Disciples were comfortable with this shift, especially since it coincided with, and perhaps resulted from, an academic interest in German liberal scholarship among prominent leaders. From 1904 until the late twenties, debates raged between the slowly diverging parties, most often found in the publications *Christian Century* (expounding the views associated with the Disciples) and *The Christian Standard* (associated with those later designated as Christian Churches). The primary symptom, and therefore center of most discussions, was open membership—and baptism by extension. However, the real issue concerned biblical authority. A conservative view of inspiration resulted in a firmer stance on the importance of immersion and hence closed membership.[8]

---

5. See Morrison, *Baptism*, 74–89; England, *One Baptism*; and Carpe, "Baptismal Theology."

6. Again see Morrison, *Baptism*. Note pp. 5–8, where he specifically attributes the need for penning his book to the "legalistic and literalistic assumptions" of immersion-baptism, and, somewhat inaccurately, identifies this "dogma" as stemming from Alexander Campbell.

7. See in particular Robinson, *Doctrine*.

8. P. H. Welshimer, among others, identified the more significant issue in the *Christian Standard*, 4 December 1926, 655. This still holds true as evidenced in Jack Cotterell's preface to his *Baptism*: "We must approach the Bible with the conviction that the original meaning of most texts, as intended by their authors and as understood by their first recipients, is recoverable to a high degree of probability. Also, we must take this originally intended meaning as the definitive, authoritative one" (Cotterell, *Baptism*, 8).

The Christian Churches, therefore, hold to adult believer's baptism as the means by which one comes into contact with the saving blood of Jesus Christ. This they share in common with their more conservative sister, the Churches of Christ. Some differences, though minor, do exist. The closer relationship with the Disciples allowed for a stronger emphasis on ethics with new birth. Immersion apart from a transformed life has no benefit. On the other side, the Christian Churches distance themselves from the more legalistic approaches characteristic of some in the Churches of Christ. With an eye toward this N. J. Aynsworth wrote:

> I cannot pass without saying that the setting forth of immersion as a mere legal condition of salvation is a woeful cheapening of baptism on its spiritual side; and it will hardly take place unless the preacher's own religion has already stiffened into legalism. A legal conversion and a legal Christian life is a wretched travesty on Christianity, and is obnoxious to all the thunders of Christ's invective against the legalism of his day.[9]

Among the Churches of Christ, which already practiced closed membership, serious questions arose at this time as to how one should regard those who actually received adult immersion from other groups who lacked the same exact understanding of baptism. David Lipscomb held any immersion of an adult believer to be valid regardless of any knowledge on the baptizand's part that forgiveness of sins was so imparted. Such was the work of God, not the one submitting to God's will.[10] Unhappy with this position, Austin McGary established a journal, *Firm Foundation*, to compete with Lipscomb's *Gospel Advocate*. Through this medium McGary and others strongly advocated the exclusion from fellowship of anyone baptized without prior knowledge of the rite's purpose. Membership within the body of Christ could only come with rebaptism correctly administered and for the valid reasons.[11] This difference of opinion still exists among Churches of Christ, yet even among congregations granting some latitude they often attempt visually to maintain some level of distinction. For example, in membership directories many will mark with an asterisk those individuals having received an "acceptable" form of baptism.

---

9. Aynsworth, *Moral and Spiritual Aspects*, 97.
10. For more recent commentary, see Allen, *Rebaptism*.
11. For a summary of this period, see Foster, "Churches," 87–90.

Three other developments during this period also deserve mention. First, the Restoration Movement's interest in first century Christian models and the later "aberrations" has generated considerable historical interest. Everett Ferguson has provided the most significant work in this area, just recently publishing perhaps the definitive study on the subject.[12] Of related interest have been significant archeological discoveries, most notably the Dead Sea Scrolls—the literature of a baptizing community in Palestine—and the numerous ancient *miqvoth* (baptisteries for Jewish ceremonial bathing) in Jerusalem.

Second, there has been a distinct move toward a greater theological appreciation of baptism. In many early works, the deeper theological ideas associated with new birth were present, but the focus on mode left them subdued. Although theology certainly plays a role in any discussion of baptism, the emphases on language (Greek grammar and word usage) and practice (biblical interpretation and early church history) dwarfed all other topics. Recent works have remedied this.[13]

Third, the last three decades have seen a renewed interest in re-unification. Baptism has had a prominent position among the issues discussed by the different Restoration Movement factions. The ongoing dialogue has produced a broader recognition of all it entails.[14]

BIBLICAL-THEOLOGICAL FOUNDATIONS

Taken individually, nothing is unique about the mode, manner, recipients, or purposes of baptism in the Restoration Movement. Most Christian traditions will find some point(s) of agreement. Instead, it is the unique combination of these that mark Restoration churches as different.

With most Christians, Restoration churches baptize in water. Βαπτίζω and its cognates connote water unless an author specifies a different element such as "fire." More importantly, the Jewish washings that prefigured Christian baptism required water. The other contemporary Jewish groups enjoining followers to participate in religious washings, probably all of an eschatological nature, did the same.[15] Evidence

---

12. Ferguson, *Baptism*.

13. In particular, see Hicks and Taylor, *River*, and relevant sections in Childers and Aquino, *Unveiling*, and Ferguson, *Church*.

14. One product of this dialogue is Fletcher, *Baptism*.

15. This is true of John the Baptist, Banus, the dissenters at Qumran, and the community of the Fourth Sibyl.

indicates that water remained the norm for early Christianity until the development of Gnosticism in the early second century. The stark dualism introduced by Gnostics and others overly influenced by Greek philosophies of the day resulted in some heretical groups separating "spiritual" activity from "physical" elements.

Water baptism, however, in no way lessens the spiritual nature of or emphasis on the work of God in baptism. The New Testament closely associates the giving of the Spirit with water and specifically baptism in water.[16] Luke–Acts clearly portrays this with the parallels drawn between Jesus' baptism in Luke 3 and the inaugural community's baptism in Acts 2.

Even in those places in Acts where anomalies occur, marking groups whose membership in God's people might be questioned by conservative Jewish believers (Samaritans, ch. 8; Gentiles, chs. 10–11; and second generation disciples of John the Baptist, ch. 19), Luke closely conjoins the two. For example, even after the reception of the Spirit by those in Cornelius's household, Peter commands them to be baptized in water (10:47). Furthermore, in Peter's defense of this action, Luke replaces the word "water" with "God," signifying in a remarkable way the role of deity in and behind this ritual (11:17).[17]

Water has played a salvific role throughout history, most often in connection with cleansing or purification. This begins on a global scale with the creation and flood narratives of Genesis (see also 1 Pet 3:19–21 and 2 Pet 3:5–6). Similarly, priests in Jerusalem, pilgrims preparing to worship, and Gentile military officers like Naaman and Cornelius, have availed themselves of the saving power of God through washing in water. Jesus himself submitted to baptism in water for "all righteousness" (Matt 3:13–15) and now baptizes believers with the Spirit usually at the time of, but always in connection with, their baptism in water.

Important thinkers in our tradition have put forward linguistic, historical, and theological reasons for immersion. First, βαπτίζειν means to dip or immerse. The earliest readers and hearers of the gospel message would have had that as the primary referent. Not only does the word itself denote immersion, but those biblical narratives that provide

---

16. Matt 3:16; Mark 1:10; Luke 3:21–22; John 3:3–5; (compare 4:13–14 and 7:37–39); Acts 2:38; 9:17–19; 10:44–48; 19:5–6; 1 Cor 6:11; 10:1–4; 12:13; Titus 3:5.

17. Μήτι τὸ ὕδωρ δύναται κωλῦσαί τις τοῦ μὴ βαπτισθῆναι τούτους. This becomes: Ἐγὼ τίς ἤμην δυνατὸς κωλῦσαι τὸν θεόν.

a larger context reveal a practice that required a descent into and ascent out of a locale with significant amounts of water, thus providing a venue favoring the word's normal meaning.[18]

Historically, the washings of the Jews, especially the priestly washings, which served as the precursors to Christian practice, required submersion. Not surprisingly, the early church as best we can tell unanimously baptized in the same manner. Even with the later developments of infant and deathbed baptisms, Christianity held to immersion. Even though practitioners in the early medieval period raised concerns about the relative safety of dipping such young or ailing members, immersion remained common in the Catholic Church until the fourteenth century and certain Reformers revived the practice in the sixteenth century. It has continued unbroken in the Greek Orthodox Church.[19] Immersion also visibly connects the believer with the death, burial, and resurrection of Jesus. This appears at least implicit in Rom 6:3–4 and Col 2:12.

Scripture does not provide details about the ages of those receiving baptism. Commentators have drawn, though, certain conclusions based on the biblical narratives. First, the very location of John's ministry as well as that of others along or near the Jordan River, including Jesus and his disciples, would have presented a major obstacle for the very young. Second, since the process includes a response of faith with a confession, it presupposes one old enough to believe and verbally communicate that belief. Third, when the Bible does specify baptizands, it speaks of adults. Fourth, the very practice of the priestly washings came with certain expectations about who could and could not respond. Entrance into the priestly service of the Temple required adulthood.[20]

We also know the early church administered baptism to adults. Patristic discussions and the evidence from ancient Christian funerary practices provide a relatively full picture of the practice. The rather strong language of John 3, "No one can enter the kingdom of God without being born of water and Spirit," eventually generated considerable angst among parents living in a world of high infant mortality. In response, emergency baptisms occasionally took place for offspring not

---

18. See Matt 3:6, 16; Mark 1:5, 10; John 3:23; 10:40; Acts 8:38–39.

19. For greater detail about the Reformation period with important corrections concerning Anabaptist practice, see Harrison, "Renewal," 95–112. On baptism in the Orthodox tradition, see the article by Steenberg in this volume.

20. See Num 4:30 and 8:24.

likely to survive. Still, what we know as "infant baptism" did not develop until much later. Tombs before the fifth century list the date of a child's baptism within weeks of death. Those who attained adulthood received baptism at a considerably later period in their lives, presumably at a time when they could believe in and confess the name of Jesus. Hence infant baptism was the exception rather than the rule.

Investigations into the origins of Christian baptism have correctly focused on Jewish practice. Until recently, scholars remained divided as to its actual origin, whether proselyte baptism or priestly washing. Two things now decisively favor the latter: the discovery of the Dead Sea Scrolls (DSS) and the critical investigation of rabbinic literature.

First, baptizing groups reacted strongly against what they perceived to be blasphemies perpetrated by the Jerusalem priesthood. Working from passages like Exodus 19, Jewish dissenters deduced that if the priests had abdicated their responsibility as the spiritual leaders of Israel, the nation itself needed to become a holy priesthood. Groups therefore retreated for practical and/or eschatological reasons to the Jordan River (Jesus, John, and Banus) or its vicinity (the DSS community) and called Israel to repent.[21]

Second, scholars now recognize the danger of assuming that later rabbinic materials preserve reliable information for reconstructing the thoughts and practices of Second Temple Judaisms. This holds true even for passages attributed to rabbis of the first century, for many tended to throw their beliefs onto important predecessors in order to validate contemporary practices. Thus, the one passage in the Mishnah quoted in support of proselyte baptism, although attributing the debate to rabbis of the late first century, may in fact be relating a later development. More decisively, however, the passage does not speak of proselyte baptism at all; it merely discusses whether a recently circumcised Gentile can participate in the ritual washings preparatory to the Passover celebrations. The earliest evidence for proselyte baptism proper comes at least four hundred years after the founding of Christianity, and therefore may have developed in imitation of Christian practice.

The priestly origins of the rite establish the basic purposes of baptism: repentance, forgiveness of sins, and the Lord's presence. One sees this most clearly with the High Priest's preparation for the Day of Atonement. He immerses himself for ritual purity for the task of enter-

---

21. The locations of the other known discipling groups remain unclear.

ing into the Holy of Holies (Lev 16:2-4). Similarly, the Dead Sea Scrolls community, a group of priestly men retreating into the wilderness to await spiritual revival, immersed themselves for forgiveness and to await the imminent coming of the Lord.[22] Within the biblical narrative, John the Baptist, a person of priestly stock, also comes proclaiming a baptism of repentance in preparation for the Lord's arrival (Matt 3:1-12; Mark 1:2-4; Luke 3:1-18).

Christian baptism follows these predecessors. The New Testament frequently associates repentance and forgiveness with baptism.[23] The significant shift for Christianity comes with the third element: baptism no longer serves an anticipatory role. Whereas all other priestly washings prepared one for coming into the Lord's presence, Christian baptism realizes it. One's sins are forgiven at baptism so that the Lord's presence might enter into the believer. What was once a future hope with the priestly and Johannine washings becomes a reality through the reception of the Holy Spirit.

Recognizing the historical development of Jewish baptismal practices does not in any way negate baptism's value. On the contrary, its Old Testament antecedents provide continuity with and supply clarity to the New Testament language associated with it.

The significance of baptism for earliest Christianity cannot be overstated. Among the biblical passages that speak of what "saves," the New Testament places baptism in the company of grace, confession, faith, works, and the blood of Christ—significant company indeed.[24] Around baptism developed creedal statements ranging from the simplest confession, "Jesus is Lord,"[25] to proclamations of new creation in Paul's churches (see below). It likely served as the subject of early hymns (Eph 5:14). Baptism even appears among the seven "ones" in Eph 4:4-6, an epitome of the Christian faith working from and augmenting the Shema (Deut 6:4-5), Israel's most sacred text.[26]

22. Cf. 1QS III:2-12 and V:13-14.

23. Matt 3:2-6; Mark 1:4; Luke 3:3; Acts 2:38-41; 22:16. See further the discussions below.

24. 1 Pet 3:21-22. For the others see Eph 2:5-8; Rom (3:28), 10:9; (Jas 2:24); and (Rom 3:24-25) respectively. (Passages within parentheses use δικαιόω rather than σώζω.)

25. See, for example, Rom 10:9; 1 Cor 12:3; and the later addition with an expanded formula found in some Bibles at Acts 8:37.

26. Note also the remarks in Heb 6 where the author sidesteps a discussion of "baptisms" yet considers them a foundational element of Christianity. Baptisms are

For this reason, writers within the Restoration Movement today focus more on the meaning of baptism than on the what and the how. The historical and linguistic reasons for adult believer immersion are well rehearsed and well known, but what value does the "correct" form have without an understanding of its real meaning? Although some within the Stone-Campbell heritage (and other groups) might argue the form properly administered guarantees salvation, most would consider that a reversion to legalism.

In terms of form equaling function, immersion necessitates a doctrine of the priesthood of all believers. This must be the starting point even though the connection is more often implicit than explicit.

The brief exhortation of Heb 10:19–25 dramatically depicts what this means. The presence of the Lord begins and ends the pericope. Christians currently have access to the true sanctuary, i.e., the Holy of Holies, having had their bodies "washed with pure water." Yet they also anxiously await the approaching day of promise. Made holy by the blood of Jesus and having been cleansed of an "evil conscience" (forgiveness of sins), they focus on "love and good deeds" (repentance).

The same ideas surface in 1 Peter but with the added link to Creation. Although this letter is correctly no longer regarded as a baptismal catechism by scholars, baptism continually hovers in the background. Here the call to priesthood gets voiced in the midst of language about new birth. The priest must be holy as God is holy (1:14–16). Those serving as priests also offer spiritual sacrifices (2:4–10), identified in part as a godly lifestyle conjoined with a "good conscience" lived in relationship to other people, including those outside the household of God (2:11—4:19).[27]

The most frequently recurring language associated with baptism in the New Testament comes from the story of Creation. This occurs in

---

listed on a par with repentance, faith, the resurrection, and eternal judgment (vv. 1–2). Concerning the plural, commentators have interpreted it variously: It could refer to baptism as one among several Jewish ritual washings or in contrast to Gentile religious ablutions. If purely intramural, then this could refer to triune immersions as with the Greek Orthodox Church or multiple recipients. For additional information, see Attridge, *Hebrews*, 164–65.

27. Rom 12:1—15:13 exhorts the Christians in Rome to offer sacrifices in similar terms (i.e., offering bodies as living sacrifices is equated with living in good relationship with other Christians in 12:3–13 and 14:1—15:13, with outsiders in 12:14–21, and the governing authorities in 13:1–14). However, Paul does not connect this idea as closely to baptism as 1 Peter, but cf. Rom 13:12–14. Paul also elsewhere equates his ministry with priestly service; see Rom 15:14–16 and Phil 2:14–17.

theological discussions relying upon the significance of baptism as well as liturgical material incorporated into biblical compositions.

At baptism God provides new birth—a "new creation" or a "re-creation."[28] Although God created male and female in his image, the introduction of sin into human history marred or destroyed this component of life. Baptism breathes the Spirit of God back into mortal bodies. This finds its strongest expression in Jesus' dialogue with Nicodemus in John 3. Being born from above becomes a desideratum for entrance into God's reign (vv. 3–7). Thematic connections between water and Spirit extend throughout the rest of the Fourth Gospel, intensifying the connection between new birth and Spirit.[29] This reaches its climax with John's version of Pentecost in chapter 20, where Jesus, just as at the very beginning, breathes the life-giving Spirit into his new creations (vv. 22–23).

Baptismal contexts in the Pauline epistles also mirror this. Thus the "old self," marred by sin, can be put to death by God through baptism and exchanged for a new birth from above (Eph 4:20–24 and Col 3:1–11). This birth results in a new, true human being who shares God's very own nature, the Holy Spirit, and grows towards the full stature of Christ. One thus abandons that humanity shaped and determined by the first Adam and joins the perfected humanity shaped and determined by the second Adam, namely Jesus Christ (Rom 5:12—6:14).

This new creation separates the believer from the otherwise overwhelming power of sin.[30] Death reigns in the humanity descended from the First Adam (Rom 5:12–21). The only means of escaping the mortal

---

28. Often writers use "regeneration" to express this concept, taken from Titus 3:4–7. Although "re-creation" looks awkward and is open to misunderstanding without a hyphen, it resonates more clearly with the first chapters of Genesis.

29. John 1:26–33; 2:6–10; 3:5–7, 22–26; 4:1–30; 5:2–14; 7:37–39; 9:5–11; 13:1–15; 15:3; 18:11; 19:28–30. Note in particular the connection to Jesus' death made through the prediction in 7:38, the pouring of water and wine on the altar during the Festival of Tabernacles when Jesus made this pronouncement, and its fulfillment upon the piercing of his side when water and blood flow from his belly (19:34). R. Alan Culpepper summarizes John's use of symbolism thus, "Although baptism seems to remain the normative practice for those entering the new life, the fourth evangelist qualifies its importance by tying it to the wider symbolic value of water, belief, and the work of the Spirit" (*Anatomy*, 193–94); see also Dodd, *Interpretation*, 137–40.

30. This also separates and protects one from the spiritual powers arrayed against God's people. Baptism unites the believer with the spiritual victory in the heavenly realms won by Christ's death on the cross. See, for example, Col 2:8–15.

grip of sin is to exchange one form of humanity for another—to choose birth into the world of the Second Adam, putting aside the old self and its weaknesses. Thus sin, a natural corrupting element within the lives of mortals, becomes an unnatural intruder in the world of those led by the Spirit (Rom 6:1—8:17). Paul even applies this to Jewish life apart from Christ (7:14-24). The Law of Moses, although inherently good and spiritual (7:12, 14), remains inferior because of the powerful impulses of sin.[31] In other words, the Law of Moses is prescriptive—it can only tell us what we should and should not do; the Law of Christ is descriptive—it embodies a new ontological reality. The former explains who we cannot be, the latter who we are. The difference is not in the content of the "Laws" but in the constitution of their recipients. "Therefore there is no condemnation for those who are in Christ Jesus, for the Law of the Spirit of life (i.e., the life-giving Spirit from Gen 1-2) in Christ has set us free from the Law of sin and death" (Rom 8:1). As a result, only those who have become members of the true humanity, descended from the Second Adam, can fulfill the righteous decrees of the Law (Rom 8:4).

The Creation story also played a significant role in catechesis, at least in Pauline churches. In three letters to three different churches dealing with three very different sets of problems composed at three different periods we find recurring baptismal language.[32] This shared phrasing suggests an established block of material, probably liturgical, accompanying Christian initiation. The standard and perhaps earliest formulation occurs in Gal 3:26-28, "Neither Jew nor Greek, slave nor free, male and female." The last phrase comes straight from Gen 1:27 (LXX) and reflects Jewish (Middle Platonic) beliefs that the ideal/spiritual human lacked gender. Thus in baptism the inferior demarcations of the created world lose their power and the believer enters the ideal, spiritual realm where gender distinctions play no role.

The contrast between baptism and circumcision in Col 2 also belongs in this category.[33] Working from a body of Jewish Scriptures speak-

---

31. Paul addresses the relevant interrelationships in Rom 6–7: sin–grace (6:1–14), grace–law (6:15—7:6), and law–sin (7:7—8:17).

32. Gal 3:26-28; Col 2:9-11 and 1 Cor 12:13. Despite the truncated formula of 1 Cor 12:13, Paul discusses the full triad in the seventh chapter (male–female vv. 1-16, Jew–Greek vv. 17-20, and slave–free vv. 21-24).

33. This hardly provides evidence of infant baptism, as the context mentions a body of teaching and a response of faith (v. 7) as well as adult responses toward the dangers of syncretism (vv. 6-23). Instead, it is a metaphor for dying with Christ.

ing of circumcision as a holistic response to God rather than a legalistic one (see Deut 10:16, for example, and an application of this idea in Acts 7:51), the Colossians are reminded of their total devotion to God as empowered first (both in time and significance) through baptism. Rather than the cutting off of a very small portion of the flesh in circumcision, baptism severs one completely from the "old" self. Baptism thus fulfills the true purpose of circumcision (one of heart rather than flesh) and far surpasses it in power (the entire body rather than a minuscule fold of skin). As Lightfoot says,

> Baptism is the grave of the old man, and the birth of the new.[34] As he sinks beneath the baptismal waters, the believer buries there all his corrupt affectations and past sins; as he emerges thence, he rises regenerate, quickened to new hopes and a new life. This it is, because it is not only the crowning act of his own faith but also the seal of God's adoption and the earnest of God's Spirit. Thus baptism is an image of his participation both in the death and resurrection of Christ.[35]

A further development in early Christian thought either began or greatly expanded in Asia Minor where writers likened baptism to the ritual bath of the bride-to-be. In the Household Code of Ephesians, Jesus presents the church to himself as a bride without wrinkle or blemish having been purified through the washing of the water, which is the Word (5:25–27). The bridal imagery permeating the Fourth Gospel duplicates it, with a striking parallel with washing and Word.[36] Baptism thus prepares and purifies the community of believers for an intimate relationship with her Lord. From Paul's perspective, this is the true meaning of

---

34. The author wrote at a time when "man," in his own speech and the language of his Bible, often referred to the totality of humanity. In Col 2 one finds ἄνθρωπος, a gender neutral term best rendered "person" in English. Considering the language of re-creation and the concept of a genderless existence associated with baptism, both of which appear in this passage, the gender neutral language found in more recent English translations is welcome.

35. Lightfoot, *Colossians and Philemon*, 184.

36. The verbal parallels come closest in John 15:3, but the wedding theme, along with a connection between water and word, is interwoven through the Gospel's narrative. Thus Jesus transforms the Jewish waters of purification at the wedding in Cana (ch. 2), John the Baptist speaks of himself as the "best man" (3:22–30) in a context of purifying water, and John evokes the wedding stories of Genesis with his account of Jesus meeting the Samaritan woman at the well (ch. 4).

"the two shall become one flesh."[37] This builds on the idea already inherent in baptism that it is preparatory to entering into the Lord's presence. Although those baptized receive the Lord's Spirit, it serves as a "down payment" guaranteeing the consummation and fullness to come when the Lord Jesus Christ returns (2 Cor 1:22; 5:12; Eph 1:14). This metaphor reaches a vivid climax with the marriage of the Lamb in the Book of Revelation.

This metaphor has ethical implications as well. The wedding garb of God's people in Revelation not only represents the cleansing power of Christ's blood but his work in their daily activities—"the holy deeds of the saints" (19:8). Something similar takes place in Ephesians where new birth results in both cleansing and moral/ethical transformation (4:17—6:9). Perhaps the Household Code with its portrayal of the sacred marriage of Christ and the church intentionally concludes this section of the letter.

Due to the ascendancy of Reason during the Enlightenment and also attempts to wrest power out of the hands of clerics, some Reformers emptied the sacraments of their potency, most notably by reducing them to mere symbols. This view predominates even today with many viewing baptism as "an outward sign of an inward grace." This, however, does not do justice to the mysteries of God's work.

The New Testament writers emphasize that Christ is the one baptizing when one submits to God's will, regardless of the particular individual submerging the penitent convert. This message begins with John the Baptist and continues with the descriptions of early Christian baptism in Acts.[38] Paul also strongly connects the efficacy of baptism to the work of God or Christ and compares it to significant points within salvation history where God decisively acted on behalf of his people (1 Cor 10:1-5). This precludes baptism becoming a human work on the one hand and a mere physical emblem on the other. Any washing without the decisive authority, activity and presence of the Father, Son, and Spirit merely becomes a soaking.[39]

---

37. After quoting Gen 2:24, Paul states, "This mystery is great, but I am speaking of Christ and the church" (Eph 5:31-32).

38. Matt 3:11; Mark 1:8; Luke 3:16; Acts 1:4-5; 2:4-18; 11:15-17.

39. This, at least in part, is the meaning of the phrase "in the name of the Father, the Son, and the Holy Spirit" in the Great Commission (Matt 28:18-20), sometimes mistaken even today as a magical formula that guarantees the efficacy of baptism.

Scripture also vividly portrays baptism as a real unification with the death, burial, and resurrection of Jesus. We are crucified and buried "with Christ" (Rom 6:4; Gal 2:19; Col 2:12). It is not our own death that saves, but his. And we are raised with him in his resurrection to walk in a new life. Because of this our lives are "hidden" in Christ, only to be revealed for what they truly are at the Parousia (Col 3:3–4).

The language and theology of the Reformation needs to be revisited. Grace is not merely inward nor baptism merely outward.

PASTORAL CONCERNS

The fact is that we only know of the early church's baptismal practices from texts specifically theological and pastoral in nature. The authors of the New Testament directed their works to insiders, those already baptized in the name of Jesus. Detailed explanations of the ritual and topical expositions of its meaning had no place in the body of these works. Even the few narrative details in the Gospels and Acts have their own theological and pastoral aims. Every explicit and implicit reference to baptism applies to life in the kingdom.

With its descent, burial in water, and ascent, baptism concretely immerses the penitent believer into the story of Christ. The full ramifications of this can easily be overlooked. Understandably we gladly welcome God's pronouncement at baptism that we are his children. We revel in the outpouring of his Spirit. Jesus' baptism becomes our baptism. Initial joy can fade, though, when adherence to Jesus becomes uncomfortable or even perilous. Yet this anointing shared with the *beginning* of Jesus' ministry also calls us to share its *end*. After all, Jesus challenged his followers to take up their crosses and to follow him.[40] This too belongs to baptism.

The Second Gospel much more than the others pursues this particular implication. In the introduction (1:1–15), Mark organizes the material chiastically, bracketing the whole with "gospel" or "good news" (vv. 1, 15). The next pairing occurs with the word "desert" (vv. 4, 12) while "baptism" dominates the center (vv. 4–8 and 9–11). In this way Mark challenges the reader up front: The "good news" not only includes the glorious initiatory experience of baptism, it must also embrace "desert" moments.

---

40. See, for example, Mark 8:31–35; 9:30–35; 10:32–45.

Mark likewise frames the entire Gospel. Employing inclusio, another ancient literary device, he begins and ends his volume with a "tearing" (1:10 and 15:38) accompanied by a proclamation that Jesus is God's Son (1:11 and 15:39). Because these verbal links occur in the stories of Jesus' baptism and crucifixion, the two meld; baptism and crucifixion are inextricably combined.

Mark further reinforces this at a critical juncture in the narrative. After their request to obtain the two greatest positions in the imminent kingdom, Jesus asks James and John whether they can be baptized with the baptism with which he will be baptized, a clear reference to his even more imminent death (10:35–40). In conjunction with a number of other themes in the Second Gospel, Mark makes it clear that any immersion that does not take into account the call to suffering, to participating with Christ in those "desert" moments, and to taking up one's cross and following the road that leads to Calvary, is no baptism at all.[41]

Although primarily reflecting on baptism's implications for the future, 1 Peter reveals traces of a similar perspective. The letter addresses those who have been born again (1:3, 23; 2:2; 3:21) and who now must live as aliens (1:1 and 2:11) in a world of competing lordships.[42] The appropriate response is to follow one's calling, specifically identified as the imitation of the true Lord, Jesus Christ, as he hung on the cross.[43] Suffering for doing good is not the last word, however. Baptism also saves, rescuing the righteous from an ungodly world and vindicating them before the spiritual powers by means of Jesus' resurrection (3:20–22).

The church today, especially in North America, needs to become reacquainted with the call to suffering service. Christ died on the cross not to spare disciples from pain and suffering, but to call them to authentic lives of self-sacrifice. Baptism unites us with the crucifixion in more ways than one.

---

41. Several other Markan themes contribute to this overall picture, including the use of "road" (ὁδός). Jesus' oft repeated directives, "Don't tell," are punctuated only twice with charges to "tell" what the Lord has done, in each case only after the emptying of a tomb (5:19 and 16:7).

42. "Lord" (κύριε) was the appropriate address for kings, governors, and slave owners in the Greco-Roman world. For purposes of exhortation 1 Peter also includes husbands within that category (3:6).

43. Note the repeated "for this reason you were called" (1 Pet 2:21 and 3:9), each followed with a scriptural exposition and a direct link to the account of Jesus' crucifixion (2:21–25; 3:10–11; and 18–19).

Baptism places the believer within a larger community. Indeed, as discussed above, the immersed belong to a completely different humanity. In light of this, the biblical authors sometimes portray baptism as an identity marker.

In Matt 3:7–10, John the Baptist excoriates many of the Pharisees and Sadducees approaching him to be baptized. Their lack of repentance and fruitless lives reveal them as the venomous offspring of vipers rather than children of Abraham. True submission to God in baptism and a faithful life mark the child of the kingdom of heaven. Those responding accordingly, Jesus will baptize in the Holy Spirit, resulting in salvation; those who are not he will baptize in fire, resulting in condemnation (v. 12).[44]

Significantly, Matthew includes baptism among the final instructions given to the church (Matt 28:18–20). Jesus' last words carry special weight. The one on whom God has bestowed all authority in heaven and earth sends forth his followers to create a peculiar people, "disciples," from every nation, a task that includes "going," "baptizing," and "teaching" (28:18–20).

The Fourth Gospel provides perhaps the starkest delineation between insiders and outsiders. Everything is black and white, defined in terms of opposing pairs like light-dark and life-death. Not surprisingly, people also fall into binary opposites. Those with saving faith stick with Jesus and plumb the depths of his words even when seemingly impossible or occasionally disgusting. Others reject Jesus outright or abandon him soon after believing.[45]

The first of many such encounters occurs with respect to baptism.[46] Entrance into God's reign requires a birth from above constituting water and Spirit. Against all expectations, Nicodemus, a Jewish religious leader more familiar with divine revelation than most, balks at the inane idea of rebirth. Incredulous, he cannot or will not move away from a superfi-

---

44. This probably explains in part Matthew's addition that Jesus received baptism to "fulfill all righteousness" (Matt 3:15). Since Jesus did not require repentance, the forgiveness of sins, nor any preparation for coming into the Lord's presence (the primary reasons for the priestly washing), baptism confirms Jesus' identity as God's Son in a way qualitatively different than its confirmation of all God's other children.

45. Interesting examples occur in John 6:60–66 and then in 10:31–59, where Jesus' teaching persuades those "who had believed in him" that he instead should be stoned for blasphemy. See also John's summary of the first half of the Gospel (John 12:37–43).

46. See n. 36 above for the connections between the stories of John 2 and 4.

cial, literal understanding of Jesus' message. This respected Jewish male therefore departs unfaithful—he remains "in the dark" and adulterous.

The story does not end there. On the opposite end of the spectrum, a nameless Samaritan woman of questionable morals approaches Jesus in broad daylight at a watering hole, the customary location for finding spouses in the Bible. Cautiously, and in stark contrast to Nicodemus, she moves beyond a superficial understanding of Jesus' message to a deeper comprehension. As a result of this encounter with the living water, the adulteress departs from Jesus faithful (4:1–26). With even greater irony, the male disciples of Jesus arrive from the town of Sychar with loaves of bread; she returns with an entire field of wheat ready for harvest (vv. 31–38).

In a picturesque way, Revelation describes the church's constituents. Throughout the book, white raiment signifies those who belong in the throne room of God. The twenty-four elders wear robes of white (4:4). At other times and places, white robes get doled out to the martyrs (6:11), those coming from the great tribulation (7:13), and the bride of Christ (19:8). The hosts of heaven attending the wedding of the Lamb also sport garments of white linen (19:14). Even those on earth who remain holy because they have not polluted their garments walk with Christ adorned in white (Rev 3:4–5). Their robes have been washed, whitened by the red blood of the Lamb. [47] They stand apart from all others.

In Galatians, Paul argues that faith rather than circumcision is the true identity marker of those who wish to be children of Abraham, descended through Isaac as the true children of promise (ch. 3). Paul then anchors his argument by reminding his readers of their baptism. Baptism places one in Christ (or rather is how one "puts on" Christ). Additionally, the teaching that accompanied their immersion reminds them that they thereby washed away all barriers. The old designations Jew and Gentile or circumcised and uncircumcised have lost their relevance (vv. 26–28). Abraham's children place their faith in the Son of God, sealed by a common teaching and a common baptism. At the close of the letter Paul reminds the Gentile believers that they follow the Law

---

47. See Rev 7:9–17. The opening doxology of the Apocalypse (1:5–6) may also connect baptism to the washing away of sins and the blood of Christ. It also would explicitly tie the whitened robes to the priesthood. (The color and context alone may do that anyway.) The original text here, i.e. the choice between λύω or λούω, is uncertain. If the latter is not original, it still attests a significant early Christian interpretation of baptism.

of Christ as opposed to the Law of Moses, they are a new creation set apart from ethnic distinctions,[48] and they are the Israel of God.[49]

Paul also touches upon this in Romans 9–11. At stake is the faithfulness of God vis-à-vis Israel. Paul argues that God has always defined "Israel" as the faithful and that all who enter, including Gentiles, must do so on the same basis, by faith. Unexpectedly, Paul does not suggest that Jesus opens a new door for Gentile inclusion. Instead Jesus has ever been the sole means of entry, even before the incarnation. Paul concludes, then, that the "gospel" was preached throughout Israel's history by such eminent spokespersons as Moses (10:5–13) and Elijah (10:14–21). In a sense, the pious Jews of the past placed their faith in Jesus Christ and, with all the baptized, confessed him as Lord (10:9). This is why not all Israel (those who *claim* a special relationship with God) are Israel (those who *believe* in his Son) and why all Israel (as God defines it) shall be saved.[50]

This raises another, related issue. Since baptism marks incorporation into the people of God, it coincidentally points to the requisite unity of that people. Although infrequently mentioned in the New Testament, this theme must have been foundational for we find it in the earliest creeds.[51]

Paul's passing reference to baptismal catechesis in 1 Cor 12:13 furthers his argument against divisiveness. The church is one body having imbibed the one Spirit. Thus Christian unity has empowerment from on high. The paranetic portion of Ephesians begins with a slightly modified version of a traditional formulation—the "seven ones" (4:4–6).[52] Under the one Spirit Paul places one body and one hope. With the one Lord come one faith and one baptism. God the Father is "over," "through," and "in" all. The wholeness of deity and Christian practice attest the need for Christian unity.

---

48. In 1 Cor 7 Paul also uses "new creation" in contrast to circumcision and uncircumcision. Note especially that this occurs within a discussion of the traditional baptismal triad (see below).

49. Gal 6:12–16, see also v. 2.

50. Rom 9:1–8, especially v. 6, and 11:25–27.

51. 1 Cor 12:13; Gal 3:26–28; Eph 4:4–6; and Col 2:9–11.

52. He alters the first triad because of his ecclesiological focus. The Spirit would have originally stood as the first element. Paul frequently marks a shift from theology to paranesis with παρακαλῶ.

Unity with Christ demands community with his people. On the one hand, today's prevailing culture of rugged and exaggerated individualism desperately needs to hear this message. There is no such thing as an individual Christian. On the other hand, those who thrive on dissension and divisiveness, sometimes even "in the name of the Lord," and others who so easily abandon their community of faith at the smallest slight, need to reflect on the significance of their inclusion in the one body through the one Spirit at baptism.

The New Testament most often brings baptism to bear on the necessity of living as people who no longer belong to this world. Those who have repented, had their sins washed away, and received the Holy Spirit lead dramatically different lives, but they still find themselves tempted to participate in a surrounding culture tainted by sin.

The preaching of John the Baptist and its ethical character provide the starting point in the Gospels, especially in the expanded treatments of Matthew and Luke. But John's baptism, even though administered for repentance and the forgiveness of sins, lacked the power necessary for complete transformation. This only Christ could provide.

The Book of Acts narrates the fulfillment of John the Baptist's prophecy. At Pentecost and thereafter, Jesus baptizes those who place their faith in him. This has a recognizable effect. Those who receive the Spirit display a lifestyle consistent with kingdom ethics (2:40-47 and elsewhere). Those rejecting the Spirit, no matter how sincere and pious, look quite different (such as the Sanhedrin in 7:51-53 and even some believers in 5:1-10 and 8:13-21).

Paul reminds the saints in Rome that baptism united them with the death of Christ where sin received its deathblow. The old person has died so that the new creation, made in the image of Christ, might live a new life (chs. 5-6, especially 6:1-11). Believers therefore have an obligation to live in the Spirit (ch. 8) and not to allow sin to reign in God's new creation (ch. 6).

In 1 Corinthians, a list of sins epitomizes the types of people who cannot inherit the kingdom of God. At the same time, many of the Corinthian converts had previously engaged in precisely these ungodly behaviors. The difference came with their washing, sanctification, and justification (6:9-11). As a result, they should no longer participate in deeds of darkness nor should they tolerate those within the community of faith who do (5:1—6:8).

According to Ephesians, those who have been made alive with, raised with, and seated with Christ now live in the Spirit in a manner radically different than when they had aligned themselves with the "ruler of the power of the air" (Eph 2:1–7). Having been born again they have put off the old person, characterizing them as disobedient children (2:2), and put on Christ and their "new person" to become beloved children of God (4:20–24 and 4:31—5:2). In chapters four and five Paul contrasts former behavior with kingdom life. For example, those who once used their hands to steal for themselves now put those hands to work to provide for others (4:28). Colossians likewise employs baptism as a reminder of the concrete nature of the new life (Col 3:8–15), but baptism also has a certain antagonistic relationship with other theologies, whether Greek or Jewish. The believer joins Christ in triumphal procession, celebrating his victory over all other spiritual forces (2:6–15). (As in Ephesians, the demonic powers can have a deleterious effect on human behavior.)

The only baptismal reference in the Pastoral Epistles also addresses Christian ethics. Once having lived ignorantly like the rest of the world, Christians now must imitate their Savior—his goodness and love of humanity. This is due to the fact that Christ saved them through "washing" and the renewal by the "Holy Spirit" that Christ poured upon them (Titus 3:1–7).[53]

According to 1 Peter, life in the present must reflect the nature of the God who created us through imperishable seed (1 Pet 1:22—2:3). This displays itself in a transformed life recognizable to, even if unappreciated by, outsiders.[54] Baptism relates to a "good conscience" (3:21). In this regard the parallel construction in 3:16 (and perhaps 2:19) is noteworthy. The phrase "doing good" recurs throughout these discussions as well (2:12–15, 18–20; 3:2–6, 13–17; cf. 4:19). Baptism serves as a catalyst for a proactive stance in the world.

Baptism invites us to participate in eternity. Immersion unites us with Christ's Passion and God's people in the past, reminds us of our true identity in the present, and connects us to the future.

Although few entertain any longer the idea that 1 Peter served as a baptismal catechesis, the ritual lies in the background of most of the letter. The opening paragraph blesses the God who caused us to be born

---

53. The language of inheritance in Titus 3:7 also parallels Pauline language elsewhere regarding baptism as an identity marker.

54. See 1 Pet 2:12, 15, 19, 21; 3:1–2, 9, 14, 16–17; 4:14–16.

again into three eschatological realities: a living hope, an imperishable inheritance, and a prepared salvation (1:3–5). Immersion provides assurance about the future.

Paul reminds us that the Spirit believers receive is merely a "down payment" of a consummation yet to appear (2 Cor 1:22; 5:12) and that the ascent out of the baptismal font prefigures a final resurrection (Rom 6).[55]

The canon closes with the following observation of John in Revelation:

> Blessed are those who have washed their robes so that they will have the right to the tree of life and may enter through the gates into the city. Outside are the dogs and witches and fornicators and murderers and idolaters and everyone who loves and practices falsehood. (22:14–15)[56]

Paul's tone in 1 Corinthians should serve as a warning to those who would make too much of baptism. The Christians in Corinth divided the church based on prominent individuals, personal achievements, elevating certain spiritual gifts over others, and social status. In the introduction (chs. 1–4), Paul distances himself from anything that might allow people to boast about any special religious relationship with him. He expresses thanks that he only baptized a relatively small number while sharing the gospel in that city (1 Cor 1:14–16). Apparently some Corinthians idolized those who spoke more eloquently or who had larger numbers of converts, so Paul downplays his own role and that of others so that Christ might be properly elevated. With an amusing wordplay, Paul reminds the Christians that salvation belongs to God. The roles of planter (Paul as evangelist) and irrigator (Apollos as successful baptizer) are merely ancillary to what only God can accomplish (3:5–9).

Baptism resurfaces in 1 Corinthians as part of Paul's teaching about Christians' consumption of food sacrificed to idols (chs. 8–10). Some Corinthians, eager to maintain social connections (eating at temples was the equivalent of today's "power lunch"), attempted to rationalize participation in the pagan world by refusing to recognize the existence of

---

55. An enigmatic reference to baptism for the dead appears in 1 Cor 15:29. Whatever its particular meaning, it also connects immersion with the eschatological resurrection.

56. It is recognized that Revelation does not appear in all Christian canons and that its actual placement in the order of books is an accident of history.

other gods and goddesses (an idea they derived from Paul's own teaching). They implied that the reality of Christian rituals such as baptism and the Eucharist provided divine, almost magical, protection against any external spiritual evils. Paul responds by reminding the Corinthians of biblical history. The Israelites too had been baptized and celebrated the Lord's Supper while in the wilderness (vv. 1–6). Regardless, once they began playing around with idolatry they lost their valued position and fell under divine judgment. Corpses strewn about the desert serve as a sufficient reminder of the need for total devotion to God.[57]

Baptism is not a work. It is not magic. To view it as such can have serious consequences.

CONCLUSION

Although the Restoration Movement breathed the air of the Enlightenment and positively welcomed the victories of "the common man" signaled by the American and French Revolutions, this allowed for a fresh reexamination of central Christian doctrines. As a result, Stone-Campbell churches have a rich understanding of baptism worth including in larger discussions about the rite's purposes and meaning.

Baptism immerses one into a process of salvation that begins with the "new birth," but grows toward the "full stature" of Christ occurring as a result of God's will for and work in the lives of his people. Baptism requires little on our part—faith and confession. That one does not baptize oneself (active or middle voice) but is baptized (passive voice), in contrast to other Jewish washings, draws attention to the fact that one submits completely to another—it is birth "from above," it is being buried "with Christ," it is being raised from the dead by God who so raised Jesus in order that we might live in newness of life and be empowered by his Spirit for a ministry of holiness. God is the Creator and we the created. For these reasons there is a ready answer to the question posed at the beginning of the chapter. Baptism is rightfully categorized as "most important."

---

57. It is likely that the healing of the lame man in John 5:1–15 plays a similar role. Whereas the stirred waters of the Jewish *miqvah* failed to heal, Jesus, the source of "living water," makes him whole again. The following narrative, however, suggests this person hardly qualified as a disciple. Jesus sought him out and threatened that, despite his purification, things would become worse than before without repentance and a changed life.

FURTHER READING

Campbell, Alexander. *The Christian System*. 2nd ed. Pittsburg: Forrester and Campbell, 1839.

Morrison, C. C. *The Meaning of Baptism*. Chicago: Disciples Publication Society, 1914.

9

Baptism among Pentecostals

STEVE STUDEBAKER

NESTLED AMID MOUNTAINS AND alpine forests, the cool waters of Medicine Lake in Northern California are where I was baptized. At the time and in the recall of memory, the natural beauty of the surroundings infused the experience with a mystical quality that my Pentecostal theology of water baptism does not. For three years, my family attended a Pentecostal church with a broken baptismal. During the period we were a part of that church, no effort was made to fix the baptismal, no one seems to have missed the use of the baptismal, and to my knowledge no one in the church was baptized there or anywhere else. Such a state of affairs in a Roman Catholic or Lutheran church, for example, would be unthinkable. Consequently, the first challenge for a Pentecostal theology of water baptism is that Pentecostalism, at least within North America and except for Oneness Pentecostalism, has an underdeveloped theology and practice of water baptism. An additional challenge for the task of this chapter is that although Scripture says, "there is one body and one Spirit ... one Lord, one faith, one baptism, one God and Father of all" (Eph 4:4–5), we need to recognize that Pentecostalism contains, at the levels of practice and doctrine, many baptisms. Therefore, we need to trust that the grace of the one Spirit, one Lord, and one God and Father ultimately transcends the diversity of Pentecostal practices and doctrines of water baptism. In light of the diversity of global Pentecostalism and my affiliation with the Assemblies of God (a Classical Pentecostal denomination), this analysis focuses on the Pentecostal ways of understanding water baptism within the North American forms of the Pentecostal movement, which include Classical Pentecostalism, the Charismatic movement, and Oneness Pentecostalism. With the above challenges and scope in mind, this article sets out to accomplish the following: first, to portray the diverse nature of Pentecostalism; second, to outline the challenges the diversity of the movement poses to an effort to set forth a Pentecostal theology of water baptism; and third, to describe the understanding of water baptism within Classical Pentecostalism, the Charismatic movement, and Oneness Pentecostalism.

PENTECOSTALISM(S)!

The rise and global expansion of Pentecostalism is one of the most notable stories of Christianity in the twentieth century and first years of the twenty-first century. Pentecostalism, in its various forms, has attracted more than 602 million adherents. Within the span of a century, Pentecostalism grew from scattered bands of revival seekers to a global movement that comprises nearly one third of Christians worldwide. Although Pentecostalism started primarily as a movement within North American conservative Protestantism, it has now become a global phenomenon that transcends confessional boundaries. Indeed, most Pentecostals now live outside of North America. For instance, as of 2007 the worldwide number of Pentecostals, Charismatics, and Third Wavers or charismatic-type Christians was approximately 602 million, and roughly two-thirds of these were non-white and non-Western. Furthermore, the majority of those classified as Pentecostal in these statistics would not be considered as such in the Classical Pentecostal sense (of the 602 million perhaps about 15 percent are Classical Pentecostals).[1]

The worldwide Pentecostal groups operate in spiritual gifts and participate in charismatic forms of worship, ministry, and personal spiritualities, but do not necessarily hold to a unified set of doctrines even in respect to Pentecostalism's most celebrated doctrine of Spirit baptism and the practice of speaking in tongues.[2] For example, the South American Chilean Pentecostal movement and the large Brazil for Christ Evangelical Pentecostal Church (*Igreja Evangélica Pentecostal "Brasil*

---

1. Barrett, Johnson, and Crossing, "Missiometrics 2007," 32.

2. Matthew S. Clark notes that the issue of tongues has not played the *sine qua non* role of identifying authentic Pentecostalism among South African Pentecostals as it has among Western Pentecostals. See Clark, "Initial Evidence," 208.

para Cristo") embrace the experience of Spirit baptism, but do not insist on the doctrine of initial evidence. Among Pentecostal groups in Britain and Europe, such as the Elim movement, the doctrine of initial evidence has never been accepted as the exclusive sign of Spirit baptism, and among groups that do formally hold to the doctrine, such as the Assemblies of God in Great Britain and Ireland, it is losing widespread support.[3] Moreover, theological diversity also characterizes Pentecostal views on water baptism. The diverse character of Pentecostal movements presents significant challenges to an attempt to identify *the* Pentecostal view on water baptism.

PROBLEMS FOR A PENTECOSTAL THEOLOGY OF WATER BAPTISM

The first problem for discussing *the* Pentecostal theology of water baptism is that it does not exist. The Pentecostal movement is not coincident with any one denomination, theological perspective, or doctrine. Pentecostalism is a global movement that encompasses distinct Pentecostal denominations and Christians within the traditional Protestant churches and the Catholic Church. Although the habit has been to portray Pentecostalism as originating in the North American revivals led by Charles Fox Parham in Topeka, Kansas and William J. Seymour in the Azusa Street Mission in Los Angeles, California, recent studies on global Pentecostalism have highlighted the global points of origin for the Pentecostal movement and thereby have effectively challenged the habit of North American interpretations of Pentecostalism to privilege the North American sources of the movement.[4] In support of global origins for Pentecostalism, Allan Anderson cites the revivals in Korea (1903), China (1908), and India (in Tamil Nadu in 1860–1865, in Travancore in 1873–1881, and with Pandita Mukti's Mission in 1905–1907); all of which predated and/or were not connected with the Azusa Street Revival. He also highlights that news of Mukti's Indian revival and other Pentecostal revivals in Venezuela and Norway sparked the Pentecostal revival in Chile that led to the formation of the Chilean Methodist Pentecostal Church under the leadership of Willis

---

3. Anderson, *Pentecostalism*, 65, 73, 94–95.

4. Anderson, "Revising," and Creech, "Visions of Glory." For an interpretation that supports the traditional North American source of the global Pentecostal movement, see Robeck, "Pentecostal Origins from a Global Perspective."

Hoover.⁵ Thus, the origins and radiating centers of influence for early Pentecostalism were not exclusively North American.

The historical and theological reality is that the Pentecostal movement is pluriform, which makes the undertaking of defining Pentecostalism a difficult task. As Harold Hunter points out, "the ubiquity of the Pentecostal-Charismatic movement as it launches into the twenty-first century outdistances current attempts of classification and clarification."⁶ The result of the diversity of the Pentecostal movement is that no single view within Pentecostalism can function as *the* Pentecostal or meta-Pentecostal understanding of water baptism. Even the Classical Pentecostal theology of water baptism cannot be articulated without equivocation. For example, the International Pentecostal Holiness Church is a Classical Pentecostal denomination and has allowed infant baptism, even if they practiced it infrequently (or perhaps never).⁷ Furthermore, Cecil Robeck and Jerry Sandidge point out that some Pentecostal churches, such as "the Iglesia Methodista Pentecostal (Chile), the Iglesia Pentecostal de Chili, the Mülheim Association of Christian Fellowships of Germany, and the Yugoslavian Kristova Duhovna Crkva Malokrštenih," practice infant baptism.⁸

A second problem is that Pentecostal theology has not produced a unique theology of water baptism. For the most part, the Pentecostal views on water baptism are derivative. On the one hand, the majority of the early Pentecostals who became members of the first North American Pentecostal denominations, such as the Assemblies of God, Pentecostal Assemblies of Canada, the Church of God, and the International Church of the Foursquare Gospel, adopted a believer's baptism understanding of water baptism. On the other hand, most Pentecostal-Charismatic believers in Protestant churches and the Catholic Church adopt the view of water baptism of their host church. Even among the recent and innovative Pentecostal theological projects, such as those by Frank D. Macchia and Amos Yong, significant advances in a Pentecostal theology of water baptism have not been set forth in a detailed way (I will address the pro-

5. Anderson, "Revising," 152–56.
6. Hunter, "Reflections," 320.
7. Ibid., 332.
8. Robeck and Sandidge, "Ecclesiology," 532. Robeck and Sandidge's article was originally presented in 1988 as part of the third quinquennium (1985–1989) of the international Roman Catholic/Pentecostal Dialogue in Emmetten, Switzerland.

posals of Macchia and Yong in the section on the Classical Pentecostal view of water baptism).

A third problem is that the derivative nature of Pentecostal notions of water baptism seems to be linked to Pentecostalism's focus on Spirit baptism and/or charismatic experience and spiritual gifts. Until the 1990s, the theological issue of Spirit baptism, the normativity of speaking in tongues as the initial evidence of Spirit baptism, and the perennial role of spiritual gifts in the church predominated Pentecostal scholarship. Consequently, Pentecostal scholarship tended to be preoccupied with hermeneutical issues related to the exegesis of Luke–Acts. Dialogue with non-Pentecostal scholars revolved around defending the Pentecostal perspectives on the above issues. Illustrative of the character of this phase of Pentecostal theological reflection are the seminal texts by James D. G. Dunn, *Baptism in the Holy Spirit* (1970), who critiques the Pentecostal understanding of Spirit baptism, and Roger Stronstad, *The Charismatic Theology of St. Luke* (1984), who supports the Pentecostal view of Spirit baptism by interpreting Luke–Acts in terms of redaction criticism. The point is that Pentecostals generally have not given a theology of water baptism sustained attention.[9] The exception to this are Charismatic theologians within the traditional Protestant and Catholic Churches who have sought to understand the relationship between water baptism and Spirit baptism, but again the effort has been to explicate Spirit baptism's meaning within the received theology of water baptism.

PENTECOSTAL VIEWS OF WATER BAPTISM

The modern Pentecostal movement has three primary forms that have developed diachronically and now co-exist. These three variations are Classical Pentecostalism, the Charismatic movement, and the Third Wave or Neocharismatic movement. Although rejecting traditional trinitarianism, Oneness Pentecostalism fits within the category of Classical Pentecostalism. The following section focuses on the Classical and

9. Thus the scant documentary sources available. Robeck and Sandidge list only two book-length treatments on water baptism: Gortner et al., *Water Baptism*, and Beall, *Newness*. In the process of researching for this essay, I was unable to uncover more recent book-length treatments. Even more telling of the dearth of Pentecostal theological reflection on water baptism is the fact that Robeck and Sandidge's journal article should be a key resource for anyone seeking to explore in detail a Pentecostal theology of water baptism, and particularly the historical sources of it within the Pentecostal movement. See Robeck and Sandidge, "Ecclesiology."

Oneness Pentecostal and Charismatic views on water baptism. The essay does not address water baptism within the Third Wave. The Third Wave is an elusive group in respect to definitions and categorizations. It is most known by the notable leaders and revival centers within the movement, such as John Wimber (1934–1998) and the Vineyard churches; John Arnott and the Toronto Airport Vineyard Christian Fellowship; John Kilpatrick and the Brownsville, Florida revival, and more recently, Todd Bentley and the Lakeland, Florida revival. The Third Wave also can refer to the more or less evangelical churches in the UK and North America that have integrated, in varying degrees, charismatic worship styles and spiritualities, but have not adopted a distinct Pentecostal theology or theology of water baptism. For this reason, I have decided to focus on the Pentecostal movements in North America that have in some sense a distinct, even if embryonic, Pentecostal theological tradition or have sought to integrate their theologies of Spirit and water baptism.

CLASSICAL PENTECOSTAL VIEW(S) OF WATER BAPTISM

Classical Pentecostalism effectively began 1 January 1901 when Agnes Ozman (1870–1937) experienced a baptism in the Holy Spirit with the sign of speaking in tongues. Ozman was a student of Charles Fox Parham (1873–1929) at Bethel Bible School in Topeka, Kansas. Parham had Wesleyan-Holiness roots and founded the school to prepare missionaries for the great end-time revival that he believed would break forth in the new millennium and usher in the return of Christ. A student at Parham's Houston Bible Institute, William J. Seymour (1870–1922) was a black Holiness preacher who became the chief leader of the Azusa Street Revivals in 1906–1909 and 1911–1912, which is the more well-known beginning of North American Pentecostalism. The Azusa Street Revival effectively began 9 April 1906, when Edward Lee spoke in tongues at home while Seymour prayed for him. Seymour rushed to the Asberry residence at 214 Bonnie Brae Street to report the news and several others soon received the gift of tongues. Revival erupted and within a week the Asberry home could not contain the increasing throngs who came to observe and participate in the new revival. The search for a larger venue led Seymour to the dilapidated two-story building at 312 Azusa Street. Under Seymour's leadership, Azusa Street became the focal point and a pilgrimage site for the two periods of revival that launched the Pentecostal movement.

During the early years, controversies erupted that led to splits within Pentecostalism, which later became institutionalized in the formation of the first Pentecostal denominations. This first controversy was over the relationship between Spirit baptism and sanctification. In the initial phase of the Pentecostal movement, a majority of its supporters were from Wesleyan-Holiness backgrounds. When they came into the Pentecostal experience, they retained the Wesleyan-Holiness distinction between conversion and entire sanctification and added to it the experience of Spirit baptism for empowered ministry. Moreover, the Classical Pentecostal understanding of Spirit baptism as a distinct work that empowers the recipient for ministry has clear antecedence in late-nineteenth century Reformed evangelical revivalists such as Reuben A. Torrey (1856–1928) and Dwight L. Moody (1837–1899). The resulting combination of holiness sanctification and Reformed Spirit Baptism was a theology of three works of grace—conversion/justification, entire sanctification, and Spirit baptism.

In 1911, William Durham's (1873–1912) "Finished Work of Calvary" theology and Seymour's Holiness doctrine of sanctification came into sharp conflict. Although Durham received Spirit baptism at Azusa Street in 1907, he returned to Azusa, while Seymour was away on a preaching tour, and preached against the three stage holiness sequence of conversion, sanctification, and Spirit baptism, and advocated in its place a two stage paradigm of conversion-sanctification (doctrine of progressive sanctification) and Spirit baptism. Durham insisted that sanctification is part of the salvation provided by Christ on the cross (hence, finished work of Calvary) and that Spirit baptism is the only subsequent work of grace. When Seymour returned to Azusa and Durham spurned his appeal to desist in critiquing holiness theology, Seymour banned Durham from Azusa. Durham in turn began to preach in a nearby building and a majority of the Azusa participants followed him.

In the wake of the Durham controversy, the Azusa revival and Seymour's leadership in the Pentecostal movement gradually waned and within several years the divide between Holiness and Finished Work Pentecostals ossified institutionally in the formation of the first Pentecostal denominations. A collateral affect of the Durham affair and the formation of the first Pentecostal denominations was the replacement of the interracial texture of the Azusa revivals with predominantly racially segregated groups. The holiness denominations that formed are the Pentecostal Holiness Church (now International Pentecostal Holiness Church), Church of God in Christ, and the Church of God (Cleveland). The Finished Work denominations are the Assemblies of God, the Pentecostal Assemblies of Canada, and the International Church of the Foursquare Gospel. Despite the difference over the doctrine of sanctification, the doctrine that Spirit baptism is an experience subsequent to conversion that empowers for ministry and that speaking in tongues is its proper evidence unites the two and three stages groups as Classical Pentecostals. Moreover, Classical Pentecostals tend to hold to a similar understanding of water baptism.

Pentecostals prefer the terminology of ordinance to sacrament to describe water baptism (and the Lord's Supper). For many Pentecostals, "sacrament" conveys magical notions of the communication of grace. However, the Pentecostal rejection of baptismal regeneration rests, at least in part, on a misunderstanding of *ex opere operato* in Catholic theology and the fact that the Lutheran practice of infant baptism presumes the gift nature of faith and grace. For example, Myer Pearlman critiques sacramental efficiency, when he states, "water baptism in itself has no saving power."[10] The Pentecostal theologian Larry D. Hart better expresses the relationship between the faith and the divine agency dimensions of sacramental efficiency when he says that "only as an act of Spirit-enabled repentance and faith is baptism efficacious."[11] Thus, "sacramental" views of water baptism (e.g., Lutheran and Catholic) do not assign "saving power" to water baptism *per se*. In sacramental theology, a sacrament is a tangible item that signifies and communicates something else. Christian sacraments signify and effect or confer grace by the power of God at work in and through the elements. They do not do so in a magical way nor are they inherently holy or significant in a religious sense. As signs, they are physical elements that signify a spiritual dimension of grace. They communicate grace to human beings because God chose them to do so. As a consequence of their divine institution, they infallibly accomplish their divine purpose, which is the conveyance of grace to the participant. When the sacraments are received in faith they confer grace to the recipient by the work of Christ.[12]

10. Pearlman, *Doctrines*, 355.

11. Hart, *Truth*, 586.

12. For further elaboration on the nature of sacramental efficiency, see Studebaker, "*Ex opere operato*," 328–30.

For example, a Mother's Day card is paper and ink, but also much more. When the mother opens it, the card represents and conveys to her in some measure the love of her child. Or, when lovers exchange kisses, they express and give their love to each other through them. A sacrament of God's grace is similar, but its instrumental function is more profound. In the above examples, the card and the kisses communicate love between people, but in a restricted sense compared to a sacrament's communication of divine grace. The reason is that God is Spirit and omnipresent and consequently can dwell within a human person in a more intimate way than a human person can experience unity with another human person. Thus, when a person receives the grace of Christ in a sacrament, the presence of Christ is there in an ontological and personal sense that surpasses the personal presence conveyed by symbols in human-human interaction.

In recent years, and particularly facilitated by ecumenical dialogues, advances have been achieved in Pentecostal appreciation and understanding of sacramental theology. One example is that both parties in the Roman Catholic/Pentecostal international dialogue agreed that "God's gift precedes and makes possible human receiving of the benefits of the sacraments [and] there is mutual affirmation that water baptism requires faith."[13] A second one is the work of Frank D. Macchia that has shown that Pentecostal spirituality, and especially speaking in tongues, is a sacramental way of experiencing the eschatological and redemptive presence of God.[14] Yet, I suspect that although Pentecostal professional theologians will readily recognize that Catholics affirm the precedence of grace and faith for sacramental efficiency, at the popular or lay level of the churches such ecumenical understanding is less common.

The terminology of ordinance also reflects the Pentecostal belief that participation in water baptism is primarily an act of obedience.[15] E. S. Williams (quoting an unnamed source) reflects the obediential character of an ordinance when he defines it as, "that which is decreed or

---

13. Kärkkäinen, *Spiritus*, 206. For a full description and analysis of the discussion of water baptism in the Roman Catholic/Pentecostal Dialogue, see *Spiritus*, 199–233. *Spiritus* provides a thorough treatment of the first three quinquennia (1972–1989) and Kärkkäinen's discussion of the fourth phase of the dialogue (1990–1997) is available in *Ad ultimum terra*.

14. Macchia, "Tongues," 61–76.

15. Hunter, "Reflections," 329.

ordained of God; established rule; a prescribed practice of usage."[16] The logic is that since Christ was baptized, and he commanded his followers to be baptized, then Christians should be baptized to follow the example of Christ and to obey his command.[17] Of course obedience to Christ is an important Christian virtue, but this way of thinking about water baptism is essentially moralistic. The event of water baptism offers little to the Christian life other than fulfilling a prescription of moral obedience. Pearlman expresses the awkward Pentecostal perspective on water baptism when he recognizes that "we cannot say that the rite is absolutely essential to salvation. But we may insist that it is essential to full obedience."[18] The thin theology of water baptism corresponds to its peripheral place in the life of many Pentecostal churches; as Robeck and Sandidge point out, "baptism has an ambiguous role among Pentecostals."[19] Thus, without a deep theology of water baptism, the practice of water baptism becomes functionally irrelevant in many Pentecostal churches.

In addition to being an ordinance, water baptism is a symbol of an accomplished experience of grace. Some Pentecostals draw on the Augustinian phrase that water baptism is an "outward and visible" expression of an "inward and invisible" reality.[20] Entailed in the symbolic understanding of water baptism is the rejection of sacramental efficiency.[21] Raymond Pruitt states that "the signs and symbols themselves do not impart spiritual grace, but are expressions of what has been imparted through our relationship with Christ."[22] Thus, water baptism outwardly symbolizes the accomplished and previous inward experience of the grace of Christ. Michael Dusing clarifies that "baptism symbolizes a great spiritual reality (salvation) which has revolutionized the life of a believer; nevertheless, the symbol itself should never be elevated to the level of that higher reality."[23] For Pentecostals water baptism is a symbol

---

16. Williams, *Systematic Theology*, 3:149.

17. Dusing, "New Testament Church," 558. The joint statement by the Oneness and Trinitarian Pentecostals carries on this perspective; see Society for Pentecostal Studies, "Oneness–Trinitarian Report," 208.

18. Pearlman, *Doctrines*, 355.

19. Robeck and Sandidge, "Ecclesiology," 508.

20. Pruitt, *Fundamentals of the Faith*, 239–40.

21. Gee, "Baptism and Salvation," 8–9.

22. Pruitt, *Fundamentals of the Faith*, 240.

23. Dusing, "New Testament Church," 562.

of an accomplished fact or experience of grace. Ernest Williams argues on the basis of Matt 28:18–19 that Jesus commanded his disciples first to go and to make disciples and then to baptize them. And further maintains that the pattern of Acts shows that "baptism followed faith."[24] The recipient of water baptism is a believer who has already repented of sin and experienced the grace of Christ.

Reflecting the Classical Pentecostal view of water baptism, the "Oneness–Trinitarian Pentecostal Final Report," states "we . . . consider baptism as distinct from salvation but as still necessary as an act of obedience in which conversion by faith/repentance in Christ is expressed and confirmed. We recognize this act as deeply spiritual . . . and richly theological in meaning."[25] But just before the above statement, the Final Report notes that an issue that divides the Oneness Pentecostals and the Classical Pentecostals is:

> The relationship of water baptism and salvation; specifically, the Oneness Pentecostal understanding of water baptism as essential to salvation and the Trinitarian Pentecostal tendency to regard baptism as a sign of salvation that is not essential to it.[26]

The paradox and tension is that although Pentecostals primarily see water baptism as a symbol of an inner experience of grace, which is not essential to salvation, they also see water baptism as a symbol that dramatizes in a very tangible way the experience of dying with Christ to sin and rising within him to new life. Recognizing, if not theologically articulating, the deep significance of water baptism for the Christian life, Myer Pearlman refers to water baptism as a "sacred drama."[27] Again, Robeck and Sandidge are on the mark when they state, "[B]y making it a rule to be obeyed without a context, it becomes an issue of secondary importance. It becomes a symbol of something that is believed *not* to be there at all, the presence of Christ, and the church must look elsewhere to find that presence."[28] Thus, for Pentecostals, water baptism is a rich theological and spiritual experience, but ultimately one unnecessary for salvation.

---

24. Williams, *Systematic Theology*, 3:151.
25. Society for Pentecostal Studies, "Oneness–Trinitarian Report," 209.
26. Ibid.
27. Pearlman, *Doctrines*, 356.
28. Robeck and Sandidge, "Ecclesiology," 527.

Underlying the symbolic perspective of water baptism is a theology of divine immediacy. Pentecostals maintain that all people have direct access to the presence and grace of God. As Myer Pearlman states, "New Testament Christianity is not a ritualistic religion; at the heart of it is man's direct contact with God through the Spirit."[29] Frank Macchia also notes that from a Pentecostal perspective notions of sacramental efficiency seem to institutionalize and formalize the work of the Spirit and undermine the "cherished belief in the unmediated gracious presence of God conveyed directly to the believer by the Holy Spirit."[30] For Pentecostals, the forgiveness and grace of God can be had with the expression of faith without the need of ecclesiastical means.

Pentecostals also believe water baptism signifies the death, burial, and resurrection of Christ.[31] By participating in water baptism, the believer publicly identifies with the death and resurrection of Christ. The "public" qualifier is important because water baptism does not in any way cause or effect the salvific union or identification of the believer with Christ, but rather publicly dramatizes an accomplished experience of grace and consummated relationship with Christ.[32] Furthermore, the symbolism of death and resurrection is a key reason that Classical Pentecostals typically advocate immersion rather than sprinkling as the mode of water baptism. The submergence and emergence of the believer in and from the waters of baptism symbolize the believer's participation in the death and resurrection of Christ and especially of the believer's death to sin and new life of righteousness.[33]

Water baptism also includes a public identification of believers with Christ's church. Following Matt 28:19, trinitarian Pentecostals practice a trinitarian confession of faith in water baptism.[34] The exception to the trinitarian pattern is of course Oneness Pentecostals, who baptize in the name of Jesus only on the basis of Acts 2:38. Pentecostals see water baptism as a testimony to the world that they have confessed Jesus as their Lord and Savior and that henceforth they belong to his kingdom.

---

29. Pearlman, *Doctrines*, 352.

30. Macchia, "Tongues," 61–62.

31. Gee, "Baptism and Salvation," 11; Gortner, "Importance of Water Baptism," 39, 43–43; and Pruitt, *Fundamentals of the Faith*, 240.

32. Dusing, "New Testament Church," 559, 562.

33. Pearlman, *Doctrines*, 356 and Williams, *Systematic Theology*, 3:150.

34. Gortner, "Apostolic Formula."

Pearlman declares that "by the rite of baptism the convert, figuratively speaking, publicly dons the uniform of the kingdom of Christ."[35] Water baptism identifies the believer as one who has participated in the grace of Christ and become a member of the community of Christ.[36] Yet, as Robeck and Sandidge maintain, the corporate identification of the believer with the body of Christ is an underdeveloped and under-recognized aspect of water baptism within Pentecostalism.[37] The influence of the evangelical and Holiness tradition on Pentecostalism leads it to favor individualistic understandings of the nature of conversion and the Christian life. For example, in North America, Pentecostals emphasize church attendance as a mark of Christian obedience, but do not have a highly developed ecclesiology and sense that the larger, even worldwide, body of Christ, informs the individual's Christian identity.

The conditions of water baptism are repentance and faith in Christ. The conditions of repentance and faith are the reasons Classical Pentecostals exclude infants from receiving water baptism (although as noted above, the International Pentecostal Holiness Church does not prohibit infant baptism). James Lee Beal's interpretation of the practice of baptism in Acts 2 and 16 expresses a common Classical Pentecostal perspective on infant baptism:

> It is clear from these accounts and others that the apostles of Jesus Christ taught that baptism in water is the God-required act of obedience that testifies of a genuine repentance and faith. They did not teach that infants should be brought to the waters of baptism. Baptism was part of the believer's response to God's offer of salvation, along with repentance, faith, and receiving the gift of the Holy Spirit. Infants could not repent or believe the Word and spiritually respond to God. Therefore, they were not baptized.[38]

An additional reason for rejecting infant baptism is the uncertain status of the infant as a sinner in need of forgiveness. Pentecostals often adopt the notion that human persons prior to the age of accountability and the ability to make a conscious profession of faith in Christ are saved.[39] In

---

35. Pearlman, *Doctrines*, 356.

36. Hart, *Truth*, 585, 587; Higgins, Dusing, and Tallman, *Introduction to Theology*, 173–74; Horton, *Systematic Theology*, 559; and Pruitt, *Fundamentals of the Faith*, 240.

37. Robeck and Sandidge, "Ecclesiology," 524–32.

38. Beall, *Newness*, 80.

39. Hunter, "Reflections," 333.

other words, people are not held accountable for faith in Christ until they have the intellectual and moral capacity to understand the gospel and accept it. Myer Pearlman and Ernest Williams (who approvingly cites Pearlman), suggest that since children prior to the age of accountability have "no sins to repent of and cannot exercise faith they are logically excluded from water baptism."[40] The theological problem with the above notion is that it seems to overlook the traditional distinction between original sin and acts of sin, and the idea that grace most fundamentally treats the guilt and corruption caused by original sin. Moreover, Ernest Williams maintains that "infants who die before accountability begins are saved through the redemption which is in Christ Jesus." The problem with saying they are saved by Christ presupposes that the infants are sinners in need of grace, but the theological case Williams and Pearlman build to exclude the necessity for infant baptism presupposes they are without sin (e.g., "infants have no sins to repent of").[41]

In recent years, Frank D. Macchia and Amos Yong have made innovative and suggestive proposals for a Pentecostal theology of water baptism. Although Macchia and Yong are not strictly Classical Pentecostals, their background is Classical Pentecostalism and their efforts in part seek to encourage the Classical Pentecostal tradition to embrace more expansive theological visions. With that in mind, the discussion of their contributions to a Pentecostal theology of water baptism fits well as the conclusion of this section on the Classical Pentecostal theology of water baptism.

Macchia portrays water baptism as a public performance of the believer's Spirit baptism that confesses their solidarity with the death of Christ, their participation in the resurrection of Christ in their new life, and their anticipation of participation in the eschatological kingdom.[42] Even though Macchia is open to a more sacramental way of thinking about grace, and sees water baptism as more than primarily an act of obedience (and in doing so invests the rite with more theological significance than does traditional Pentecostalism), he continues the traditional Classical Pentecostal emphasis that water baptism is an act that celebrates something that has already taken place. He compares the relationship between baptism and regeneration to the one between a marriage

40. Pearlman, *Doctrines*, 355 and Williams, *Systematic Theology*, 3:153.
41. Williams, *Systematic Theology*, 3:153.
42. Macchia, *Baptized in the Spirit*, 249.

ceremony and the love shared between two people. Macchia suggests that the "wedding ceremony confirms and fulfills a commitment between two hearts joined together in love."[43] His rejection of infant baptism on the basis that baptism "depends on the rite being a performance of our commitment to the crucified and risen Christ in faith and obedience," nevertheless, shows that he sees regeneration and salvation as primarily an experience that precedes water baptism (i.e., baptism is a "*performance of our commitment* to the crucified and risen Christ").[44] The result is that Macchia remains within the believer's baptism trajectory of the Classical Pentecostal theology of water baptism.

Yong proposes that baptismal regeneration coheres with Pentecostal theology as long as the efficacy of the rite derives from the activity of the Spirit and presupposes the faith of the participant. Yong presses Pentecostals to see baptism and the sacraments more broadly, in more than merely symbolic terms. He maintains that Pentecostals can embrace a view of the sacramental mediation of grace if they emphasize that sacramental efficacy depends on the invocation and working of the Spirit in the sacramental elements and presupposes the faith of the participant.[45] In his perspective, baptism enacts participation in the death and resurrection of Christ *and* the reception of the Holy Spirit.[46] He proposes that baptism can be understood as an event in which the Spirit enacts "the life and grace of God to those who need and receive it by faith."[47] Baptism is an invitation to enact participation in the death and resurrection of Christ, but also is an actualization of that enactment. In other words, baptism is the concrete way the believer enacts their identification with Christ and is an event in which the believer experiences the grace of Christ through the operative power of the Spirit in the event and through the elements that constitute the sacramental event. Although Yong's proposal is innovative, its current state of development is more suggestive than explicated.

43. Ibid., 250.
44. Ibid.
45. Yong, *Spirit Poured Out*, 157–60.
46. Ibid., 159.
47. Ibid., 160.

CHARISMATIC VIEWS OF WATER BAPTISM

The Charismatic movement was the first major development after the consolidation around the doctrine of Spirit baptism achieved in Classical Pentecostalism. The Charismatics share much in common with the Classical Pentecostals, but are unique in that that they come from mainline Protestant denominations and the Catholic Church, and although they affirm Spirit baptism, they are less stringent on speaking in tongues as its initial evidence. For the first half of the twentieth century the North American Pentecostal movement remained a distinct subgroup within Protestant Christianity. However, in the 1950s, Christians within the traditional mainline Protestant churches and the Roman Catholic Church not only came into the Pentecostal experience, they remained within their churches. Prior to the Charismatic Renewal, church leaders and congregants who participated in Pentecostalism most often left their traditional churches and joined Pentecostal ones. Harald Bredesen (1918–2006), a Lutheran minister, broke that trend.

At a Pentecostal summer camp in 1946, Bredesen received Spirit baptism and retained his Lutheran ordination. He subsequently became a central figure in the Charismatic Renewal movement. Demos Shakarian's (1913–1993) Full Gospel Business Men's Fellowship International, founded in 1951, also facilitated the spread of the Charismatic movement. The organization became an important gateway for Spirit-filled businessmen to introduce their non-Pentecostal colleagues to Spirit baptism and charismatic spirituality. One of the more visible events in the rise of the Charismatic Renewal was Dennis Bennett's (1917–1991) embrace of the Pentecostal experience. Bennett was rector of St. Mark's Episcopal Church in Van Nuys, California. On Passion Sunday 1960, he announced to his congregation that he had received Spirit baptism and spoke in tongues. The leadership of the church immediately called for his resignation, which he tendered during the third service of the same day. Soon afterwards, he accepted the invitation to serve as vicar in St. Luke's Episcopal Church in Seattle, Washington, where he remained until he retired in 1981. Bennett represents the broader experience of the mainline churches with the Charismatic Renewal—initial shock and subsequent integration. By the early 1960s, all of the major mainline Protestant denominations had people receiving Spirit baptism and speaking in tongues *and* remaining within those churches as renewal communities.

The Catholic Charismatic Renewal began in 1967 at Duquesne University, Pittsburgh, PA and the University of Notre Dame, South Bend, IN. Throughout the 1970s, the renewal spread from America to Europe, Australia, Latin America, and Korea. Early leaders in the movement included Ralph Martin (1942–), Stephen Clark (1940–), and Léon-Joseph Cardinal Suenens (1904–1996), who was the papal representative to the Catholic Charismatic movement and helped to keep the movement within the ecclesiastical structures of the Catholic Church. Notre Dame continued to be a center for the renewal through the 1970s by its sponsorship of an annual conference that at its height in 1976 drew 30,000 participants. From its beginning through the 1970s, covenant communities served as centers of renewal and cultivated leaders and publications for the movement. Among these were the Word of God in Ann Arbor, MI; People of Praise in South Bend, IN; Alleluia in Augusta, GA; Emmanuel in Brishbane, Australia; Emmanuel in Paris, France; and Chemin Neuf in Lyon, France. In the 1980s leadership passed from the community centers to diocesan leaders. Like their fellow Protestant Charismatics, Catholic Charismatics saw their fresh experience of the Spirit as a renewal of their traditional Catholic faith, rather than as something that would lead them to leave it. Indeed, they saw their movement as a product of the reforms initiated by the Second Vatican Council and an answer to Pope John XXIII's prayer that the council might usher in a new Pentecost.

Charismatic Pentecostals typically endorse their denomination's view of water baptism. For illustrative purposes, I here present the Catholic Charismatic understanding of the relationship between water baptism and Spirit baptism. Although the *Malines I* document does not speak for all Catholic Charismatics, it provided an official endorsement and theological guide for understanding the Catholic Charismatic Renewal. In 1974, Léon-Joseph Cardinal Suenens appointed Kilian McDonnell to prepare a theological account of the Charismatic Renewal in conjunction with an international team of Catholic theologians and pastoral leaders that met in Malines, Belgium. After further consultation with leading Catholic theologians, the team assembled at Malines and signed the document now known as *Malines I*.[48]

Catholic Charismatics embrace the Catholic doctrine of water baptism and, therefore, affirm that the believer receives the grace of Christ in

---

48. McDonnell, *Presence, Power, Praise*, 3:13–70.

the rite of water baptism. *Malines I* states, "in the New Testament it is by receiving the sacrament of Baptism that one becomes a member of the body of Christ because in Baptism one receives the Spirit."[49] Although Oneness Pentecostals also believe in the necessity of water baptism for salvation and see it as coincident with salvation, the Catholic understanding is distinct from the Oneness view. Water baptism is necessary in Oneness Pentecostalism because it is the preeminent act of repentance and obedience to Christ. However, the Catholic view places the emphasis on water baptism as the means of the grace of Christ. Certainly it is an act of obedience, yet the focus of the rite is not the obedience of the human person, but rather the activity of God to confer grace on the person through the rite (hence, *ex opere operato*).

The key teaching of *Malines I* in respect to water baptism and Spirit baptism is the distinction between the theological and experiential senses of Spirit baptism. Catholic charismatic theology does not alter the Catholic teaching that water baptism is the sacrament of Christian initiation and, therefore, the gateway for the full range of the grace of Christ. Consequently, it maintains that Spirit baptism is received in water baptism. The reception of the Spirit in water baptism is the theological sense of Spirit baptism. The experiential sense of Spirit baptism refers to the common practice among Christians to have a powerful release of the grace received in baptism after, in some cases even many years after, their water baptism. In this sense, the experience of Spirit baptism can be understood as a "renewal of baptismal consciousness and realities."[50] Although when Catholic Charismatics speak of Spirit baptism, they generally refer to the conscious experience of the actualization of the Spirit received in water baptism; they also assume the full presence of the Spirit of Christ from the event of water baptism.[51] Thus, the charismatic experience of Spirit baptism does not mean that the Christian has received something they had not previously had in a theological sense, but only in a phenomenological or experiential sense.

The coincidence of water baptism and Spirit baptism sharply distinguishes the Catholic Charismatic theology of Spirit baptism from the Classical Pentecostal view. Classical Pentecostals believe that Spirit baptism is a distinct reception of the Spirit that is subsequent to salvation

---

49. Ibid., 3:25.
50. McDonnell, "Holy Spirit and Christian Initiation," 58.
51. McDonnell, *Presence, Power, Praise*, 3:39–40.

and wholly unrelated to water baptism and even conversion/initiation. In contrast, a leading Catholic Charismatic theologian, Kilian McDonnell, maintains that "by all considerations Paul considered water baptism the locus of the giving and receiving of the Spirit . . . Paul knew of no post-baptismal rite which conferred the Spirit."[52] The Catholic Charismatic view, even though it recognizes the legitimacy of subsequence in terms of the conscious experience of Spirit baptism, insists that a person receives the Holy Spirit/Spirit baptism in water baptism.

Locating the theological meaning of Spirit baptism in the sacrament of water baptism is the most common Catholic charismatic view, nevertheless Francis J. Sullivan has developed an alternative one. Drawing on the theology of Thomas Aquinas, Sullivan maintains that the graces of Spirit baptism are not entirely contained within water baptism and a subsequent release of the grace of water baptism. Spirit baptism can be an experience of grace that is in some sense distinct from the grace of water baptism. He affirms the reception of the Spirit in the sacrament of water baptism, but also suggests that the Holy Spirit may produce new works in the believer that are theologically and experientially distinct from the grace of water baptism.[53]

ONENESS PENTECOSTALISM'S THEOLOGY OF WATER BAPTISM

Oneness Pentecostalism emerged within the early Pentecostal movement over a new understanding of the nature of and formula for water baptism. The beginning of the movement can be identified as the camp meeting in Arroyo Seco, near Los Angeles, in April of 1913. In a sermon on baptism, Robert E. McAlister suggested that the apostles baptized in the name of the Lord Jesus Christ rather than using the trinitarian formula of Matt 28:19, because the "Lord-Jesus-Christ" is the theological equivalent of "Father-Son-and-Holy Spirit."[54] Later that evening, John G. Schaepe was purported to receive a "revelation" on baptizing in the name of Jesus. The movement began to grow quickly through evangelistic activities and the integration of independent Pentecostal churches and fledgling Pentecostal denominations and networks. By 1916, the

---

52. McDonnell, "Holy Spirit and Christian Initiation," 73.
53. Crowe, *Pentecostal Unity*, 135–36.
54. Burgess and Van Der Maas, eds., *Dictionary*, s.v., "Oneness Pentecostalism."

Oneness insistence on baptism and re-baptism in the name of Jesus and its non-traditional trinitarianism led the Assemblies of God (a trinitarian Pentecostal denomination) to include a clear trinitarian confession in its Statement of Fundamental Truths and thereby to exclude Jesus Name ministers and congregations.

The Pentecostal Assemblies of the World (PAW), under the leadership of Garfield T. Haywood, was one of the earliest Oneness Denominations. Originally a multi-racial group, the white constituency sought to create two racially distinct denominations and withdrew from the PAW in 1924. The various Oneness groups struggled to maintain their membership through the 1930s, and finally most of the white groups united to form the United Pentecostal Church Incorporated in 1945. It remains the largest Oneness Pentecostal denomination. Worldwide, Oneness Pentecostalism includes a membership of approximately 14 million in over 425 organizations.[55]

Oneness Pentecostalism derives its name from its rejection of the doctrine of the Trinity. They prefer a modalist approach to the Trinity that sees God as one eternal being without internal distinction of persons. Their preference for a modalistic understanding of God derives from their belief that it is biblical and that it avoids what they perceive as the corruption of monotheism, and the polytheism or subordinationism inherent in traditional trinitarianism.[56]

According to Oneness theology, the terms Father, Son, and Holy Spirit are titles that Scripture uses to indicate the different roles of the one God in salvation history. Trinitarian language, therefore, applies only to the economic activity of God and does not connote eternal distinctions within the one God.[57] The one God foreordains to come among humanity in the Incarnation. The title "Father" refers to the foreordination of God, the divine origin of the redemptive work of God in the Incarnation, and the absolute transcendence of God. The title "Son" points to the coming of God in the Incarnation. The name "Holy Spirit" connotes the presence of God in the lives of believers to actualize grace.[58] Moreover, the titles simultaneously apply to Jesus as the revelation of

---

55. Ibid., s.v., "Oneness Pentecostalism."

56. Society for Pentecostal Studies, "Oneness–Trinitarian Report," 216, and Reed, "*In Jesus' Name*," 237, 252–53.

57. Reed, "*In Jesus' Name*," 265–73.

58. Society for Pentecostal Studies, "Oneness–Trinitarian Report," 215.

the one God. David Reed summarizes the relationship between the titles and uni-personal identity of Jesus as God in the following way: "the Oneness christocentrism becomes apparent because as humanity Jesus is the Son, and as Spirit (i.e., in his deity) he reveals, indeed *is* the Father, and sends, indeed *is* the Holy Spirit as the Spirit of Christ."[59] The critical point is that the titles of Father, Son, and Holy Spirit illumine the distinct redemptive roles of the one God and do not indicate eternal distinctions or persons within the one God; in other words, the titles are not names of divine persons.[60] God has one personal identity.[61] Consequently, the one God has one name; the Name of Jesus. To understand the religious significance of the name of Jesus for Oneness Pentecostals, one can compare it to the role that reverence for the name Yahweh plays within Judaism.[62] The revelation of the name of Jesus does not connote merely a title or transitory work, but is the proper and holy name of God that at once "bears the divine reality in person, character and purpose, without violating the divine transcendence."[63]

In Oneness Pentecostal theology, water baptism is the second part of the tripartite experience of salvation. Oneness Pentecostals maintain that salvation has three facets: repentance, water baptism in Jesus' name, and Spirit baptism. Although each aspect is distinct experientially, they are theologically part of the one salvific event. In the "Oneness–Trinitarian Pentecostal Final Report", the Oneness team affirmed that repentance, water baptism, and Spirit baptism "are closely associated and often nearly simultaneous, but theologically they are distinct events."[64] Salvation begins with faith that finds its concrete expression in repentance and obedience.

The primary expression of repentance and chief act of obedience in the experience of salvation is baptism in the name of Jesus. Water baptism is a necessary step in the process of salvation because it is a necessary act of obedience. Christ commands all who have faith in him

---

59. Reed, "In Jesus' Name," 263.
60. Ibid., 260.
61. Ibid., 256–57.
62. Ibid., 235–45, 250–52.
63. Ibid., 248.
64. Society for Pentecostal Studies, "Oneness–Trinitarian Report," 210.

to be baptized. For Oneness Pentecostals, a faith that does not obey the command of Jesus Christ to be baptized in his name is inconceivable.[65]

Although Oneness Pentecostal theology affirms the necessity of water baptism for salvation, they do not hold to baptismal regeneration. The efficacy of water baptism resides in the power of the name of Jesus that is confessed in the event of water baptism. In effect, the repentant believer receives the grace of Jesus in the experience of water baptism. However, the water is not the medium, but more the occasion for the conferral of grace. Oneness theology, therefore, does not teach baptismal regeneration, but it does seem to see the removal of sins and regeneration as coincident with water baptism.[66]

The third and culminating part of the conversion-initiation experience is Spirit baptism. The inclusion of Spirit baptism in conversion sharply distinguishes the Oneness Pentecostal theology of Spirit baptism from the Classical Pentecostal teaching. Oneness Pentecostals reject the Classical Pentecostal theology of Spirit baptism as an experience distinct from and subsequent to conversion. Oneness Pentecostals also see speaking in tongues as an indispensible experience of salvation. They do not believe that speaking in tongues saves the believer, but rather that anyone who is saved will necessarily be baptized in the Spirit and consequently will speak in tongues. Thus, tongues are the initial physical evidence of Spirit baptism and thus integral to the experience of salvation.[67] Classical Pentecostals and Oneness Pentecostals agree that speaking in tongues is the initial physical evidence of Spirit baptism, but differ on the necessity and placement of Spirit baptism in the order of redemption (*ordo salutis*). Classical Pentecostals see Spirit baptism as an experience that is subsequent to conversion, and although vitally important for empowered ministry, ultimately unnecessary for salvation, whereas Oneness Pentecostals locate Spirit baptism in conversion and see it as one of the three essential dimensions of salvation.

Focusing more specifically on the event of water baptism, Oneness soteriology teaches that the grace received in water baptism has three aspects. The first is the remissions of sins. Oneness theology finds a correlation between the imagery of the baptismal water cleansing the believer of sins and Old Testament water purification rituals in the

---

65. Reed, "In Jesus' Name," 314–15.
66. Ibid., 316–17.
67. Society for Pentecostal Studies, "Oneness–Trinitarian Report," 220.

Tabernacle of Moses and the redemption the nascent people of Israel received through the water of the Red Sea.[68] Water baptism is also a sign of spiritual circumcision.[69] Circumcision functioned as a sign of inclusion in the covenant between Israel and God. Similarly, water baptism identifies a person with the death and resurrection of Christ. Finally, water baptism signals the inner transformation wrought in the believer by grace. Drawing on John 3:5 and Acts 2:38, Oneness theology coordinates spiritual renewal or the new birth with the rite of water baptism. Water baptism, then, is the event in which the believer receives the forgiveness of sins, regeneration, and the power to live in holiness and obedience to Jesus.[70] The clear connection between water baptism and the forgiveness of sins and the new birth of conversion are characteristics that Classical Pentecostals will continue to find incompatible with their understanding of the relationship between conversion-initiation and water baptism.[71]

The Classical and Oneness Pentecostal views on water baptism reflect significant differences, yet at the same time they share important similarities. They explain the importance of water baptism in terms of an act of obedience. To be sure, Oneness Pentecostals see it as the chief initial act of obedience in a way that Classical Pentecostals do not, but nonetheless they both understand its significance as an act of obedience to the command of Christ and not as a means of grace. They also agree that water baptism identifies believers with Jesus Christ and publicly initiates them into the community of the church.

CONCLUSION

One cannot speak of *the* Pentecostal theology of water baptism any more than one can speak of *the* Pentecostal view of most any doctrine. Pentecostalism is not monolithic, but is rather a worldwide movement that comprises diverse theologies and practices. In recognition of the global diversity of the Pentecostal movement, this essay describes the most common approaches to water baptism among Pentecostals and Charismatics within North America. The Classical Pentecostal view is

---

68. Reed, "In Jesus' Name," 318.

69. Ibid., 243–44.

70. Ibid., 318–19.

71. For instance, see William W. Menzies's response (commissioned by General Superintendent George Wood of the Assemblies of God) to the Oneness–Trinitarian Pentecostal Final Report, 2002–2007, "Trinitarian Pentecostal Response," 230–31.

a form of believer's baptism and, aside from slight nuances, is nearly an entirely derivative doctrine from the believer's baptism tradition. People in the Charismatic movement assimilated their experience and theology of Spirit baptism into their traditional church theologies, and thus do not have a distinct *Pentecostal* view of water baptism. The Oneness Pentecostals have articulated the most distinctive theology of water baptism within North American Pentecostalism. They see it neither only in terms of believer's baptism nor in a fully sacramental view, but nonetheless consider it as a necessary act of Christian repentance and faith in the experience of conversion/initiation.

FURTHER READING

Classical Pentecostal–Assemblies of God

Statement of 16 Fundamental Truths http://www.ag.org/top/Beliefs/Statement_of_Fundamental_Truths/sft_full.cfm.

Assemblies of God Statement on Infant Baptism, Age of Accountability, Dedication of Children, endorsed by Assemblies of God's Commission on Doctrinal Purity and the Executive Presbytery: http://www.ag.org/top/Beliefs/gendoct_11_accountability.cfm.

Oneness Pentecostal–United Pentecostal Church International

Doctrinal Statement: "Why We Baptize in Jesus' Name" http://www.upci.org/doctrine/baptism.asp.

Conclusion

Author Responses

One of the objectives of this project was to provide scholarly articles that not only presented the theological views of the rite across a broad range of Christian traditions, but also fostered continued scholarly and pastoral discussion across confessional and communal boundaries. To our way of thinking, one of the best ways to accomplish such a goal was to conclude this volume with the observations and conclusions of the contributors themselves. We asked each scholar to read the other contributors' articles and then to provide brief reflections upon what they read. Our hope was that through these scholarly reflections a number of talking points would rise to the surface that could provide opportunities for continued dialogue on the place of baptism in Christian theology and practice.

It is not likely to be a surprise that some of the questions raised in these reflections pertain to issues such as the mode of baptism (affusion or immersion), the age and/or intellectual maturity of the baptized (infant or adult), and whether or not water baptism is even necessary. These issues have been and still remain important matters for discussion in the conversation regarding the theology and practice of baptism in the broader Christian tradition. However, in both the preceding chapters and the reflections here, a number of additional issues have been raised by nearly all of the contributors. These include issues of church history, Christian anthropology, hamartiology, hermeneutics, authority, pastoral theology and practice, and Christian identity (of both the individual and the community). In one way or another, the scholars involved in this project have shown that these issues, though not necessarily about baptism *per se*, factor significantly in the shaping of a theology and practice of baptism.

REFLECTIONS FROM THE ORTHODOX TRADITION

Irenaeus M. C. Steenberg

The wide-ranging offerings of the contributors to this volume raise a number of interesting issues on which one might comment in reply—perhaps first among these being the sheer scope for discussion, when baptism is considered across so wide a spectrum of groups that practice it. Just what is implied in this act is a point of radical variation across the traditions represented in this book: an issue that raises yet further questions on what is shared and what is in fact quite different in the varied groups bearing the name "Christian" in the twenty-first century.

One issue seems to me especially worthy of reflection, namely, how baptism is seen to relate to the intellectual capacity of the human person, and the manner in which this is tied into understandings of human sin. We might proceed by asking, in what manner is sin understood to affect the condition of the human constitution, such that baptism may effectively act upon it at various ages of a person's maturing physical and intellectual life?

A remark made by Hayes in his chapter on baptism in the Anglican Communion sets a helpful comparative stage. Tracing out the practice of infant baptism from a historical perspective, he comments that a view of "original sin" dating back to St. Augustine sets the essential framework.[1] Here Orthodox would pause, for while the Orthodox Church has always insisted upon the historical and theological precedents for the baptism of infants, such a linking to an Augustinian concept of "original sin" sits quite at odds with customary Orthodox expressions of sin and human nature. While St. Paul, of course, accurately observes that death originates in sin, and that all are mortal and thus all are in some direct manner touched and affected by sin, the automatic assignment of sin *to the level of nature* as the means of explaining how these two observations fit together, is not something that Orthodox theologians (including a majority of the early and eastern Fathers of the Church) have ever found terribly convincing. Indeed, the very idea that a newborn infant possesses original sin as a kind of "thing," or natural and quasi-physical possession that can be taken away from him by some ritual act, most Orthodox would see as an objectification and materialization of sin that comes dangerously close to Gnosticism. Augustine may have pondered

---

1. See Hayes, "Baptism in the Anglican Communion," 112.

the possibilities of such a natural connection of sin to the constitution of the creature (though most expressions of Augustinian original sin go far further on the point than he ever would have condoned), but this is precisely one of the grounds on which Orthodoxy has viewed aspects of his legacy with a degree of reserve.

Perhaps surprisingly, I am much happier with the view (on this sole point!) of the English Separatist John Smyth, who rejected the extreme form that doctrines of original sin had taken in the early seventeenth-century West, and argued instead that children are born in innocence[2]—a point resonant with Orthodoxy, which, for example, does not pronounce prayers of absolution over the body of a deceased infant in the funeral service, given a belief in the innocence of the newborn child. Of course, Smyth was to take this older confession in a direction no Orthodox could condone: that therefore baptism should not be permitted of infants, since—purportedly—one of the main *raisons d'être* of infant baptism (the removal of original sin) does not apply. Instead, both in his works and by his example, Smyth moved the age of baptism into adulthood, or at least intellectual maturity. If it is not an act of washing away in-built sin, it must be an act of covenantal confession, which can only be entered into by one of rational mind and consenting heart.

Yet this seems, to me, to avoid one extreme by going to another: from sin as an in-built, almost material reality passed on from one generation to the next, to sin as an almost exclusively intellectual activity—ultimately requiring, despite the best efforts of Smyth and his cohorts to produce a scriptural warrant for adult believer's baptism, a denial of the clear practices of the New Testament.

Surely an authentic Christian anthropology and doctrine of sin must stand in the middle, recognizing that sin is always inherently an act, not a substance, but also understanding that it affects even those whose intellectual maturity has not yet attained the level of consent, of engagement, of reasoned participation. Thus the mystery of baptism takes up the infant, innocent in her creation yet still marred by the sin of the world, washes her clean and joins her to the mystery of Christ's redemptive life.

---

2. As discussed by Cross, "Baptism among Baptists," 139.

REFLECTIONS FROM THE ROMAN CATHOLIC TRADITION

Gerard Kelly

In this response I wish to draw attention to an important pastoral issue that was raised both directly and indirectly by a number of authors, namely the question of baptismal identity in the West today. Vissers puts the issue most starkly when he notes that "baptismal identity creates the basis for Christian worship, discipleship, ethics, spirituality, and mission. It embodies our justification, sanctification, and vocation."[3] He concludes his essay by commenting that the present situation of churches affords "a new opportunity to think together about the theology and practice of baptism."[4] These ideas resonate with me, as I also wrote about identity in my own essay. Vissers, however, brings out the pastoral imperative arising from the current situation. He frames baptismal identity in terms of relationship—with God, with the people of God, and with the world. This suggests to me that there could be much benefit in the churches taking baptism and baptismal identity as a starting point for the development of pastoral plans. I acknowledge that there could be suspicion of this in some quarters if it were perceived that sacrament rather than word was the bedrock of a pastoral plan. Such a suspicion, however, would represent old thinking. There is enough consensus in the chapters of this book that baptism has its effects by means of word and Spirit that no one should any longer have to choose between word or sacrament.

Cross made an observation about some Baptists that helped me think in terms of both/and rather than either/or, when he referred to attempts to avoid the spirit-matter dualism and to "restore a healthy view of God as Creator and matter as the means in and through which he works for the salvation of his bodily creation, humanity."[5] This also highlights a further aspect of today's pastoral challenge, where people live in an environment that places emphasis on the material and the bodily. In some cases this has destructive consequences. A healthy Christian identity in the twenty-first century should integrate the spiritual and the material. Perhaps churches can help people work out how to be in relationship with God, the people of God, and the world in such a way that they are faithful to the gospel into which they are baptized but without

---

3. Vissers, "Baptism in the Reformed Tradition," 76–77.
4. Ibid., 108.
5. Cross, "Baptism among Baptists," 145.

denying that they live in a world that often gives more prominence to the material than the spiritual. Cross draws attention to the close connection between baptism and discipleship, which he notes is often called catechumenate in other traditions. In other words, baptism frames a whole life, and is not just a single moment. Many churches are learning that ritual is an important element in baptismal catechesis, both before and after baptism. Ritual involves the material and the bodily.

There is a presupposition lurking in the foregoing discussion, and it is the need for vibrant Christian communities where the baptismal life is modeled and supported. Studebaker offers an interesting observation that within North America, "Pentecostals emphasize church attendance as a mark of Christian obedience, but do not have a highly developed ecclesiology and sense that the larger, even worldwide, body of Christ, informs the individual's Christian identity."[6] Kolb makes a similar point when indicating that for Lutherans, "incorporation into the church dare never be understood as merely external membership in an institution."[7] The glorification of the individual is a mark of modern life. Yet there are many signs that people are hungry for community, and that they find it in the church. A rich theology of baptism can offer us a way to be less focused on the institutional and juridical aspects of the church, and to consider it as a *koinōnia* or communion. In this way it will look quite different than a club or a free association of like-minded people, but rather be a community called and gathered by God where we live the saving grace we have received.

The pastoral imperative that all our churches are facing may help us develop even deeper convergences on baptism. This will happen when our concern for Christian identity through baptism leads us to a fresh consideration of the theological differences that have traditionally separated us.

REFLECTIONS FROM THE LUTHERAN TRADITION

Robert Kolb

Almost all Christians regard baptism as *the*—or at least a significant—entry point into the church. Baptists regard it as a defining mark of their understanding of what it means to be Christians, and all Christians use

6. Studebaker, "Baptism among Pentecostals," 214.
7. Kolb, "The Lutheran Theology of Baptism," 69.

the word to assert something about their identity as children of God. Christians call it mystery, sacrament, rite, ritual, sign, reality, a form of the re-creative Word of God, combining some terms, rejecting others. Baptism is a theme that runs throughout the New Testament; some see it implicitly mentioned more in the New Testament than explicitly in allusions to new life in Christ. Clearly, baptism formed a vital element in the early church's existence and its understanding or definition of the Christian faith. The essays in this volume demonstrate that it has never ceased to be that.

But baptismal waters divide as well as unite the church today. Several essayists in this collection remind readers that within their own traditions a wide spectrum of views of baptism has emerged over time. A volume such as this offers an arena for healthy exchange of ideas from various Christian confessions of the faith from which all can profit and learn.

These essays make clear that Christians have argued past each other quite often in discussing baptism because their particular understandings of this sacrament or rite—fundamental definitions of what it is and does (and who does the acting) differ—arise from different presuppositions, within contrasting and often conflicting conceptual frameworks. For instance, when, some thirty years ago, Baptist and Lutheran theologians came together to dialogue, they found more agreement than popular views on both sides would lead one to suspect.[8] Nonetheless, they found significant differences in their understanding of who is the primary and who is the secondary actor in baptism. Their discussions of baptism also revealed differences in their understanding of sin.

The essays in this volume reveal that baptism serves as a microcosm of the whole body of biblical teaching. How a particular group formulates its teaching and traditions regarding baptism reflects much about its conception of God, of sin and evil, of justification in God's sight, and of human responsibility toward him and toward his creation. Baptism also plays a critical, if often unrecognized, role in shaping our views of the community of Christ's people, the church, in local congregations and in the world-wide community of faith. Historical studies help us all to understand how our own positions as well as those of other traditions were determined not only by searching the Scriptures but also by concerns that reflected the challenges and oppositions of certain other

---

8. See Millar, "Common Statements," 103–8.

voices or of specific cultural situations. Such historical responses may have been justified at the time of their formulation and may still be helpful, valid expressions of the truth, but understanding why we formulate our ideas may clarify our own thinking and also assist in meeting traditional concerns with fresh language that does not offend and separate.

These essays make it clear that all Christians struggle implicitly or explicitly with the mystery of the continuation of sin and evil in the lives of those who have come to faith in Christ. No attempt to master and control this mystery succeeds. Each of us is concerned about "backsliding" or "apostasy" and about the consolation of uncertain, despairing consciences. So our address of these concerns at a doctrinal level profoundly affects the ways in which we approach the pastoral or spiritual care of both those who defy the baptismal promise (whether seen as God's or ours) and those who have strayed and suffer brokenness of conscience because of it, reduced to insecurity about God's commitment to them because of their failed commitment to him.

This volume can initiate fruitful interchange regarding a number of topics. Is baptism a form of God's Word, or a human rite, or—and in what ways—both? How does God use certain elements of his created order in delivering salvation? Answers range from "as signs that only symbolize and point to his disposition in heaven" on one end of a spectrum to "as effective means of bringing about his will" on the other. Why do the baptized, and even the unbaptized who have professed faith in Christ, stray and fall away, and how can the recollection of their baptism help the former come to repentance?

Ephesians 4:5 declares that we as Christ's church have one baptism. This calls us to careful and diligent theological work on the task of seeking and expressing the truth and gift of baptism with one voice.

REFLECTIONS FROM THE REFORMED TRADITION

John Vissers

It is a privilege to be counted among the contributors to this volume on baptism in the Christian tradition and to offer a brief reflection on the very fine essays by my colleagues. In general I am struck not only by differences in the theology and practice of baptism across the various traditions represented in these chapters, but also by the diversity within individual traditions. It is also interesting to note the overlap and interdependence of traditions, as for example, in my case, between the charismatic Pentecostal view and Reformed Christians who would understand themselves as charismatic Christians; or the indebtedness of Martin Bucer and John Calvin to Martin Luther on baptism; or the recent convergence among Reformed and Eastern Orthodox theologians on participation in Christ. I am also struck by the fact that each of the essays illustrates, if not proves, my thesis that the theology and practice of baptism in a particular tradition reveals not only how a tradition understands a particular Christian practice; it shows how the tradition construes Christian identity and existence. In this sense, baptism illumines the whole.

Studebaker's essay offers Reformed Christians a timely reminder that we often undervalue the person and work of the Holy Spirit in our understanding of Christian faith and life in general, and perhaps also in the way we understand baptism. Our Trinitarian and christological focus may well require a more robust pneumatology. Studebaker's positive evaluation of the term "sacrament" is welcome. It is difficult, I must confess, to see how there can be convergence between a Reformed (Trinitarian) understanding and that of Oneness Pentecostalism, but that may be an agenda for the future. I was also interested to note that Studebaker avers that Pentecostalism does not inherently require a theology and practice of believer's baptism.

Kelly's essay on baptism in the Roman Catholic Church nicely emphasizes that Christian identity is rooted in our participation in the life, death, and resurrection of Jesus through baptism. But I wonder about the recent Roman Catholic revision of baptism under the rubric of Christian initiation rite. I say this because I question whether the description of baptism as an initiation rite like those common to all societies is a helpful starting theological point. It is certainly representative of attempts by modern Roman Catholic theologians to ground theology in common human phenomena. But does this not make baptism a particular religious expression of general human experience? Or is it meant to describe baptism as the transcendent reality for which all humans long? That said, Kelly's emphasis on the importance of faith in baptism is welcome. He also nicely emphasizes the necessity of the church. But of course the assumption is that the church into one which must be baptized finds its true institutional expression under Rome.

Niccum's essay on baptism in the Restorationist Movement illustrates how baptism is shaped by social, cultural, intellectual, and political factors. I suspect that what is true of the Restorationist Movement and the American experiment is true for the rest of us. This essay also provides, as one might expect from a New Testament scholar in the Restorationist tradition, a rigorous and robust re-reading of the New Testament texts. It reminded me that each tradition has made certain hermeneutical decisions when reading the founding texts on baptism. Macy's article on Baptism and Quakers drove this point home because I was forced to consider what was, for me, a quite radical re-reading of the texts on baptism in order to see baptism as first and foremost a spiritual reality. A comparative study of each essay's use of the Bible in this volume would be illuminating: Which texts are chosen as primary and why? Which texts interpret which texts? To what extent is the historical-critical method employed? What is the theological hermeneutic at work?

In the essays by Hayes (Anglican), Kolb (Lutheran), and Steenberg (Orthodox) I found myself swimming in familiar waters. The essay by Hayes reinforced the diversity that can exist in a particular tradition and also the manner in which theologies and practices of baptism are so forcefully shaped by historical and cultural contexts. The indebtedness of my own Reformed tradition to Lutheranism and Orthodoxy is evident throughout my essay. The issues of human agency and freedom in relation to divine agency and freedom continue to bubble just beneath the surface of much baptismal theology.

Cross's essay on baptism among Baptists helpfully reminded me of the distinction between believer's baptism and adult baptism. If Baptists practice the former, then it raises questions from paedobaptists concerning the appropriate age at which children should be presented for baptism. What is the difference between a child who is baptized at age four or five, and an infant who is baptized? I also continue to be struck by the fact that Baptists alone, of all the traditions represented in this collection, have made a particular theology and practice of baptism the distinctive mark of denominational identity. Going forward, that may be an important theological and pastoral issue that requires attention in ecumenical discussion. To what extent is the very essence of a church's identity and existence determined by its theology and practice of baptism?

REFLECTIONS FROM THE ANGLICAN TRADITION

Alan L. Hayes

The contributions in this book demonstrate that Christians, even within their own church families, have been stunningly diverse in their practices and understandings of baptism. The diversity arises largely because baptism is the point at which a broad and complex array of theological, liturgical, pastoral, and social considerations converge. A change in my view of faith, salvation, scriptural hermeneutics, church order, Israel, Christ and culture, time, or signs will probably change my view of baptism.

In particular, a lesson that I take from this book is that a Christian community's practice and understanding of baptism reflect the historical situation or situations in which these have taken shape. Seventeenth-century Baptists, we read in this volume, were repudiating an approach to baptism that was entangled in the contemporary social reality of Christendom. Luther was repudiating a medieval German Christianity that incorporated ancient ritual practices. Early Pentecostals, who came out from a variety of denominations, derived or adapted their understandings of baptism from the teachings of their former traditions. The Quaker founder George Fox might have gone in a different direction had he been fortunate enough to discover that rarity, a religiously serious Anglican minister. Reformed theologians in the first generation were particularly concerned in their teaching on baptism to highlight and protect the new and controversial theology of justification by faith. An early leader of the Restoration movement was influenced by his avid reading of John Locke. Current Roman Catholic practice is rooted in the Second Vatican Council, in departure from the Council of Trent. Orthodox Christians base their approach to baptizing Christians who are converted from other churches on St. Basil's response to Cathari converts, not on St. Augustine's response to Donatist converts.

Now, some contributors to this volume might worry about this way of putting things. I might seem to be saying that a theology of baptism is the function of the passing circumstances of its historical origins. If that were so, some of my fellow contributors might want to reply that in providing a historical perspective on their tradition's approach to baptism, as they were asked to do, they were not agreeing to reduce it to a historical artifact, and they were not discounting its truth claims.

My position is a little more complex. Following the language of the Anglican divine Richard Hooker, I would distinguish the substance of Christian initiation from the things accessory. The substance of Christian initiation is—well, even to state it propositionally within the limits of the English language is to move away from the substance to things accessory; but the substance is imperfectly evoked by a phrase like "entering into a new relationship with Jesus Christ." Things accessory include our ecclesial processes, procedures, rituals, theological emphases, liturgical formulas, and linguistic events (such as doctrinal statements). The substance is common to all; the things accessory are diverse, being variously formed under the influence of particular historical purposes and contexts.

The Acts of the Apostles gives plentiful examples of a diversity of baptismal practices to meet particular circumstances. In Acts 2:38, baptism is followed by the gift of the Spirit, while in 10:47, the gift of the Spirit is followed by baptism. Sometimes baptism by itself is sufficient Christian initiation, but in 8:16 and 19:6 it needs to be supplemented by the laying on of hands. In 8:37 the Ethiopian eunuch proclaims Christ first, then is baptized; but in 9:8, Paul is baptized first, then proclaims Christ. Sometimes individuals are baptized alone, but in 16:31–34 an entire household is baptized after only one of them professes faith. Usually baptism in the name of Jesus is required to be recognized by the church, but for Apollos in 18:25, baptism in Jesus' name seems to be unnecessary, since he has received John's baptism. Over all, then, the assumption of the Acts of the Apostles is that the substance of Christian initiation is the same from case to case, though the things accessory vary pretty dramatically.

As well, through the twenty centuries following Acts, Christians have continued to practice a considerable diversity of things accessory to baptism, forged to meet a variety of historical circumstances, and not infrequently surviving them. The unity of substance that underlies this diversity of form—Paul's "one Lord, one faith, one baptism"—will be most clearly visible to Christians who have learned to use history as an analytic tool, and not as an apologetic weapon. In other words, if we are to move past our divisions and forward to the discernment of the Lord's body, we will require wisdom (leavened by love) as to when, where, and why our Christian views and practices of baptism have diverged. We will also require some humility to recognize the historical conditioning of some of our own certainties. Historical perspective is more needful than theological disputation, for doctrine can divide, but modesty about our own commitments, and a sympathetic historical understanding of the commitments of others, can situate us within the warmth of Christ's prayer "that all may be one."

REFLECTIONS FROM THE BAPTIST TRADITION

Anthony R. Cross

Each tradition represented in this volume strives to be faithful to God's revealed word, but what we all struggle with are, in many ways, hermeneutical issues: how we go from our understanding of New Testament baptism to applying it today; and how we assess the validity of the developments that have unquestionably taken place over 2,000 years. The issues cannot be solved simply by exegesis, for even among Baptists we understand the New Testament's teaching in different ways. We would do well to remember Paul's teaching that "now we ... know only in part" (1 Cor 13:12), and this should lead to greater humility and openness to listen to other Christians' interpretations of the Scriptures.

Baptists can agree with the repeated view throughout these chapters that faith is essential to baptism, but they do not accept the notion of vicarious faith. For the overwhelming majority of Baptists, believer's and infant baptism are two different baptisms that express two completely different understandings of becoming a Christian and being a Christian. For us, it is the person's faith that is essential as the human side of the divine-human encounter, not the faith of the church, parents, or godparents. No one can believe for another. This is not to fall prey to an excessive individualism (though this is often a danger for Baptists and Evangelicals), but to express agreement with Tertullian's dictum that "people are made, not born Christians."[9] Nor is it to deny the prevenient grace of God, who is the giver of the gift of saving faith (Eph 2:8), and neither is it to sideline the corporate dimension, the church, "For in the one Spirit we were all baptized into one body" (1 Cor 12:13). In fact, Baptists still have a great deal to learn from other traditions on the corporate aspects and responsibilities of being a Christian and the need for nurture in the faith at all ages of a person's spiritual pilgrimage. We are exploring ways

9. Tertullian, *Apology*, 18.

to develop and strengthen our nurture, not just of young believers, but of all believers. To this end, an increasing number of Baptists are exploring dimensions of the catechumenate, both pre- and certainly post-baptism. Baptists are also learning much, not least from paedobaptists, about the place of children within the orbit of the church, and the developments of the service of infant presentation and blessing are liturgical expressions of this.

A constant Baptist response to moves towards unity, such as that embodied in *Baptism, Eucharist and Ministry*, is that we share a vision of Christian *unity*, not *uniformity*, and that it is in the deeper realities of which baptism (and the Lord's Supper) are visible and efficacious signs, and to which they bear witness, that such unity is properly to be found. This is by no means to minimize the importance of baptism and Eucharist, but enables Baptists to share fellowship (expressed by a growing number of Baptists who practice forms of open membership) with those from other baptismal traditions and those, such as the Friends and Salvation Army, who see things very differently.

It is appreciated when acknowledgement has been made that Anabaptists (and Baptists) have been persecuted for their beliefs, but we must be alert to the way we have at times disparaged and even condemned the beliefs and practices of those who disagree over this central rite of the Christian church. For such we ask forgiveness. Perhaps the key example of this is in so-called rebaptism, but we ask those of other traditions to understand that in the same way they regard their baptism as a matter of deep theological conviction, so too do Baptists in their practice of the baptism of believers. Such is not done to offend paedobaptists, but faithfully to honor our Lord and God.

On a personal note, what strikes me about the contributions to this book is the importance that all Christian traditions give to the theology and practice of baptism, and the non-confrontational tone in which these articles have been written. While we do not all agree, it is nevertheless important for the different Christian traditions to engage in explorations such as this for, as the pastor of the Pilgrim Fathers, John Robinson, is famed as saying, the Lord has "more truth and light yet to break forth out of his holy Word."[10] The result of my own study of Baptist baptismal theology and practice is that it has benefitted much from ecumenical encounter and dialogue, and it is the hope of many Baptists that this

---

10. Cf. Winslow, *Hypocrisie Unmasked*, 97.

continues as we learn more of the riches of baptism from others and they from us.

REFLECTIONS FROM THE QUAKER TRADITION

Howard R. Macy

This book project has improved my education, and I am glad. I thank the editors for their invitation to write and I thank the other contributors for their thoughtful and informative articles. By describing both historical theology and contemporary practice, the authors highlight similarities and differences between traditions. They also show development and dissent within traditions and, even more strikingly, widely varied practices not only between traditions but also with a single stream. All of this has enriched my understanding.

Sometimes Friends comment that if the New Testament clearly required water baptism, its instruction would be clearer and the approaches to baptism would be less diverse. No doubt that underestimates sincere Christians' propensity to disagree and diverge over time. Yet in that context and in the light of these readings, I still wonder at the high degree of confidence that conflicting traditions have that their particular theology and practice of baptism is rooted in Jesus' teaching, the New Testament, and the practice of the earliest church.

The various descriptions of infant baptism revealed a broad spectrum of practice. All who treated it here recognize infant baptism as a later development in Christianity, not directly rooted in New Testament teaching and practice. Authors also show significantly varied understandings of infant baptism, from saving evil infants from eternal damnation to including children in God's covenant promise and in the Christian community. I found it interesting to learn how the breakdown of Christendom and the growth of both empire and missions created new challenges for understanding infant baptism alongside adult baptism and the baptism of converts.

Historically, Quakers would agree with Anabaptists that the church gathers those who choose to follow Christ. Yet Friends have also warmly enfolded children into the community of faith. For example, "birthright membership" recognizes children born into Friends families. In some periods this was abused, however, when the community neglected to ask "birthright" members to make mature decisions to follow Christ. Now

Quakers do not use the term "birthright" as often, but many Friends meetings practice baby or child "dedications" in which the congregation both recognizes parents who intend to nurture their children to follow Christ and promises to support parents and share in this vital service.

I warmed to the pastoral concern expressed in several chapters about the question of re-baptism. Though an ecumenical age may prompt more open conversation here, I sensed that the struggles and proposed solutions about re-baptism showed compassion for individual Christians who, for whatever reasons, move from one community of faith to another. Surely it would bless the whole church were this spirit to increase.

I also warmed to the commitment, expressed in several articles, to "living baptismally" (Kelly's phrase).[11] I share the conviction that baptism is entering a new life, a life worthy of Christ, a life in Christ, a life guided and empowered by the living Christ. In the spirit of George Fox's words "possess what you profess,"[12] the Friends tradition calls people to such transformed living. The prophets press in on me, too, from Samuel's sharp rebuke to Saul that "obedience is better than sacrifice" (1 Sam 15.22) to Micah, who reminds us that God does not expect extravagant rituals of worship, but requires simply that we act justly, love compassion, and walk humbly with God (Mic 6:1–8). Baptism, whether by water or by "the Holy Spirit and fire," is to receive, enter into, and live out the love of God in the power of Christ.

REFLECTIONS FROM THE RESTORATIONIST TRADITION

Curt Niccum

Even a mere survey of the contributions in this book must impress the reader with the centrality of baptism in Christian thought. On the other hand, one could hardly miss the numerous differences. Certainly these two realities affirm the need for this volume and continued dialogue. The ultimate aim? Unity. One church. One baptism. At the bare minimum, though, such conversations should broaden understanding, deepen faith, and sharpen practice.

In each essay I found insights, especially when material stood in tension with my own beliefs and practices: Baptism as initiation into

---

11. Kelly, "Baptism in the Roman Catholic Church," 27.
12. Cf. Nickalls, Cadbury, and Nuttall, *Journal of George Fox*, 4.

the larger community of faith presents certain challenges to those who reserve it for adult believers. Required programs of study before baptism or Confirmation provide greater safeguards for unity in faith but clash with the biblical narratives where one finds the spontaneous impulse of the Holy Spirit in conversion. "Spiritual" baptism highlights the transcendence of Christ's work but nearly drains the baptismal font, used consistently by Christ's earliest disciples, of any meaning. Although not persuaded, I am not unmoved. In other words, my theology of baptism still remains firmly anchored within the Restoration Movement, but it is richer than before.

However rewarding at one level, these conversations draw attention to more fundamental issues. What authority, for example, should we give to Scripture? All mainline denominations recognize that Christians come to know Christ through the work of the Holy Spirit in the Bible, in the church, and in the individual. But are these equal? Does one deserve preeminence? Although overly simplistic, one can group baptismal practices by what Christians recognize as their primary authority. Restoration Movement and Baptist churches highly esteem Scripture. Church tradition plays a greater role in Catholicism and Orthodoxy. Quakers and some Pentecostals elevate the personal experience of the Spirit. Again, all Christians accept the manifold work of the Spirit, yet how various churches weigh the Spirit's testimony affects baptismal practice. Of particular note in this respect are the developments in Catholic baptismal theology since Vatican II, one consequence of which is a greater appreciation for scriptural traditions.

Beyond the issue of authority, Christians also disagree over interpretation of the Bible. In every essay the same passages appear; nevertheless they receive widely divergent readings. Just note the explanations of the Great Commission (Matt 28:18–20) that range from liturgical legalism to dismissal as early aberration or late interpolation. Obviously more than baptism needs our attention.

Progressing through the chapters I found less and less satisfying the language of baptism as "outward sign." Perhaps most eloquently and influentially formulated by Augustine, the idea surfaced much earlier, molded in part by Greek anthropology and stark dualism. In my opinion, this has resulted in a false dichotomy between "body" and "spirit," ripping apart the very elements of creation: God took flesh, breathed into it spirit, and a living soul resulted (i.e., soul = body + Spirit). God does not concern himself with just one third of each person he creates; he cares for the whole. When healing a lame man whom four friends had lowered through a roof, Jesus refused to conform to the semantic distinction the religious observers wished to impose. To say, "Your sins are forgiven" is to say, "Get up and walk." The former does not indicate a "spiritual" ministry just as the latter does not signify a "physical" one. Jesus saved a soul that day.

I think the sacraments, too, have power because of God's merciful willingness to work with those he created exactly as he created them. Here I stand against my own tradition, for I regard the Lord's Supper, the Eucharist, to be more than crackers and juice. They are more than symbol; they are spiritual food and drink (1 Cor 10). Likewise, baptism in water also is conjoined with Spirit. The language of "outward sign" seems to convey that God does not work or manifest his power in physical elements, or at least the phrase is often interpreted so. Creation begs to differ (Rom 8).

REFLECTIONS FROM THE PENTECOSTAL TRADITION

Steve Studebaker

I want to thank all of the contributors to the volume for their fine representation of their respective traditions' views on baptism. I have two areas of reflection.

First, the Orthodox position sees baptism as entry to being "in Christ." However, what does this view mean for people, especially Evangelicals in North America, who have a conversion experience and by all appearances are "in Christ," but who may not be baptized for many months or even years after their conversion, let alone that their baptism is not within an Orthodox ecclesial context? Of course, the problem of this practice among Evangelicals is that it appears entirely at odds with the significance placed on baptism in the early church. Nevertheless, it is common among Evangelicals and thus the question: Does a person need to receive and participate in the sacramental event in order to receive the grace signified, and according to sacramental theology, communicated and mediated by the sacrament? If the answer is "yes," then that position seems to question the legitimacy of the experience of grace by those who have not received baptism (I do not think Steenberg implicitly or explicitly suggests this conclusion). If the answer is "no," then baptism as a means of grace seems to be marginalized and indeed reduced to a superfluous option. This highlights the problem in my Pentecostal tradition. We emphasize so much the direct relation a person can have with Christ and minimize and sometimes denigrate the traditional means of grace, except for Scripture, that baptism becomes functionally optional and perhaps irrelevant—remember the story of my Pentecostal church with the broken baptistery! This attitude is clearly out of step, not only with the dominant practice of the churches prior to the modern era, but with the New Testament. Jesus delineated only three (at the most) religious rites—Lord's Supper, baptism, and maybe foot washing. The centrality of baptism in the Orthodox, Catholic, Lutheran, and Anglican traditions seems more consistent with Scripture, but also stands in tension with the way many contemporary evangelical and Pentecostal Christians experience Christ's grace. I am convinced that the Pentecostal theology and practice of baptism is vacuous, but am not convinced that a strong sacramental mediation of grace is therefore necessary for receiving grace. Moreover, although I probably have a more elastic view of the "one Church" than does Steenberg, and would not restrict authentic baptism to its contours as he does, I do appreciate his willingness to maintain, as he admits, a view that is unpopular in the contemporary ecumenical ethos, which often implicitly encourages churches to scuttle their theological commitments for the sake of a contrived unity. Unity that requires churches to dispense with, deny, or reject their unique theologies and practices is obsequious at best and disingenuous at worst.

Second, Kelly suggests that since the church is a sacrament, then "the church is the place of saving encounter with the risen Jesus; it mediates the saving grace of Christ."[13] I agree that the church is a sacrament and mediates grace, but I am not convinced that it is an exclusive instrument of grace. In Acts, the Samaritans receive the gospel, and presumably Christ's grace, outside of the recognized boundary of the church; hence, the Jerusalem church dispatches Peter and John to ratify the Samaritan's inclusion in the church. Acts also portrays Gentiles—e.g., Peter at Cornelius's household and Paul and Barnabas in Antioch—receiving the gospel outside the recognized boundary of the church. Central to this issue is: What constitutes the church? It may very well be that the church was not circumscribed by the Jerusalem leadership's understanding of the church and that the church, and hence the "place"

---

13. Kelly, "Baptism in the Roman Catholic Church," 46.

of the mediation of the grace of Christ, is anywhere Christians preach the gospel and administer the sacraments and people receive the gospel and the sacraments. However, at least initially, the Jerusalem church did not recognize these instances of ministry and reception of the gospel as taking place in the church. Thus, while I agree that the church mediates the grace of Christ through its ministries, I do not think that the Holy Spirit's ability to mediate Christ's grace is circumscribed by institutional ecclesial boundaries.

Bibliography

Allen, Jimmy. *Rebaptism: What One Must Know to Be Born Again.* West Monroe, LA: Howard, 1991.
Allison, C. FitzSimons. *The Rise of Moralism: The Proclamation of the Gospel from Hooker to Baxter.* Vancouver, BC: Regent, 1966.
Ambrose. "On the Sacraments." In *The Awe-Inspiring Rites of Initiation: The Origins of the R.C.I.A.*, edited and translated by Edward Yarnold, 98–149. Collegeville: Liturgical, 1994.
Anderson, Allan. *An Introduction to Pentecostalism: Global Charismatic Christianity.* New York: Cambridge University Press, 2004.
———. "Revising Pentecostal History in Global Perspective." In *Asian and Pentecostal: The Charismatic Face of Christianity in Asia*, edited by Allan Anderson and Edmond Tang, 147–73. Asian Journal of Pentecostal Studies Series 3. Baguio City, Philippines: Regnum, 2005.
Anderson, Oscar A. *Baptism and Its Relation to Lutheran Evangelism.* Minneapolis: Augsburg, 1955.
Anderson, Paul N. "Jesus and Transformation." In *Psychology and the Bible.* Vol. 4. *From Christ to Jesus*, edited by J. Harold Ellens and Wayne G. Rollins," 305–28. Westport, CT: Praeger, 2004.
———. "Was the Fourth Evangelist a Quaker?" *Quaker Religious Thought* 76 (1991) 27–44.
Andreae, Jakob. *Acta colloquii Montis Bellisgartensis.* Tübingen: Gruppenbach, 1587.
Arand, Charles P. *That I May Be His Own. An Overview of Luther's Catechisms.* Saint Louis: Concordia, 2000.
Armstrong, John H. *Understanding Four Views on Baptism.* Grand Rapids: Zondervan, 2007.
Attridge, Harold. *Hebrews.* Philadelphia: Fortress, 1989.
Augustine. "Sermon 8 (Denis)." In *Saint Augustine: Commentary on the Sermon on the Mount with Seventeen Related Sermons: The Fathers of the Church.* Vol. 11. Translated by Denis J. Kavanagh. Washington, DC: The Catholic University of America Press, 1951.
———. "Tractate on the Gospel of John 80.3." In *St. Augustine: Tractates on the Gospel of John 55–111: The Fathers of the Church.* Vol 90. Translated by John W. Rettig. Washington: The Catholic University of America Press, 1994.
Aynsworth, N. J. *Moral and Spiritual Aspects of Baptism.* St. Louis: Christian Publishing, 1902.
Baker, Frank. *John Wesley and the Church of England.* 2nd ed. London: Epworth, 2000.
Baptism, Eucharist and Ministry. Faith and Order Paper 111. Geneva: World Council of Churches, 1982.

Baptist Union of Great Britain web site. "Declaration of Principle." No Pages. Accessed May 25, 2010. Online: http://www.baptist.org.uk/baptist_life/what_is_a_baptist/dec_of_principle.html.

"Baptist Union of Scotland" and "Baptist Union of Sweden," in *Churches Respond to BEM: Official Responses to the "Baptism, Eucharist and Ministry" Text*, edited by Max Thurian, 3:230–45 and 4:200–213. 6 vols. Faith and Order Papers 129, 132, 135, 137, 143, and 144. Geneva: World Council of Churches, 1986–88.

Barrett, David B., Todd M. Johnson, and Peter F. Crossing. "Missiometrics 2007: Creating Your Own Analysis of Global Data." *International Bulletin of Missionary Research* 31 (2007) 25–32.

Barth, Karl. *Church Dogmatics*. IV. *The Christian Life (Fragment)*, edited by G. W. Bromiley and T. F. Torrance. Translated by G. W. Bromiley. Edinburgh: T. & T. Clark, 1960.

———. *The Epistle to the Romans*. Translated by E. C. Hoskyns. London: Oxford University Press, 1933.

———. *The Teaching of the Church regarding Baptism*. Translated by Ernest A. Payne. London: SCM, 1948.

Bavinck, Herman. *Reformed Dogmatics*. Vol. 4. Edited by John Bolt. Grand Rapids: Baker, 2008.

Beall, James Lee. *Rise to Newness of Life: A Look at Water Baptism*. Detroit: Evangel, 1974.

Beasley-Murray, G. R. "Baptism Controversy—'The Spirit Is There.'" *Baptist Times* 10 (December 1959) 8.

———. *Baptism in the New Testament*. Exeter: Paternoster, 1972.

———. "The Problem in Infant Baptism: An Exercise in Possibilities." In *Festschrift Günter Wagner: International Theological Studies Contributions of Baptist Scholars*, 1, edited by Faculty of Baptist Theological Seminary, 1–14. Berne: Peter Lang, 1994.

Bebbington, D. W. *Evangelicalism in Modern Britain: A History from the 1730s to the 1980s*. London: Unwin Hyman, 1989.

Believing and Being Baptized: Baptism, So-called Re-baptism, and Children in the Church. Didcot: Baptist Union of Great Britain, 1996.

Bergsten, Torsten. "Baptism and the Church: Baptist Faith and Practice in a Biblical and Ecumenical Light." *Baptist Quarterly* 18.3–4 (July and October 1959) 125–31, 159–71.

Best, Thomas F., ed. *Baptism Today: Understanding, Practice, Ecumenical Implications*. Collegeville: Liturgical, 2008.

Boismard, M.-E. *L'Énigme de la lettre aux Éphésiens*. Paris: Gabalda, 1999.

Bonhoeffer, Dietrich. *Act and Being. Transcendental Philosophy and Ontology in Systematic Theology*. Translated by H. Martin Rumscheidt. Minneapolis: Fortress, 1996.

———. *Discipleship*. Translated by Barbara Green and Reinhard Krauss. Minneapolis: Fortress, 2001.

———. *Sanctorum Communio. A Theological Study of the Sociology of the Church*. Translated by Reinhard Krauss and Nancy Lukens. Minneapolis: Fortress, 1998.

Brenz, Johannes. *Catechismus*. 1535. Reprinted, Wittenberg: Schwenck, 1563.

Bridge, Donald and Phypers, David. *The Water That Divides*. Downers Grove: InterVarsity, 1977.

Brinkel, Karl. "Die Lehre Luthers von der *fides infantium* bei der Kindertaufe." ThD diss., University of Jena, 1955.

Bromiley, Geoffrey W. *Children of Promise: The Case for Baptizing Infants*. Grand Rapids: Eerdmans, 1979.

Burgess, Stanley M., and Eduard M. Van Der Maas, editors. *The New International Dictionary of Pentecostal and Charismatic Movements: 2002 Revised and Expanded Edition*. Grand Rapids: Zondervan, 2003.

Burreson, Kent J. "The Saving Flood: The Medieval Origins, Historical Development, and Theological Import of the Sixteenth Century Lutheran Baptismal Rites." PhD diss., University of Notre Dame, 2002.

Byrne, Brendan. *Romans*. Sacra Pagina 6. Collegeville, MN: Liturgical, 1996.

Cabasilas, Nicolas. *The Life in Christ*. Yonkers, NY: St. Vladimir's Seminary Press, 1974.

Calvin, John. *Institutes of the Christian Religion*. Westminster: Westminster Press, 1960.

Campbell, Alexander. *The Christian System*. 2nd ed. Pittsburgh: Forrester & Campbell, 1839.

———. *Debate on Christian Baptism*. Buffalo: A. Campbell, 1824.

———. *Debate on Christian Baptism*. Lexington: Skillman, 1844.

Carpe, William. "Baptismal Theology in the Disciples of Christ." *Review and Expositor* 77 (1980) 89–100.

Chadwick, Owen, editor. *The Mind of the Oxford Movement*. London: Adam & Charles Black, 1960.

Chauvet, Louis-Marie. *Symbol and Sacrament: A Sacramental Reinterpretation of Christian Existence*. Translated by Patrick Madigan and Madeleine Beaumont. Collegeville: Liturgical, 1995.

Chemnitz, Martin. "Concerning Baptism." In Chemnitz's *Examination of the Council of Trent Part II*, trans. Fred Kramer, 119–77. Saint Louis: Concordia, 1978.

———. *Examen Concilii Tridentini*, edited by Eduard Preuss. Berlin: Schlawitz, 1861.

———. *Examination of the Council of Trent*, translated by Fred Kramer. Saint Louis: Concordia, 1971–1986.

———. *Loci theologici . . . quibus et Loci communes d. Philippi Melancthonis perspicue explicantur*. Frankfurt: Spies, 1591–1592.

Childers, Jeff W., and Aquino, Frederick. *Unveiling Glory: Visions of Christ's Transforming Presence*. Abilene: ACU Press, 2003.

The Church of England web site. "Christian Initiation: Entering into a New Relationship with God." No pages. Accessed April 2009. Online: http://www.cofe.anglican.org/lifeevents/baptismconfirm/sectiona.html.

Clark, Matthew S. "Initial Evidence: A Southern African Perspective." *Asian Journal of Pentecostal Studies* 1 (1998) 203–17.

Coffey, John. "From Helwys to Leland: Baptists and Religious Liberty in England and America, 1612–1791." In *The Gospel in the World: International Baptist Studies in Baptist History and Thought, 1*, edited by D. W. Bebbington, 13–37. Carlisle: Paternoster, 2002.

Cohn, Norman. *The Pursuit of the Millennium*. 3rd ed. Oxford: Oxford University Press, 1970.

Coleman-Norton, P. R. *Roman State and Christian Church*. 3 vols. London: SPCK, 1966.

Colwell, John E. *Promise and Presence: An Exploration of Sacramental Theology*. Milton Keynes: Paternoster, 2005.

Cooper, William A. *A Living Faith: An Historical Comparative Study of Quaker Beliefs*. Richmond, IN: Friends United Press, 1990.

Cotterell, Jack. *Baptism: A Biblical Study*. Joplin: College Press, 1989.

Council for Christian Unity. *Pushing at the Boundaries of Unity: Anglicans and Baptists in Conversation.* London: Church House, 2005.

Creech, Joe. "Visions of Glory: The Place of the Azusa Street Revival in Pentecostal History." *Church History* 65 (1996) 405–24.

Cross, "The Adoption of Believer's Baptism and Baptist Beginnings." In *Exploring Baptist Origins*, edited by Anthony R. Corss and Nicholas J. Wood, 1–31. Centre for Baptist History and Heritage Studies 1. Oxford: Regent's Park College, 2010.

———. *Baptism and the Baptists: Theology and Practice in Twentieth-Century Britain.* Studies in Baptist History and Thought 3. Milton Keynes: Paternoster, 2000.

———. "The Evangelical Sacrament: *Baptisma semper reformandum*." *EQ* 80 (2008) 195–217.

———. "Spirit- and Water-Baptism in 1 Corinthians 12.13." In *Dimensions of Baptism: Biblical and Theological Studies*, edited by Stanley E. Porter and Anthony R. Cross, 120–48. JSNTSup 234. Sheffield: Sheffield Academic, 2002.

Cross, Anthony R., and Philip E. Thompson. "Introduction: Baptist Sacramentalism." In *Baptist Sacramentalism*, edited by Anthony R. Cross and Philip E. Thompson, 1–7. Studies in Baptist History and Thought 5. Milton Keynes: Paternoster, 2003.

Crowe, Terrence R. *Pentecostal Unity: Recurring Frustration and Enduring Hopes.* Chicago: Loyola University Press, 1993.

Culpepper, R. Alan. *Anatomy of the Fourth Gospel.* Philadelphia: Fortress, 1983.

Dix, Gregory. *Theology of Confirmation in Relation to Baptism.* London: Dacre, 1953.

Documents on the Liturgy 1963–1979: Conciliar, Papal, and Curial Texts. Collegeville: Liturgical, 1982.

Dodd, C. H. *The Interpretation of the Fourth Gospel.* Cambridge: Cambridge University Press, 1953.

Doig, Allan. *Liturgy and Architecture: From the Early Church to the Middle Ages.* Farnham, Surrey, UK/Burlington, VA: Ashgate, 2008.

Dowey, Edward. "Heinrich Bullinger." In *Encyclopedia of the Reformed Faith*, edited by Donald K. McKim, 44. Louisville: Westminster John Knox, 1992.

Dunn, James D. G. *Baptism in the Holy Spirit.* Philadelphia: Westminster, 1970.

———. "Sacraments." In *Unity and Diversity in the New Testament: An Inquiry into the Character of Earliest Christianity*, by J. D. G. Dunn, 150–73. 2nd ed. Valley Forge, PA: Trinity Press International, 1990.

Dusing, Michael L. "The New Testament Church." In *Systematic Theology*, edited by Stanley M. Horton, 525–66. 2nd ed. Springfield, MO: Logion, 1995.

Elert, Werner. "Anchoring the Christian Life in Baptism." In *The Christian Ethos*, translated by Carl. J. Schindler. Philadelphia: Muhlenberg, 1957.

———. *The Structure of Lutheranism.* Vol. 1. Translated by Walter A. Hansen. Saint Louis: Concordia, 1962.

England, Stephen. *The One Baptism: Baptism and Christian Unity with Special Reference to Disciples of Christ.* St. Louis: Bethany, 1960.

Ferel, Martin. *Gepredigte Taufe, eine homiletische Untersuchung zur Taufpredigt bei Luther.* Tübingen: Mohr/Siebeck, 1969.

Ferguson, Everett. *Baptism in the Early Church: History, Theology, and Liturgy in the First Five Centuries.* Grand Rapids: Eerdmans, 2009.

———. *The Church of Christ: A Biblical Ecclesiology for Today.* Grand Rapids: Eerdmans, 1996.

Fiddes, Paul S. "Baptism and Creation." In *Reflections on the Water: Understanding God and the World through the Baptism of Believers*, edited by Paul S. Fiddes, 47–67. Regent's Study Guides 4. Oxford: Regent's Park College; Macon, GA: Smyth & Helwys, 1996.

———. "*Ex opere Operato*: Re-thinking a Historic Baptist Rejection." In *Baptist Sacramentalism*, vol. 2, edited by Anthony R. Cross and Philip E. Thompson, 219–38. Studies in Baptist History and Thought 25. Milton Keynes: Paternoster, 2008.

———, editor. *Reflections on the Water: Understanding God and the World through the Baptism of Believers*. Regent's Study Guides 4. Oxford: Regent's Park College; Macon, GA: Smyth & Helwys, 1996.

———. "'Walking Together': The Place of Covenant in Baptist Life Yesterday and Today." In *Pilgrim Pathways: Essays in Baptist History in Honour of B. R. White*, edited by W. H. Brackney, P. S. Fiddes and J. H. Y. Briggs, 47–74. Macon, GA: Mercer University Press, 1999.

Finn, Thomas M. *Early Christian Baptism and the Catechumenate: Italy, North Africa, and Egypt*. Message of the Fathers of the Church 6. Collegeville: Liturgical, 1992.

The First and Second Prayer Books of King Edward VI, London: Everyman, 1976.

Fletcher, David, ed. *Baptism and the Remission of Sins: An Historical Perspective*. Joplin: College, 1990.

Foster, Douglas A. "Churches of Christ and Baptism: An Historical and Theological Overview." *ResQ* 43 (2001) 79–94.

Fowler, Stanley K. "Is 'Baptist Sacramentalism' an Oxymoron?: Reactions in Britain to *Christian Baptism* (1959)." In *Baptist Sacramentalism*, edited by Anthony R. Cross and Philip E. Thompson, 129–50. Studies in Baptist History and Thought 5. Milton Keynes: Paternoster, 2003.

———. *More than a Symbol: The British Baptist Recovery of Baptismal Sacramentalism*. Studies in Baptist History and Thought 2. Milton Keynes: Paternoster, 2002.

Fox, Thomas C. "Pope Benedict Answers Questions of Local Priests." Web page. *National Catholic Reporter*. Accessed March 11, 2009. Online: http://ncronline.org/node/12551.

Freeman, Curtis W. "'To Feed Upon by Faith': Nourishment from the Lord's Table." In *Baptist Sacramentalism*, edited by Anthony R. Cross and Philip E. Thompson, 194–210. Studies in Baptist History and Thought 5. Milton Keynes: Paternoster, 2003.

Freiday, Dean, ed. *Barclay's Apology: In Modern English*. Elberon, NJ: Hemlock, 1967.

Gee, Donald. "Baptism and Salvation." In *Water Baptism and the Trinity*, edited by J. Narver et al., 5–14. Springfield, MO: Gospel Publishing, n.d.

George, Timothy. "The Reformed Doctrine of Believers' Baptism." *Interpretation* 47 (1993) 242–54.

———. "The Sacramentality of the Church: An Evangelical Baptist Perspective." In *Baptist Sacramentalism*, edited by Anthony R. Cross and Philip E. Thompson, 21–35. Studies in Baptist History and Thought 5. Milton Keynes: Paternoster, 2003.

George, Timothy, and Denise George, editors. *Baptist Confessions, Covenants, and Catechisms*. Nashville: Broadman & Holman, 1999.

Gerhard, Johann. *Loci theologici*, edited by Eduward Preuss IV. Berlin: Schlawitz, 1866.

———. *Meditationes Sacrae (1606/7)*, edited by Johann Anselm Steiger. Stuttgart-Bad-Cannstatt: Fromann-Holzboog, 2000.

Gilmore, Alec, ed. *Christian Baptism: A Fresh Attempt to Understand the Rite in Terms of Scripture, History, and Theology*. London: Lutterworth, 1959.

Gortner, J. Narver. "The Apostolic Formula." In *Water Baptism and the Trinity*, edited by J. Narver Gortner et al., 47–53. Springfield, MO: Gospel Publishing, 2005.

———. "The Importance of Water Baptism." In *Water Baptism and the Trinity*, edited by J. Narver Gortner et al., 35–46. Springfield, MO: Gospel Publishing, 2005.

Gortner, J. Narver et al., eds. *Water Baptism and the Trinity*. Springfield, MO: Gospel Publishing, 2005.

Green, Michael. *Baptism: Its Purpose, Practice and Power*. London: Hodder & Stoughton, 1987.

Grönvik, Lorenz. *Die Taufe in der Theologie Martin Luthers*. Åbo: Åbo Akademi, 1968.

Gurney, Joseph John. *A Peculiar People*. Richmond, IN: Friends United, 1979.

Hageman, Howard. "Reformed Spirituality." In *Protestant Spiritual Traditions*, edited by Frank C. Senn, 55–79. New York: Paulist, 1986.

Hallesby, Ole. *Infant Baptism and Adult Conversion: An Exposition of the Relation between Regeneration in Infant Baptism and Awakening and Conversion*. Translated by Clarence J. Carlsen. Minneapolis: Messenger, 1924.

Hamor, Ralph. *True Discourse of the Present State of Virginia*. London, 1615. Reprint, Amsterdam: Da Capo Press, 1971.

Harmless, William. *Augustine and the Catechumenate*. Collegeville: Liturgical, 1995.

Harmon, S. R. *Towards Baptist Catholicity: Essays on Tradition and the Baptist Vision*. Studies in Baptist History and Thought 27. Milton Keynes: Paternoster, 2006.

Harrison, Wes. "The Renewal of the Practice of Adult Baptism by Immersion during the Reformation Era, 1525–1700." *ResQ* 43 (2001) 95–112.

Hart, Larry D. *Truth Aflame: Theology for the Church in Renewal*. 1999. Reprint, Grand Rapids: Zondervan, 2005.

Haymes, Brian. "Baptism: A Question of Belief and Age?" *Perspectives in Religious Studies* 27 (2000) 125–30.

———. "On Religious Liberty: Re-reading *A Short Declaration of the Mystery of Iniquity* in London in 2005." *Baptist Quarterly* 42.3 (July 2007) 197–217.

Haymes, Brian, Ruth Gouldbourne, and Anthony R. Cross. *On Being the Church: Revisioning Baptist Identity*. Studies in Baptist History and Thought 21. Milton Keynes: Paternoster, 2008.

The Heidelberg Catechism. http://www.ccel.org/creeds/heidelberg-cat-ext.txt.

Hicks, John Mark, and Greg Taylor. *Down in the River to Pray: Revisioning Baptism as God's Transforming Work*. Abilene: Leafwood, 2004.

Hicks, L. Edward. "Rational Religion in the Ohio Western Reserve (1827–1830): Walter Scott and the Restoration Appeal of Baptism for the Remission of Sins." *ResQ* 34 (1992) 207–19.

Higgins, John R., Michael L. Dusing, and Frank D. Tallman. *An Introduction to Theology: A Classical Pentecostal Perspective*. 1993. Reprint, Dubuque, IA: Kendall & Hunt, 1994.

The First and Second Prayer Books of King Edward VI, London: Everyman, 1976.

Hooker, Richard. *Of the Laws of Ecclesiastical Polity*. London: Everyman, 1922.

Horton, Stanley M., editor. *Systematic Theology*. Rev. ed. Springfield, MO: Logion, 1995.

Hunter, Harold D. "Reflections by a Pentecostalist on Aspects of BEM." *Journal of Ecumenical Studies* 29 (1992) 317–45.

Hütter, Leonhard. *Compendium locorum theologicorum ex Scripturis Sacris et Libro Concordiae*. Edited by Johann Anselm Steiger. Stuttgart-Bad-Cannstatt: Fromann-Holzboog, 2006.

International Commission on English in the Liturgy. *Documents on the Liturgy 1963–1979: Conciliar, Papal, and Curial Texts.* Collegeville: Liturgical, 1982.

Irons, William J. *The Judgments on Baptismal Regeneration.* London: Joseph Masters, 1850.

Jenson, Robert. "Baptism." In *Christian Dogmatics,* edited by Carl E. Braaten and Robert W. Jenson, 2:315–36. Philadelphia: Fortress, 1984.

Jeremias, Joachim. *Infant Baptism in the First Four Centuries.* Translated by David Cairns. London: SCM, 1960.

Jewel, John. *The Apology of the Church of England.* Translated by Lady Anne Bacon from *Apologia Ecclesiae anglicanae* [1562]. Vol. 3 of *The Works of John Jewel, Bishop of Salisbury,* edited by John Ayre. 4 Vols. Parker Society Publications. Cambridge: Cambridge University Press, 1845–50.

Jewett, Paul K. *Infant Baptism and the Covenant of Grace: An Appraisal of the Argument That as Infants Were Once Circumcised, so They Should Now Be Baptized.* Grand Rapids: Eerdmans, 1978.

Johnson, Maxwell E. *The Rites of Christian Initiation: Their Evolution and Interpretation.* Collegeville: Liturgical, 1990.

Johnsson, Lennart. *Baptist Reconsideration of Baptism and Ecclesiology: A Presentation of the Baptist Union of Sweden and a Study of Its Official Response to BEM in Relation to the Public Discussions Primarily amongst Its Pastors and Theologians.* European University Studies, Series 23 Theology. Frankfurt: Peter Lang, 2000.

Joint Working Group. "Ecclesiological and Ecumenical Implications of a Common Baptism: A JWG Study." In *Joint Working Group between the Roman Catholic Church and the World Council of Churches: Eighth Report.* Geneva: WCC Publications, 2005.

Jones, Keith M., and Ian M. Randall, eds. *Counter-Cultural Communities: Baptistic Life in Twentieth-Century Europe.* Studies in Baptist History and Thought 32. Milton Keynes: Paternoster, 2008.

Jones, T. Canby, ed. *The Power of the Lord Is over All: The Pastoral Letters of George Fox.* Richmond, IN: Friends United, 1989.

Kärkkäinen, Veli-Matti. *Ad ultimum terrae: Evangelization, Proselytism, and Common Witness in the Roman Catholic Pentecostal Dialogue (1990–1997).* Studien zur Interkulturellen Geschichte des Christentums 117. New York: Peter Lang, 1999.

———. *Spiritus ubi vult spirat: Pneumatology in Roman Catholic-Pentecostal Dialogue (1972–1989).* Schriften der Luther-Agricola Gesellschaft 42. Helsinki: Luther-Agricola-Society, 1998.

Kasper, Walter. "Ecclesiological and Ecumenical Implications of Baptism." *The Ecumenical Review* 52 (2000) 526–41.

Kavanagh, Aidan. *The Shape of Baptism: The Rite of Christian Initiation.* Collegeville: Liturgical, 1991.

Kendall, I. "The Evangelical Foundations of Believers' Baptism." *Evangelist* 1 (1922) 9–11.

Koch, Kurt. "Principles for a Christian Theology of Baptism." *Theology Digest* 52 (2005) 231–41.

Kolb, Robert. "God Kills to Make Alive: Romans 6 and Luther's Understanding of Justification (1535)." *Lutheran Quarterly* 12 (1998) 33–56.

———. *Make Disciples, Baptizing, God's Gift of New Life and Christian Witness.* Saint Louis: Concordia Seminary Publications, 1997.

———. "'What Benefit Does the Soul Receive from a Handful of Water?' Luther's Preaching on Baptism, 1528–1539." *Concordia Journal* 25 (1999) 346–63.
Kolb, Robert, and Timothy J. Wengert, editors. *The Book of Concord*. Minneapolis: Fortress, 2000.
Kolp, Alan. "Friends, Sacraments and Sacramental Living." *Quaker Religious Thought* 57 (1984) 36–52.
Kruger, C. Baxter. *The Great Dance: The Christian Vision Revisited*. Jackson: Perichoresis, 2000.
Lampe, G. W. H. *The Seal of the Spirit*. London: Longmans, Green and Co., 1951.
Leith, John. "Sacraments." In *The Dictionary of the Presbyterian and Reformed Tradition in America*, edited by D. H. Hart and Mark A. Noll, 225–28. Philipsburg, NJ: Presbyterian & Reformed, 2005.
Leonard, Bill J. *Baptist Ways: A History*. Valley Forge, PA: Judson, 2003.
Lightfoot, J. B. *St. Paul's Epistles to the Colossians and Philemon*. New York: MacMillan, 1882.
London Yearly Meeting of the Religious Society of Friends. *Christian Faith and Practice in the Experience of the Society of Friends*. Richmond, IN: Friends United, 1960.
Lumpkin, William L. *Baptist Confessions of Faith*. 2nd ed. Valley Forge, PA: Judson, 1969.
Luther, Martin. "Baptism." In *The Large Catechism*, in *The Book of Concord*, edited by Robert Kolb and Timothy J. Wengert, 456–67. Minneapolis: Fortress, 2000.
———. *Luther's Works*. Saint Louis: Concordia; Philadelphia: Fortress, 1958–1986.
———. *D. Martin Luthers Werke*. Weimar: Böhlau, 1883.
Lutheran Service Book. Saint Louis: Concordia, 2006.
Macchia, Frank D. *Baptized in the Spirit: A Global Pentecostal Theology*. Grand Rapids: Zondervan, 2006.
———. "Tongues as a Sign: Towards a Sacramental Understanding of Pentecostal Experience." *Pneuma: The Journal of the Society for Pentecostal Studies* 15 (1993) 61–76.
MacDonald, Margaret Y. *Colossians and Ephesians*, Sacra Pagina Series 17. Collegeville: Liturgical, 2000.
Marcel, Pierre Ch. *The Biblical Doctrine of Infant Baptism*. Exeter: James Clarke, 1953.
Mason, A. J. *The Relation of Confirmation to Baptism*. 2nd ed. London: Longmans, Green & Co., 1893.
Mathesius, Johannes. *Postilla oder Außlegung der Sontags Euangelien uber das gantze Jar*. Nuremberg: Berg/Neuber, 1565.
McBeth, H. Leon. *The Baptist Heritage*. Nashville: Broadman, 1987.
———. *A Sourcebook for Baptist Heritage*. Nashville: Broadman, 1990.
McDonnell, Kilian. "The Holy Spirit and Christian Initiation." In *The Holy Spirit and Power: The Catholic Charismatic Renewal*, edited by Kilian McDonnell, 57–89. Garden City, NY: Doubleday, 1975.
———, editor. *Presence, Power, Praise: Documents of the Charismatic Renewal*. 3 vols. Collegeville: Liturgical, 1980.
McKim, Donald. *Westminster Dictionary of Theological Terms*. Louisville: John Knox, 1996.
Melancthon, Philip. *Melanchthons Werke in Auswahl*, edited by Robert Stupperich. Gütersloh: Bertelsmann, 1955.

Menzies, William W. "A Trinitarian Pentecostal Response." *Pneuma: The Journal of the Society for Pentecostal Studies* 30 (2008) 229–32.
Miller, G. G. "A Baptist Theology of the Child." DTh diss., University of South Africa, 1992.
Millar, William R. "Common Statements." A section in "Lutheran-Baptist Dialogue." *American Baptist Quarterly* 1:2 (1982) 99–215.
Mörlin, Joachim. "Katechismus (1554)." In *Quellen zur Geschichte des kirchlichen Untterrichts in der evangelischen Kirche Deutschlands zwischen 1530 und 1600*, edited by Johann Michael Reu. Gütersloh: Bertelsmann, 1920.
Morrison, C. C. *The Meaning of Baptism*. Chicago: Disciples Publication Society, 1914.
Murray, John. *Christian Baptism*. Philipsburg, NJ: Presbyterian & Reformed, 1977.
Nagel, Norman E. "Holy Baptism." In *Lutheran Worship: History and Practice*, edited by Fred L. Precht, 262–89. Saint Louis: Concordia, 1993.
Nelle, Wilhelm, editor. *Paul Gerhardts Lieder und Gedichte*. Haumburg: Schloeßmann, 1907.
Nickalls, John L., editor. *The Journal of George Fox*. London: Cambridge University Press, 1952.
Nickalls, John L., Henry Joel Cadbury, and Geoffrey Fillingham Nuttall. *The Journal of George Fox: A Revised Edition by John L. Nickalls: With an Epilogue by Henry J. Cadbury and an Introduction by Geoffrey F. Nuttall*. Philadelphia: Religious Society of Friends, 1985.
Nischan, Bodo. "The Exorcism Controversy and Baptism in the Late Reformation." *Sixteenth Century Journal* 18 (1989) 31–51.
Noll, Mark A. *A History of Christianity in the United States and Canada*. Grand Rapids: Eerdmans, 1992.
Northwest Yearly Meeting of Friends. *Faith and Practice*. Accessed June 18, 2009. Online: http://nwfriends.org/what-friends-believe.
Old, Hughes Oliphant. "Baptism." In *Encyclopedia of the Reformed Faith*, edited by Donald K. McKim, 21–24. Louisville: Westminster John Knox, 1992.
———. *The Shaping of the Reformed Baptismal Rite in the Sixteenth Century*. Grand Rapids: Eerdmans, 1992.
Ordo Baptismi Parvulorum. Vatican: Typis Polyglottis Vaticanis, 1969.
Ordo Initiationis Christianae Adultorum. Vatican: Typis Polyglottis Vaticanis, 1972.
Orombi, Henry Luke. "What is Anglicanism?" *First Things: A Monthly Journal of Religion and Public Life* 175 (August/September 2007) 23–28.
Osborne, Kenan B. *The Christian Sacraments of Initiation: Baptism, Confirmation, Eucharist*. New York: Paulist, 1987.
Oyer, John S. *Lutheran Reformers against Anabaptists: Luther, Melanchthon, and Menius and the Anabaptists of Central Germany*. The Hague: Nijhoff, 1964.
Palmer, G. E. H. *Philokalia*. Vol. 4. Translated by G. E. H. Palmer, Philip Sherrard, Kallistos Ware. Berkshire: The Eling Trust, 1995.
Pearlman, Myer. *Knowing the Doctrines of the Bible*. 1937. Rev. ed. Springfield, MO: Gospel Publishing, 1981.
Peters, Albrecht. *Kommentar zu Luthers Katechismen*, edited by Gottfried Seebaß. 5 vols. Göttingen: Vandenhoeck & Ruprecht, 1991.
Peterson, Eugene H. *Working the Angles: The Shape of Pastoral Integrity*. Grand Rapids: Eerdmans, 1987.

Pfatteicher, Philip H. *Commentary on the Lutheran Book of Worship. Lutheran Liturgy in Its Ecumenical Context*. Minneapolis: Augsburg & Fortress, 1990.

Philipp the Younger (Baron of Winnenberg and Beihelfstein). "Vom heiligen Tauff." In *Das deutsche Kirchenlied von der ältesten Zeit bis zu Anfang des XVII. Jahrhunderts*, edited by Philipp Wackernagel, 5:34–35. Hildesheim: Olms, 1964.

Pinnock, Clark H. "The Physical Side of Being Spiritual: God's Sacramental Presence." In *Baptist Sacramentalism*, edited by Anthony R. Cross and Philip E. Thompson, 8–20. Studies in Baptist History and Thought 5. Milton Keynes: Paternoster, 2003.

Porter, Stanley E., and Anthony R. Cross. "Introduction: Baptism in Recent Debate." In *Baptism, the New Testament and the Church: Historical and Contemporary Studies in Honour of R. E. O. White*, edited by Stanley E. Porter and Anthony R. Cross, 33–39. Sheffield: Sheffield Academic, 1999.

———. "Introduction: Baptism—An Ongoing Debate." In *Dimensions of Baptism: Biblical and Theological Studies*, edited by Stanley E. Porter and Anthony R. Cross, 1–6. Sheffield: Sheffield Academic, 2002.

Procter, Francis, and Walter Howard Frere. *A New History of the Book of Common Prayer*. London: Macmillan, 1965.

Pruitt, Raymond M. *Fundamentals of the Faith*. Cleveland, TN: White Wing, 1981.

Punshon, John. *Reasons for Hope: The Faith and Future of the Friends Church*. Richmond, IN: Friends United, 2001.

Rainbow, Jonathan H. "'Confessor Baptism': The Baptismal Doctrine of the Early Anabaptists." In *Believer's Baptism: Sign of the New Covenant in Christ*, edited by Thomas R. Schreiner and Shawn D. Wright, 189–206. Nashville: B&H Academic, 2006.

Raitt, Jill. *The Colloquy of Montbeliard: Religion and Politics in the Sixteenth Century*. Oxford: Oxford University Press, 1993.

Reed, David A. *"In Jesus' Name": The History and Beliefs of Oneness Pentecostals*. Journal of Pentecostal Theology Supplement Series 31. Blandford Forum, UK: Deo Publishing, 2008.

Renihan, James M. *Edification and Beauty: The Practical Ecclesiology of the English Particular Baptists 1675–1705*. Studies in Baptist History and Thought 17. Milton Keynes: Paternoster, 2008.

Riggs, John W. *Baptism in the Reformed Tradition: An Historical and Practical Theology*. Columbia Series in Reformed Theology. Louisville: Westminster John Knox, 2002.

Riker, D. B. *A Catholic Reformed Theologian: Federalism and Baptism in the Thought of Benjamin Keach, 1640–1704*. Studies in Baptist History and Thought 35. Milton Keynes: Paternoster, 2009.

Ringwald, Bartholomaeus. "Von Stiftung und Nutz der Tauffe." In *Das deutsche Kirchenlied von der ältesten Zeit bis zu Anfang des XVII. Jahrhunderts*, edited by Philipp Wackernagel, 4:924. Hildesheim: Olms, 1964.

The Rites of the Catholic Church. Vol 1. New York: Pueblo, 1990.

Rituale Romanum: Pauli V Pont. Max. Jussu editum aliorumque pontt. Cura recognitum atque ad normam codices juris canonici accommodatum. Rome: Marietti, 1952, titulus II.

Robeck, Cecil M., Jr. "Pentecostal Origins from a Global Perspective." In *All Together in One Place: Theological Papers from the Brighton Conference on World Evangelization*, edited by Harold D. Hunter and Peter Hocken, 166–80. Sheffield: Sheffield Academic, 1993.

Bibliography

Robeck Cecil M., Jr., and Jerry L. Sandidge. "The Ecclesiology of *Koinōnia* and Baptism: A Pentecostal Perspective." *Journal of Ecumenical Studies* 27 (1990) 504–34.
Robinson, William. *The Biblical Doctrine of the Church*. St. Louis: Bethany, 1955.
Roy, Kevin. *Baptism, Reconciliation and Unity*. Carlisle: Paternoster, 1997.
Saarnivaara, Uuras. *Scriptural Baptism. A Dialog between John Bapstead and Martin Childfont*. New York: Vantage, 1953.
Sanford, Don A. *A Choosing People: The History of Seventh Day Baptists*. Nashville: Broadman, 1992.
Scaer, David P. *Baptism*. Saint Louis: Luther Academy, 1999.
Schleiermacher, F. D. E. *The Christian Faith*. London: T. & T. Clark, 1999.
Schlink, Edmund. *The Doctrine of Baptism*. Translated by Herbert J. A. Bouman. Saint Louis: Concordia, 1972.
———. *Ökumenische Dogmatik: Grundzüge*. Göttingen: Vandenhoeck & Ruprecht, 1983.
Schnabel, Eckhard J. *Early Christian Mission. I. Jesus and the Twelve*. Leicester, UK: InterVarsity, 2004.
Schreiner, Thomas R., "Baptism in the Epistles: An Initiation Rite for Believers." In *Believer's Baptism: Sign of the New Covenant in Christ*, edited by Thomas R. Schreiner, and Shawn D. Wright, 67–96. NAC Studies in Bible & Theology. Nashville: B&H Academic, 2006.
Selnecker, Nikolaus. *Institutionis Christianae religionis, Pars secunda*. Frankfurt: Lechler, 1573.
———. "Das Sacrament der Heiligen Tauffe," In *Das deutsche Kirchenlied von der ältesten Zeit bis zu Anfang des XVII. Jahrhunderts*, edited by Philipp Wackernagel, 4:255. Hildesheim: Olms, 1964.
Society for Pentecostal Studies. "Oneness-Trinitarian Pentecostal Final Report, 2002–2007." *Pneuma: The Journal of the Society for Pentecostal Studies* 30 (2008) 203–24.
Spinks, Bryan D. *Early and Medieval Rituals and Theologies of Baptism*. Liturgy, Worship and Society Series. Aldershot, UK: Ashgate, 2006.
Stein, Robert H. "Baptism in Luke–Acts." In *Believer's Baptism: Sign of the New Covenant in Christ*, edited by Thomas R. Schreiner and Shawn D. Wright, 35–66. Nashville: B&H Academic, 2006.
Stronstad, Roger. *The Charismatic Theology of St. Luke*. Peabody, MA: Hendrickson, 1984.
Studebaker, Steven M. "*Ex opere operato*: A Proposal for Lutheran and Catholic Unity." *One in Christ* 35 (1999) 326–38.
Tanner, Norman P., editor. *Decrees of the Ecumenical Councils*. London/Washington: Sheed & Ward/Georgetown University Press, 1990.
Taylor, Charles. *A Secular Age*. Cambridge, MA: Belknap, 2007.
Thompson, Philip E. *The Freedom of God: Towards Baptist Theology in Pneumatological Perspective*. Studies in Baptist History and Thought 20. Milton Keynes: Paternoster, 2009.
Torrance, James B. *Worship, Community and the Triune God of Grace*. Downers Grove, IL: InterVarsity, 1996.
"Towards Baptist Identity: A Statement Ratified by the Baptist Heritage Commission in Zagreb, Yugoslavia, July 1989," in *Faith, Life, and Witness: The Papers of the Study and Research Division of the Baptist World Alliance—1986-1990*, edited by William H. Brackney and Ruby J. Burke, 146–49. Birmingham, AL: Samford University Press, 1990.

Tranvik, Mark D. "The Other Sacrament: The Doctrine of Baptism in the Late Lutheran Reformation." ThD diss., Luther Northwestern Theological Seminary, 1992.

Trigg, Jonahan. *Baptism in the Theology of Martin Luther.* Leiden: Brill, 1994.

Ulm, Johann Conrad von. "Gesang vom H. Tauff." In *Das deutsche Kirchenlied von der ältesten Zeit bis zu Anfang des XVII. Jahrhunderts,* edited by Philipp Wackernagel, 5:352–53. Hildesheim: Olms, 1964.

Volf, Miroslav. *Exclusion and Embrace.* Nashville: Abingdon, 1996.

Walker, John, and Alexander Campbell. *Infant Sprinkling Proved to be a Human Tradition.* Steubenville: A. Campbell, 1820.

Walton, Robert C. "Zwingli, Huldrych (1484–1531)." In *Encyclopedia of the Reformed Faith,* edited by Donald K. McKim, 413–14. Louisville: Westminster John Knox, 1992.

Wellum, Stephen J. "Baptism and the Relationship between the Covenants." In *Believer's Baptism: Sign of the New Covenant in Christ,* edited by Thomas R. Schreiner, and Shawn D. Wright, 97–162. Nashville: B&H Academic, 2006.

Welshimer, P. H. [Editorial]. *Christian Standard* (4 December 1926) 655.

West, W. M. S. "Baptism: Report of the Faith and Order Consultation, Louisville 1979." *Baptist Quarterly* 28.5 (January 1980) 232–39.

———. "The Child and the Church: A Baptist Perspective." In *Pilgrim Pathways: Essays in Baptist History in Honour of B. R. White,* edited by W. H. Brackney, et al., 75–164. Macon, GA: Mercer University Press, 1999.

———. "Towards a Consensus on Baptism? Louisville 1979." *Baptist Quarterly* 28.5 (January 1980) 225–32.

The Westminster Confession of Faith. .http://www.reformed.org/documents/wcf_with_proofs/.

Whitaker, E. C. *Documents of the Baptismal Liturgy.* Revised and expanded by Maxwell E. Johnson. Collegeville: Liturgical, 2003.

White, B. R. *The English Baptists of the Seventeenth Century: A History of the English Baptists,* vol 1. 2nd ed. Didcot: The Baptist Historical Society, 1996.

White, R. E. O. *The Biblical Doctrine of Initiation.* London: Hodder & Stoughton, 1960.

Wigand, Johannes. *De Anabaptismo.* Leipzig: Defner, 1582.

Willcuts, Jack L. *Why Friends are Friends: Some Quaker Core Convictions.* Newberg, OR: Barclay, 1984.

Williams, Ernest S. *Systematic Theology.* 3 vols. Springfield, MO: Gospel Publishing, 1981.

Williams, George Hunston. *The Radical Reformation* 3rd ed. Kirksville: The Sixteenth Century Journal, 1992.

Wingren, Gustaf. *Gospel and Church.* Translated by Ross Mackenzie. Philadelphia: Fortress, 1964.

Winslow, Edward, and Howard M. Chapin. Hypocrisie *Unmasked: A True Relation of the Proceedings of the Governor and Company of the Massachusetts against Samuel Gorton of Rhode Island.* Providence: Club for Colonial Reprints, 1916. Available on Google Books http://books.google.com/books?id=IPrFff0lFyUC&lpg=PP1&ots=PHJ91guYuJ&dq=Winslow%20hypocrisie%20unmasked&pg=PA97#v=onepage&q&f=false.

Winter, Sean F. "Ambiguous Genitives, Pauline Baptism and Roman *Insulae*: Resources from Romans to Support *Pushing the Boundaries of Unity*." In *Baptist Sacramentalism*

2: edited by Anthony R. Cross and Philip E. Thompson, 77–91. Studies in Baptist History and Thought 25. Milton Keynes: Paternoster, 2008.

Wright, David, editor. *Baptism: Three Views*. Downers Grove, IL: InterVarsity, 2009.

———. "Recovering Baptism for a New Age of Mission." In *Doing Theology for the People of God: Studies in Honor of J. I. Packer*, edited by Donald Lewis and Alister McGrath, 51–66. Downers Grove, IL: InterVarsity, 1996.

———. "Scripture and Evangelical Diversity with Special Reference to the Baptismal Divide." In *A Pathway into the Holy Scripture*, edited by David F. Wright and Philip E. Satterthwaite, 257–76. Grand Rapids: Eerdmans, 1994.

———. *What Has Infant Baptism Done to Baptism? An Enquiry at the End of Christendom*. Milton Keynes: Paternoster, 2005.

Wright, S. *The Early English Baptists, 1603–1649*. Woodbridge: Boydell, 2006.

Yarnold, Edward. *The Awe-Inspiring Rites of Initiation: The Origins of the R.C.I.A.* Collegeville: Liturgical, 1994.

Yong, Amos. *The Spirit Poured Out on All Flesh: Pentecostalism and the Possibility of Global Theology*. Grand Rapids: Baker Academic, 2005.

Name Index

Allen, J., 180
Allison, C. F., 126
Ambrose, 48
Anderson, A., 203, 204
Anderson, O., 73
Anderson, P., 160, 168
Aquinas, T., 59, 80, 113, 219
Aquino, F., 181
Arand, C. P., 57
Armstrong, J. H., xv
Arnott, J., 206
Athanasius, 13, 138
Athenagoras I, xiv
Attridge, H., 186
Augustine of Hippo, 8, 41, 42, 47, 48, 49, 50, 54, 84, 105, 107, 112, 226, 234, 240
Aynsworth, N. J., 180

Baker, F., 127
Barclay, H., 124
Barclay, R., 157, 162, 163, 165
Barrett, D. B., 202
Barth, K., 67, 79, 93, 95, 98, 107, 139
Barth, M., 98, 108, 109
Basil, 17, 18, 19, 20, 21, 25, 234
Bavinck, H., 101
Beall, J. L., 205, 213
Beasley-Murray, G. R., 139, 140, 144, 147, 149, 152, 154, 155
Bebbington, D. W., 138
Benedict XVI (pope), 32
Bennett, D., 216
Bentley, T., 206

Bergsten, T., 152
Berkhoff, L., 102
Best, T. F., xiv
Beza, T., 93
Blaurock, G., 81
Blunt, R., 141
Boismard, M.-E., 40
Bonhoeffer, D., 68, 70
Bredesen, H., 216
Brenz, J., 63, 64
Brinkel, K., 57
Bucer, M., 79, 80, 83, 84, 85, 99, 117, 232
Bugenhagen, J., 62
Bullinger, H., 79, 85, 86, 103
Bunyan, J., 151
Burgess, S. M., 219
Burreson, K., 61
Byrne, B., 39

Cabasilas, N., 6, 7, 67
Cadbury, J., 239
Calvin, J., 78, 79, 85, 86, 87, 87, 88, 89, 94, 95, 98, 103, 104, 105, 106, 107, 110, 116, 122, 123, 124, 232
Campbell, A., 175, 176, 177, 178, 179
Carpe, W., 179
Chadwick, O., 127
Charles I (king), 124
Charles II (king), 125
Charles V (emperor), 63
Chauvet, L.-M., 35, 36, 46, 50
Chemnitz, M., 75

Childers, J. W., 181
Chrysostom, J., 4, 12, 24, 25
Clark, M. S., 202
Clark, S., 217
Cocceius, J., 93
Coffey, J., 151
Cohn, N., 55
Coleman-Norton, P. R., 141
Colwell, J. E., 144, 145, 146, 147, 149, 152
Cop N., 86
Cotterell, J., 179
Cranmer, T., 115, 117, 119, 120, 121, 122, 130
Creech, J., 203
Cross, A. R., xv, 136, 138, 139, 140, 142, 144, 145, 148, 155, 227, 228, 229, 233, 236
Crossing, P. F., 202
Crowe, T. R., 219
Culpepper, R. A., 187
Cyprian of Carthage, 4
Cyril of Jerusalem, 3, 7, 10, 11, 13, 22, 23, 25

Dix, G., 128
Dodd, C. H., 187
Doig, A., 5
Dowey, E., 85
Dunn, J. D. G., 164, 169, 205
Durham, W., 207
Dusing, M., 210, 212, 213

Eaton, S., 141
Edwards, J., 79, 95, 96
Elert, W., 68, 72
Elizabeth I (queen), 78, 120, 123
Emmott, E. B., 157
England, S., 179
Erasmus, 80

Ferel, M., 60
Ferguson, E., xv, 181
Fiddes, P. S., 145, 146, 147, 150, 154

Finn, T. M., 42
Finney, C., 171
Fletcher, D., 181
Foster, D. A., 180
Fowler, S. K., 146, 147
Fox, G., 158, 159, 162, 172, 234, 239
Fox, T. C., 32
Freeman, C. W., 145
Freiday, D., 157, 162, 163, 165
Frere, W. H., 117

Gee, D., 210, 212
Geddes, J., 125
George, D., 137, 138
George, T., 137, 138, 147, 154
Gerhard, J., 65
Gerhardt, P., 65
Gilmore, A., 147
Gorham, G., 127, 128
Gortner, J. N., 205, 212
Grebel, C., 81
Gregory I (pope), 112
Gregory of Nazianzus, 12, 25
Gregory of Nyssa, 7, 8, 9, 11
Grönvik, L., 53
Guder, D., 102
Gurney, J. J., 160, 162, 164, 165

Hageman, H., 79
Hall, D. J., 77
Hallesby, O., 69, 70, 71, 72, 73
Hamor, R., 124
Harmless, W., 43
Harmon, S. R., 142
Harrison, W., 183
Hart, L. D., 208, 213
Hauerwas, S., 77
Hayes, A. L., 111, 226, 233, 234
Haymes, B., 142, 150, 151, 154, 155
Haywood, G. T., 220
Heidegger, J. H., 93
Helyws, T., 138, 139, 140
Henry VIII (king), 112, 156
Heppe, H., 93, 94

Name Index

Heshusius, T., 64
Hicks, E., 176
Higgins, J. R., 213
Hippolytus, 3, 4, 34
Hodge, A. A., 97
Hodge, C., 97
Hooker, R., 122, 123, 235
Hoover, W., 204
Horton, S. M., 213
Hunter, H., 204, 209, 213
Hütter, L., 64, 65, 75

Irenaeus, 3

James I (king), 123, 124
Jenson, R., 67, 68, 70, 72, 73, 74
Jeremias, J., 69
Jewel, J., 122
Jewett, P. K., 140
John (elector), 62
John XXIII (pope), xii, 217
John of Kronstadt, 6
Johnson, M. E., 34, 43
Johnson, T. M., 202
Johnsson, L., 152
Jones, K. M., 143, 146
Jones, T. C., 162

Kärkkäinen, V-M., 209
Kasper, W., 43, 45, 47
Keach, B., 142
Kelly, G., 26, 228, 232, 239, 242
Kendall, I., 146
Kilpatrick, J., 206
Kingo, T. H., 66
Knox, J., 91
Kolb, R., 53, 57, 58, 59, 60, 63, 74, 229, 233
Kolp, A., 167
Kruger, B., 102

Lampe, G. W. H., 129
Lee, E., 206
Leith, J., 95

Leonard, B., 136, 137, 138, 141
Lightfoot, J. B., 189
Lipscomb, D., 180
Locke, J., 175, 234
Lumpkin, W. L., 137, 138, 141, 142, 155
Luther, M., 53, 54, 55, 56, 57, 58, 59, 60, 61, 62, 63, 64, 65, 66, 67, 73, 75, 80, 83, 86, 87, 88, 106, 107, 116, 117, 232, 234

Macchia, F., 204, 205, 209, 212, 214, 215
MacDonald, M. Y., 40
Macy, H., 151, 233, 238
Mant, R., 127
Mason, A. J., 128
Martin, R., 217
Marty, M., xv
Mary I (queen), 120
Mathesius, J., 64
McAlister, R. E., 219
McBeth, H. L., 138, 141, 143, 144
McCalla, W. L., 177
McDonnell, K., 217, 218, 219
McGary, A., 180
McKim, D., 103
Melanchthon, P., 61, 62, 63, 64, 117
Menzies, W. W., 223
Millar, W. R., 230
Miller, G. G., 139
Moltmann, J., 98, 102, 109
Moody, D. L., 207
Morrison, C. C., 179
Müntzer, T., 56

Nagel, N. E., 62
Nelle, W., 66
Neumeister, E., 66
Nevin, J., 97
Newbigin, L., 102
Niccum, C., 174, 233, 239
Nickalls, J. L., 159, 239
Nischan, B., 61

Noll, M. A., 95
Nuttall, G. F., 239

Old, H. O., 99
Oprenov, T. B., 146
Orombi, H. L., 131
Oyer, J. S., 55, 56
Ozman, A., 206

Parham, C. F., 203, 206
Patrick, Saint, 112
Paul XI (pope), xiv
Pearlman, M., 208, 210, 211, 212, 213, 214
Peters, A., 57
Peterson, E., 158
Pfatteicher, P. H., 62
Philipp the Younger, 65
Philpotts, H., 127, 128
Pinnock, C., 145
Pius X (pope), 129
Polanus, A., 93
Porter, S. E., xv
Procter, F., 117
Pruitt, R., 210, 212, 213
Pusey, E., 127

Rainbow, J. H., 145, 154
Randall, I. M., 143, 146
Reed, D. A., 220, 221, 222, 223
Renihan, J. M., 142
Rice, N. L., 177
Riggs, J., 80, 81, 82, 84, 85, 86, 89, 94, 97
Riker, D. B., 142
Ringwald, B., 65
Robeck, C. M., 203, 204, 205, 210, 211, 213
Robinson, J., 237
Robinson, W., 179
Roy, K., 142

Saarnivaara, U., 70, 71, 72, 74
Sandidge, J., 204, 205, 210, 211, 213
Sanford, D. A., 142

Selnecker, N., 65
Seneca, 86
Seymour, W. J., 203, 206, 207
Scaer, D., 67, 70, 72, 74
Schaepe, J. G., 219
Schaff, P., 97
Schillebeeckx, E., 167
Schleiermacher, F., 79, 95, 96, 97
Schlink, E., 67, 68, 69, 70, 72, 74
Schnabel, E., 138
Schreiner, T. R., 140, 154
Schwarzburg-Rudolstadt, E., 66
Scott, W., 176
Scotus, D., 60, 80, 113
Shakarian, D., 216
Smyth, J., 138, 139, 140, 141, 227
Spinks, B. D., 27, 113
Stansell, R., 172
Steenberg, I. M. C., 1, 226, 233, 241, 242
Stein, R. H., 139, 149
Stone, B. W., 176
Stronstad, R., 205
Studebaker, S., 201, 208, 229, 232, 241
Suenens, L-J., 217
Sullivan, F. J., 219
Symeon the New Theologian, 8

Tallman, F. D., 213
Tanner, N. P., 44, 47
Taylor, C., 77
Taylor, G., 181
Taylor, J., 126, 127, 128
Tertullian, 3, 41, 42, 147, 236
Thompson, P. E., 145, 148
Torrence, J., 76, 102
Torrey, R. A., 207
Trigg, J., 53, 54, 58, 59
Tranvik, M. D., 62, 63, 64
Turretin, F., 93

Ulm, J., 65
Updegraff, D., 171
Van Der Maas, E. M., 219

Vissers, J., 76, 228, 231
Volf, M., 77

Walker, J., 177, 177
Walton, R. C., 80
Warfield, B. B., 97
Wellum, S. J., 140
Welshimer, P. H., 179
Wengert, T. J., 57, 58, 60, 63
Wesley, J., 126, 127
West, W. M. S., 139
Whitaker, A., 124
Whitaker, E. C., 34, 52
White, B. R., 139, 147
Wied, H., 117
Wilcuts, J., 163, 169, 172
Willimon, W., 77
Williams, E. S., 209, 210, 211, 212, 214
Williams, G. H., 56

Wimber, J., 206
Winslow, E., 237
Wingren, G., 72, 73
Winter, S. F., 152
Wollebius, J., 93
Wood, G., 223
Wright, D., xv, xvi
Wright, S., 139, 141
Wyclif, J., 113, 116, 122

Yarnold, E., 34
Yong, A., 204, 205, 214, 215

Zizioulas, J., 102
Zwingli, U., 78, 79, 80, 81, 82, 83, 84, 85, 86, 87, 88, 95, 98, 99, 145

Scripture Index

OLD TESTAMENT

Genesis
1	55, 65
1–2	188
1:27	188
2:24	190
17:1–19	103

Exodus
19	184
19–34	103

Leviticus
16:2–4	185

Numbers
4:30	183
8:24	183

Deuteronomy
4:35	13
6:4–5	185
10:16	189

1 Samuel
15:22	239

Ecclesiastes
3:2	11

Ezekiel
47:1–12	65

Micah
6:1–8	239

NEW TESTAMENT

Matthew
3:1–2	143
3:1–12	185
3:2–6	185
3:6	143, 183
3:7–10	193
3:11	143, 144, 159, 190
3:12	193
3:13–15	182
3:13–17	2, 144
3:15	167, 193
3:16	146, 182, 183
5–7	153
10:22	73
18:3	13
18:14	64
19:14	13, 64
24:13	73
28	xiii, 165, 166
28:18–19	211
28:18–20	2, 190, 193, 240
28:19	43, 55, 56, 64, 67, 73, 93, 148, 149, 153, 212, 219
28:19–20	144, 165, 166, 168

Mark

1:1	191
1:1–15	191
1:2–4	185
1:4	185, 191
1:4–5	143, 144
1:4–8	191
1:5	183
1:7–8	144
1:8	159, 190
1:9–11	144, 191
1:9–13	2
1:10	182, 183, 192
1:11	192
1:12	191
1:15	191
2	104
5:19	192
8:31–35	191
9:30–35	191
10	118
10:13	148
10:13–14	64
10:32–45	191
10:35–40	192
10:38	164
10:39	25
11:27–33	161
13:13	73
15:38	192
15:39	192
16:7	192
16:9–20	166
16:15	166
16:16	43, 44, 56, 66, 67, 144

Luke

3	182
3:1–18	185
3:3	143, 185
3:16	144, 159, 190
3:21–22	2, 144, 182
12:50	25, 164
18:15	71
18:16	13
23:42–43	168
24:13–35	36
24:45–53	166

John

1:12	148
1:26–28	144
1:26–33	159, 187
1:29–34	2, 167
1:31–33	144
1:32–33	145
2	189, 193
2:6–10	187
3	64, 122, 183, 187
3:3	148
3:5	148, 165, 223
3:3–5	69, 182
3:3–7	187
3:3–8	65
3:3–12	55
3:5	43, 127, 145, 148
3:5–7	187
3:14–15	168
3:14–16	148
3:16	148
3:22	168
3:22–26	187
3:22–30	189
3:23	183
4	189, 193
4:1–26	194
4:1–30	187
4:2	168
4:13	182
4:23	163
4:31–38	194
5:1–15	199
5:2–14	187
6:60–66	193
7:37–39	182, 187
7:38	187
9:5–11	187
10:31–59	193

John (cont.)

10:40	183
12:37–43	193
13:1–15	187
13:35	166
15:3	187, 189
15:6	73
16:13	169
18:11	187
19:28–30	187
19:34	187
20	187
20:21–23	166
20:22–23	187
20:31	148

Acts

1:4–5	160, 190
1:5	159
1:8	166
2	176, 182, 213
2:4–18	190
2:38	1, 101, 144, 145, 146, 148, 154, 182, 212, 223, 235
2:38–41	185
2:39	101
2:40	2
2:40–47	196
2:41	144, 154
2:42–45	36
5:1–10	196
5:31	67
7:51	189
7:51–53	196
8	37, 46, 112, 182
8:4–11	101
8:12	144
8:13–21	196
8:16	149, 235
8:26–40	36, 101
8:30–35	36
8:36–38	36, 144
8:37	185, 235
8:38	146
8:38–39	183
8:39	36
9:8	235
9:17–19	182
10	101
10–11	182
10:24–48	139
10:43	67
10:44–48	2, 144, 182
10:47	182, 235
10:48	149
11:14	3, 139
11:15–17	190
11:16	159
11:17	182
13:23–25	159
13:38	67
16	213
16:14–15	101, 144
16:15	3, 104, 139
16:29–34	101
16:30–33	139
16:31	3
16:31–33	144
16:31–34	235
16:33	104
17:28	6
18:8	104, 139, 144
18:25	159, 235
19	182
19:1–7	159
19:4	144
19:5	6, 149
19:5–6	182
19:6	6, 235
22:16	1, 146, 185
26:18	67

Romans

1:16	148
3:21–22	39
3:23	38
3:24	38
3:24–25	185

Romans (cont.)

3:28	148, 185
4:5–7	148
4:11	104
5–6	196
5:12	112
5:12–21	187
5:12—6:14	187
5:15	39
5:17	154
5:18–19	38
6	38, 39, 58, 100, 196, 198
6–7	188
6:1–11	100, 143, 153, 196
6:1–14	188
6:1—8:17	188
6:2–11	148
6:3	9, 14, 39, 149
6:3–4	144, 146, 183
6:3–5	146
6:3–11	54, 55, 58, 67, 68, 71, 72
6:4	9, 12, 25, 39, 56, 141, 157, 191
6:4–5	38
6:5	25
6:6	25
6:8	12
6:11	50
6:15—7:6	188
6:23	70
7:7—8:17	188
7:12	188
7:14	188
7:14–24	188
8	196, 241
8:1	188
8:4	188
8:12–13	148
8:14–17	42
8:15	42
9–11	195
9:1–8	195
9:6	195
9:19–22	73
10:5–13	195
10:9	185, 195
10:9–10	149
10:14–21	195
11:25–27	195
12	72
12:1–2	51
12:1—15:13	186
12:3–13	186
12:4–8	151
12:14–21	186
13:1–14	186
13:12–14	186
14:1—15:13	186
15:14–16	186

1 Corinthians

1	153
1–2	59
1–4	198
1:10–17	162
1:12–14	55
1:13–17	169
1:14–16	198
1:16	3, 139
1:17	144, 153, 170
3	153
3:5–9	198
5:1—6:8	196
6:9–11	148, 196
6:11	43, 146, 148, 182
6:13–14	39
7	195
7:1–16	188
7:14	112
7:17–20	188
7:21–14	188
8–10	198
10	241
10:1–2	104
10:1–4	182
10:1–5	190
10:1–6	199

1 Corinthians (cont.)

10:2	164
12:3	185
12:11	39
12:12–13	39, 153
12:12–31	151
12:13	69, 143, 144, 145, 148, 150, 153, 182, 188, 195, 236
13:12	151, 236
15:29	198
15:45	39

2 Corinthians

1:21–22	67, 140
1:22	190, 198
4:6	55
5:12	190, 198
5:17	76, 153

Galatians

2:19	191
2:20	13, 148, 157
3	194
3:2–5	148
3:6–7	148
3:14	148
3:26	146, 150
3:26–28	153, 188, 194, 195
3:27	24, 66, 146, 148, 149, 153, 157, 165
3:27–28	39, 58
3:28	55, 105
4:5	42
6:12–16	195

Ephesians

1:9	105
1:10	40
1:13	40, 41, 140
1:14	190
2	45
2:1–7	197
2:2	197
2:5–6	38, 40
2:5–8	185
2:6	41
2:8	236
2:13–16	40
2:14–16	6
2:15	49
2:19	150
2:22	44
3:2–3	105
3:17	148
4	45
4:1–6	45
4:1–16	151
4:4–5	201
4:4–6	153, 161, 185, 195
4:5	125, 145, 153, 162, 231
4:17—6:9	190
4:20–24	187, 197
4:22	153
4:24	153
4:28	197
4:30	140
4:31—5:2	197
5:14	185
5:25–27	56, 143, 189
5:26	42, 146, 165
5:31–32	190
5:32	105

Philippians

2:8	13
2:14–17	186

Colossians

1:26–27	105
2	55, 188, 189
2:6–15	197
2:6–23	188
2:7	188
2:8–15	187
2:9–11	188, 195
2:10–12	163

Colossians (cont.)

2:12	141, 146, 148, 157, 183, 191
2:11–12	140, 153
2:11–15	55, 67, 71
2:16–17	163
2:17	104
3:1–11	187
3:2–4	50
3:3–4	191
3:5–11	153
3:8–15	197
3:9	10
3:12–14	165
3:12–17	153

1 Timothy

3:16	105
4:1	73
6:12	143, 149

Titus

3:1–7	197
3:3–8	55, 65
3:4–7	187
3:5	146, 148, 182
3:5–7	148
3:5–8	56
3:7	197

Hebrews

6	185
6:1–2	112, 186
6:1–5	143
6:4–6	73
9:10	163
10:9	163
10:19–25	186

James

2:24	185

1 Peter

1:1	192
1:3	192
1:3–5	198
1:14–16	186
1:22—2:3	197
1:23	192
2:2	192
2:4–10	186
2:5	51
2:9	44, 51
2:11	192
2:11—4:19	186
2:12	197
2:12–15	197
2:15	197
2:18–20	197
2:19	197
2:21	192, 197
2:21–25	192
3:1–2	197
3:2–6	197
3:6	192
3:8–22	143
3:9	192, 197
3:10–11	192
3:13–17	197
3:14	197
3:16	197
3:16–17	197
3:18–19	192
3:19–21	182
3:20–21	104
3:20–22	192
3:21	43, 56, 68, 71, 148, 192, 197
3:21–22	185
4:14–16	197
4:19	197

2 Peter

1:4	42
3:5–6	182

1 John
2:20 6

Revelation
1:5–6 194
3:4–5 194
4:4 194
6:11 194
7:9–17 194
7:13 194
19:8 190, 194
19:14 194
22:14–15 198

EARLY CHRISTIAN LITERATURE

Didache
7 3

Dead Sea Scrolls
1QS III:2–12 185
1QS V:13–14 185

www.ingramcontent.com/pod-product-compliance
Lightning Source LLC
Chambersburg PA
CBHW070238230426
43664CB00014B/2349